The Experimental Zone

An Interdisciplinary Investigation
on the Spaces and Practices
of Collaborative Research

Séverine Marguin
Henrike Rabe
Friedrich Schmidgall

The Experimental Zone

An Interdisciplinary Investigation on the Spaces and Practices of Collaborative Research

Séverine Marguin
Henrike Rabe
Friedrich Schmidgall

PARK BOOKS

Introduction

Diverse, flexible, open: More and more companies are presenting their workplaces and methods as the "offices of the future" or "innovation spaces". In this context, office design supposedly acts as a driver of creativity and innovation. A long tradition of experimentally and creatively exploring the connection between space and knowledge exists in the field of office architecture, with key developments including the redesign of the open-plan office as an "office landscape" by the Quickborn team in the late 1950s (Kockelkorn 2008), the creation of typifications of workspaces by Francis Duffy and DEGW since the end of the 1960s (Duffy 1969; Duffy et al. 1976; Duffy et al. 1992; Duffy 1997; Laing et al. 1998; Harrison et al. 2004) and the concept of "Office Urbanism" with its "mega floor" by Hitoshi Abe in the 00s (Nobuyuki 2003). By contrast, the design of scientific architecture, i.e. the spaces in which scientific research and teaching take place, is not yet being questioned and experimented with to the same extent, although the university is the place of knowledge generation and innovation par excellence. In addition, current paradigms of interdisciplinarity and digitization present the university with new challenges. For instance, questions regarding which spaces are suitable for interdisciplinary collaborations, and the precise impact of digitization on the architecture of science arise. The latest discourses on the sites of interdisciplinary and creative knowledge production such as the media lab (e.g. Emerson et al. 2019), the Co-Working Space (Merkel 2019; Müller 2018) or the design studio (e.g. Yaneva 2009) on the one hand, and discussions surrounding creative techniques such as designing (Mareis et al. 2010) or design thinking (Brown 2009; Übernickel et al. 2015) on the other, reveal scientists' fascination with these topics. However, the question of how to design the spaces of research continues to be neglected: How can space actively promote knowledge processes?

While, in architecture, the *active space* often constitutes the implicit starting point of a design ("an atrium encourages encounters", "a design fosters diverse activities"), such a view has long been deemed outlandish by the humanities and social sciences (Niewöhner 2014). Only in the context of the "material-cultural turns" (Harrison 2013, 4), and in particular the *spatial turn*, was space rediscovered as a research object and described as active or "agentified" (Niewöhner 2014, 19). Nevertheless, not only are surprisingly few empirical investigations on concrete places of knowledge production published, but few connections between spatial discourses in architecture (Hillier and Hanson 1984; Hara 2004; Kojima 2007; Sailer and Penn 2009), in anthropology (Yaneva 2009; Niewöhner 2014; Beck 2015; Ash 2016), in sociology (Löw 2001; Delitz 2010; Steets 2015), or in interaction design (Dalton et al 2016) can also be observed. In our research project

ArchitecturesExperiments, we have tackled precisely this research gap and—in a constellation between architecture, interaction design and sociology—developed a new interdisciplinary approach to empirical spatial research.

As far as the question of knowledge production is concerned, we draw on Laboratory Studies (Latour and Woolgar 1979; Galison and Thompson 1999; Knorr Cetina 1999), and also on Workplace Studies (Suchman 1987; Knoblauch 1997; Heath et al. 2000) and Studio Studies (Yaneva 2009; Farias and Wilkie 2016). The originality of our study, however, lies in the fact that we explored a target group that has been rarely investigated to date, namely a multidisciplinary group of scientists. At the Cluster of Excellence *Image Knowledge Gestaltung. An Interdisciplinary Laboratory* of the Humboldt-Universität in Berlin, all research topics were addressed in interdisciplinary team constellations—primarily consisting of scholars from the humanities and design[1] disciplines. Increasingly in demand today, interdisciplinary research nonetheless poses immense challenges for researchers on account of different ways of working, methods and technical languages (Mejía et al. 2017; Shanken 2010; Galison 1999). In our research project, we were able to investigate the *Interdisciplinary Laboratory*'s extraordinary endeavor from within and in the making, placing a particular focus on space: What influence does space have on interdisciplinary knowledge production? Which spaces and spatial qualities are required to develop new knowledge at the interface between the disciplines? We place particular emphasis on the question of collaboration: What effect does space have on collaboration within and between existing teams as well as on the emergence of new constellations? A specific challenge was to find spatial conditions that promote collaboration but also offer opportunities for individual retreat. For this purpose, it was necessary to explore the ways in which the different *physical-virtual* research spaces relate to each other, i.e. to determine under which conditions they unfold, coexist, interrupt, dock or merge.

In order to investigate these questions empirically, we developed a novel experimental and interdisciplinary method for the investigation and design of space, so-called *experimental design-based field research*. For this purpose, a research area of 350 m^2, the Experimental Zone, was created for forty scientists[2], which was redesigned and rebuilt approximately every two months over a period of three years (figs. 0.1–3). A total of eighteen experimental settings was carried out and observed both quantitatively and qualitatively. In line with a practical theoretical approach, the materialized knowledge practices and routines, i.e. bodies and objects, were afforded special scrutiny. In this way, the effects of physical-virtual space on interdisciplinary knowledge practice could be explored in an unprecedented manner.

This book aims to share the results and challenges of this study with an interdisciplinary readership. Conceived as a hybrid of the literary traditions holding sway in the fields of architecture, design and the social sciences, it consists of five scientific chapters complemented by extensive visual material generated as a result of the design and observation of the spatial settings. The chosen format is intended to allow readers not only to retrace but also to continue the evaluation of this rich material: While the texts highlight individual images, the complete visual material is made searchable and comparable in the so-called *collections*. In **Part One**, we present our theoretical positioning: What do we mean by 'space'? What do we mean by 'physical-virtual'? How do we define 'knowledge production' and 'collaboration'? In **Part Two**, we explain the experimental approach and the specific challenges which characterize this methodological approach. With regards to the collection of data, we present our mixed-method approach and novel hybrid observation and evaluation methods. Furthermore, we have structured our interdisciplinary teamwork by means of a procedure model. As an excursus, three further researchers involved in the project—Finn Geipel, Fabian Scholz, and Christian Stein—will describe its development in a **guest contribution**. In Parts Three to Five, we present the findings of the study. **Part Three** begins with a dense description of the individual research practices. At the level of the individual workstation, we trace the physical-virtual research spaces as a dynamic habitat and elaborate its characteristics. In **Part Four**, we explore how the individual practices meet in the open

1 We use the term "design" as an umbrella term for the disciplines of design and architecture (Mareis 2010, Schäffner 2010).

2 The names of participants in the Experimental Zone were replaced by pseudonyms throughout the publication on the grounds of data protection.

space and which challenges emerge as a result of the co-presence of the heterogeneous research spaces. The analysis shows that the participants negotiate the Experimental Zone on three levels, namely in terms of territories, interactions and atmospheres. In **Part Five**, we investigate how a mere co-presence evolves into collaborations. We synthesize the spaces of collaboration according to their type and thus develop the characteristics of a collaborative habitat in the sense of a space that promotes collaboration.

The monograph thus documents our contributions to three current discourses. Firstly, we hope to provide impetus for the field of spatial theory by seeking to link relational and agentified spatial models and by overcoming the dichotomy between the physical and the virtual. Secondly, we provide empirical results for basic research on space with potential consequences for its design: By describing the conditions under which spaces of individual and collaborative research unfold, interrupt, or merge, we reveal the characteristics of an architecture that promotes interdisciplinarity. And thirdly, our project opens up new methodological perspectives, particularly in view of the fact that space, with its multiple dimensions and aspects—social, physical-spatial and digital—often proves impossible to negotiate with the methods of one discipline alone (Baur et al. 2014). In a constellation combining architecture, interaction design and sociology, we have addressed precisely this challenge and developed a new interdisciplinary approach to empirical spatial research. This enabled us to link a scientific investigation with design practice, thus paving the way for a 'design turn' in the social sciences. The project has shown that spatial research benefits immensely from the knowledge that only materializes in the making, e.g. in designing, prototyping, building, drawing, testing or using spaces. And, vice versa, empirical findings from spatial research are all the more valuable if they inspire the design of new spaces.

Gästeliste

1:20 Mode
(Experimentalzon

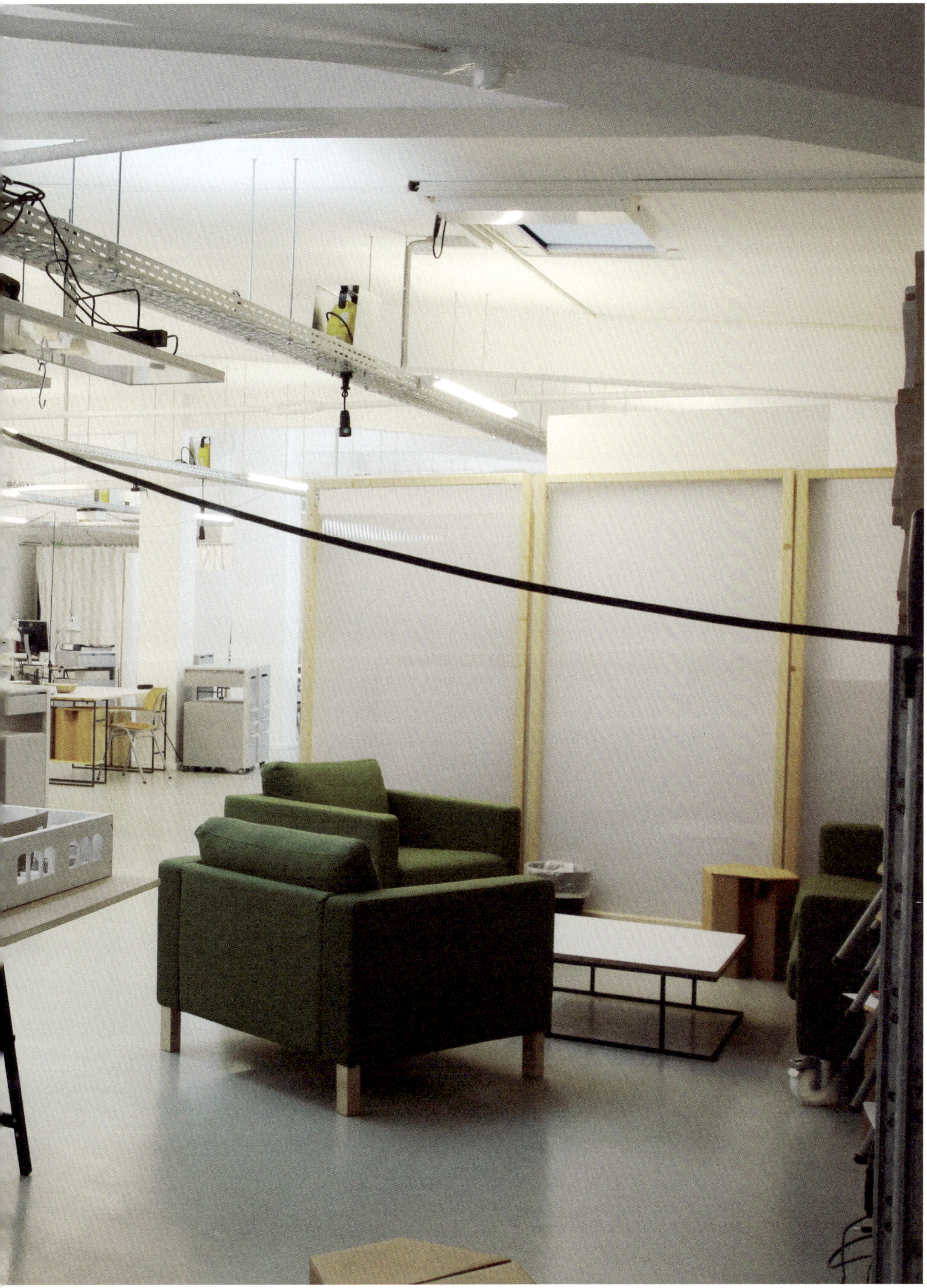

Part 1

Investigating Space, Knowledge and Collaboration: A Theoretical Framework

Our aim is to explore the interrelationship between space and knowledge practices. But how do we define "space"? And how do we interpret the concept of "knowledge"? Both notions are the subject of lively discussions. This first part serves to explain our theoretical positioning and clarify those discourses in which our investigation is embedded.

Firstly, we advocate a relational, agentified and integrative understanding of space, which takes, on the one hand, the conditionality of space and the social into account, and, on the other, overcomes the dichotomy between the physical and the virtual. Secondly, and in line with our practice theory approach, we think of knowledge as materialized and embodied: We are concerned with investigating science in the making. Thirdly, as far as theory is concerned, we embed our research object within the existing literature on spaces of knowledge production, such as Laboratory Studies and Workplace Studies. In this context, we have encountered two research gaps: Not only is there a lack of empirical studies on the interrelationship between space and knowledge practice, but those on the subject of interdisciplinary research groups from the humanities and design are also few and far between. The present study addresses precisely these two gaps. The first part concludes with a detailed description of our specific field of research, the Cluster of Excellence *Image Knowledge Gestaltung. An Interdisciplinary Laboratory*, and with an explanation of our understanding of interdisciplinarity and collaboration.

1 A Relational, Agentified and Integrative Understanding of Space

In recent decades, an intense preoccupation with the topic of space has emerged in various disciplines. While architects and architectural researchers began to take a closer look at the events, flows and processes in space (Hillier and Hanson 1984; Tschumi 1994; Hara 2004; Kojima 2007), the "Spatial Turn" led to a new relational and agentified understanding of space within the context of the cultural and social sciences (Löw 2001; Döring and Thielmann 2009; Niewöhner 2014). However, the discourse in the latter is anything but uniform. The Berlin anthropologist Jörg Niewöhner developed a genealogy of the concept of space in 20th- and 21st-century anthropology that describes the successive paradigms of space (Niewöhner 2014). The early social researchers understood space exclusively as a material and physical environment which determines human action in the sense of the absolute understanding of space. Absolute space "corresponds to three-dimensional, measurable, geometric-physical

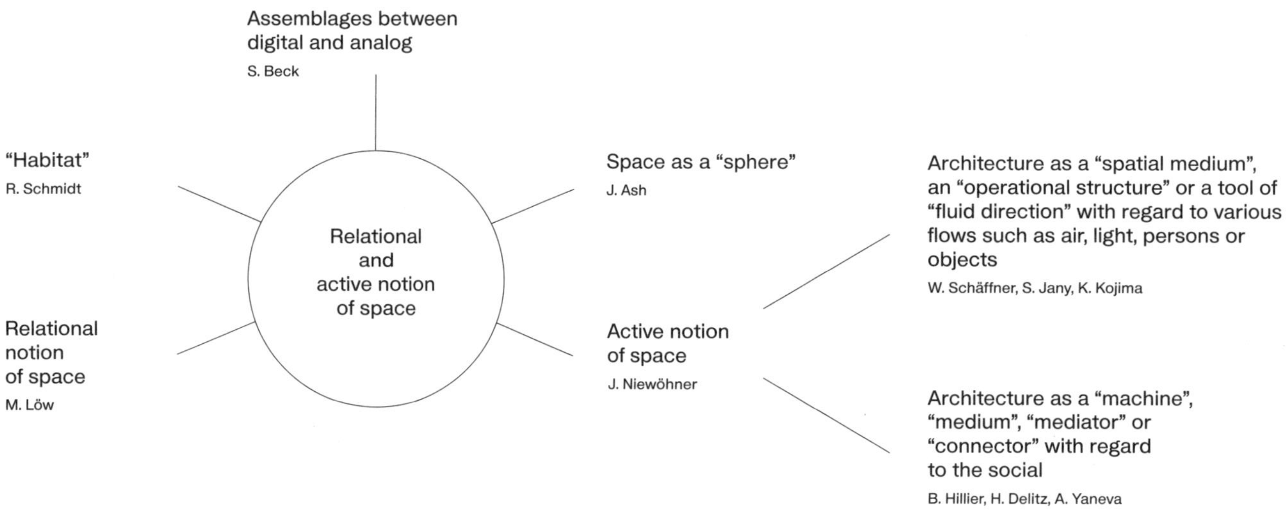

Fig. 1.1: Theoretical positioning

space: [...· space as a container"[1] (Edinger 2015, 25). In the postwar period, material space lost this prominent position: As a result of the shift from functionalism to structuralism experienced in the social sciences on the one hand, but also, as some authors point out, thanks to the political argumentations of the Second World War, which led to a negative connotation of the term "space" and to a renunciation of theoretical examinations of the same (Läpple 1991).

Since the 1980s, the concept of space has witnessed a revival, albeit predominantly as a metaphorical application for the description of practices of domination. A prominent and formative example is the definition of Pierre Bourdieu's "social space", which describes the social structure as a space of objective positions according to the volume of capital (Bourdieu 2018). Here, the notion of space must be understood as a *relative* one insofar as it only describes the arrangement of social relations to each other. The materiality of space is strongly neglected in figurative applications such as these.

An authentic renaissance of the notion of space did not occur until the late 1990s. Several theoretical models of space were developed in the social sciences, cultural studies and in architecture. The sociologist Martina Löw has established space as a sociological concept, which describes a mutual conditionality of space and the social: Space is produced through action and simultaneously affects action. Here, the understanding of space is a relational one, in Löw's words "a relational ordering of living entities and social goods" (Löw 2008, 35). With the two processes constitutive for space, *spacing* and *synthesis*, Löw attempts to take into account both the material dimension, understood as the positioning or placement of people and material and symbolic goods, as well as the dimension of perception.

Other approaches focus on the agency of space (Niewöhner 2014), which is inscribed in its materiality[2]: Some of these authors understand space as active in relation to the social, describing space or architecture as a "machine" (Hillier 1996), a "medium" (Delitz 2010, 3), or a "mediator" or "connector" (Yaneva 2010b, 144). Other authors assert that architecture actively directs and filters all sorts of elements and flows such as air, light, persons or objects, characterizing it as a tool of "fluid direction" (Kojima 2007, 134), a

1 Own translation.
2 See the concept of inscription by Latour (1987, 1997).

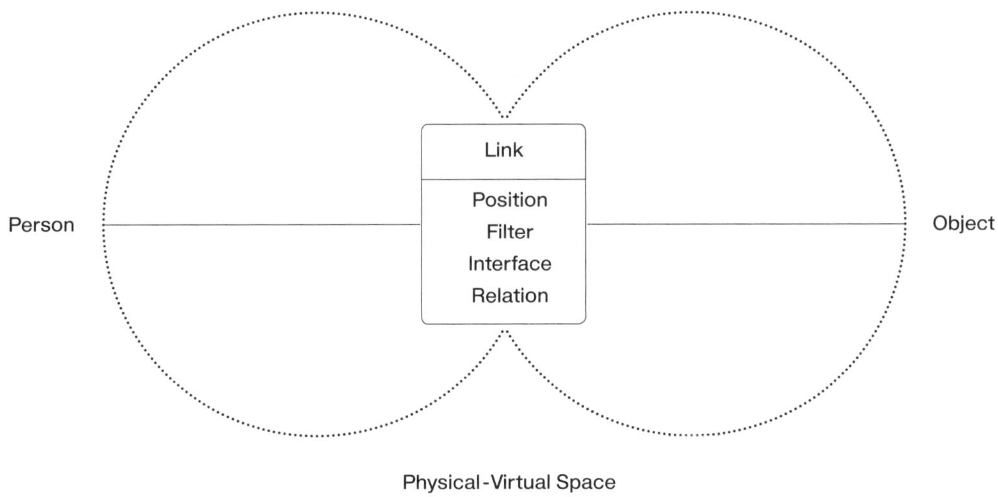

Fig. 1.2: Model of physical-virtual space

"spatial medium" (Schäffner 2010a, 137), or an "operational structure" (Jany 2015, 34).

However, we do not see any incompatible approaches here, and advocate a relational understanding of space which unfolds through the assemblages of human and non-human actors and is activated through practice (fig. 1.1). Here, we position ourselves close to the sociologist Robert Schmidt and his work on the "agency of space"[3] (Schmidt 2012, 130). Availing himself of an investigation on the spatial-material and symbolic order of a programmers' office, he elaborated the performative effects of office spaces and office artifacts by describing them "as active entities that participate in working practices through specific, productive contributions, form office people whose talents and abilities develop, help shape social life in the office, and realize a wealth of far-reaching symbolic meanings" (Schmidt 2012, 133). Schmidt further distinguishes two perceptions of the agency of space, describing office interiors on the one hand "as intentionalist design objects and materialized permanent purposes [and, on the other hand· as participants in practices" (Schmidt 2012, 154). In our analysis, we espouse a combination of both interpretations which includes both the original, purposefully designed affordance of the artifacts and the "practical performativity [of space· that emerges from the interaction with the participants, and therefore amounts less to a persuasive motivation than to a physical mobilization of the office subjects" (idem).

In the context of these agentified and relational notions of space, we consider it important to address another dimension of space in the light of our research on the topic of knowledge production. The majority of research practices are performed using computers or digital media. As a result, an analysis of the effects of space cannot be limited to the architectural or physical-material space. But how can one consider virtual space? A highly diverse, heterogeneous literature on the subjects of cyberspace, the virtual sphere, the virtual world, virtual reality, augmented reality, hyperreality, etc., exists. These concepts all refer to an immaterial space that is a product of computer technologies, each emphasizing a particular dimension. Even though these notions are currently in high demand, they are not particularly helpful when it comes to an analysis of the working space of researchers. They are all based on

3 Own translation of this and the following quotes by Robert Schmidt (2012).

the dichotomy between real and virtual, analog and digital. We would like to question this dichotomy or additive understanding of space, and propose the idea of an *integrative*[4] or *physical-virtual space* (fig. 1.2). Physical and virtual "spaces" are no longer understood as independently existing expanses of space, but, instead, as aspects of a single integrative space. As such, these two aspects of space cannot be perceived individually, but can only be experienced together.

Following the anthropologist Stefan Beck, we seek to probe further and move beyond this dichotomy of behind and in front of the screen.[5] We do not regard the virtual as another type of space existing in parallel to physical space, but understand both as an integrated, permeated continuum. In his theory of practice 3.0, Beck calls for the "assemblages of human and non-human elements in concrete action contexts"[6] to be examined at the interface between digital and analog (Beck 2015, 11).

Based on his considerations, we asked ourselves the following: At what point does an assemblage become space, and what are the properties of this spatial arrangement? Not all assemblages form spaces. When are the assemblages activated and when do they become space? And when are the spaces deactivated? Here, we identify three main characteristics:

1.
The human and non-human elements are positioned in a certain order contiguous to each other: E.g. the computer screen faces the person, the keyboard is positioned between both. If the screen is facing away from the person, the assemblage consists of the same elements, but creates either no research space or a different one. This is what Löw terms "spacing". By contrast, we include digital elements in the assemblages.

2.
In order for the assemblage to become a space, it must be "activated" by the acting person. In addition to the mental construction of space (a person thinks of space as space and actually constructs it as such, which Löw terms "synthesis performance"), we place practice at the center of this activation: Space unfolds in the enactment of practice (Mol 2003; Schmidt 2012). Only through the action, i.e. the gestures, does it become consistent.

3.
Lastly, the assemblage must facilitate a certain immersion of the acting person with the space enclosing and separating them from their surroundings. The precise nature of this invisible border within this immersive dimension and the point at which it becomes effective, or not, remains unclear. This is discussed in more detail in the presentation of the empirical materials (→ see Parts Three, Four and Five).

We conduct spatial research in the field of knowledge production. What do we mean by knowledge production?

2 A Practice-theoretical Analysis: Science in the Making

The aim of our research project is to question the effect of space, as an actor, on knowledge production. What is the role played by space in the process of knowledge creation? We understand knowledge in the narrower sense of "scientific knowledge" as opposed to everyday knowledge (Berger and Luckmann 1969). Due to our particular target group, consisting of scientists and designers, we speak here predominantly of researching specialist knowledge, whether in the natural sciences, humanities or design. In this sense, we conduct "research on research" and are interested in how scientific and design-related findings are produced. The production of specialist knowledge has been and remains the subject of numerous writings, particularly in the fields of the history of science and philosophy, as well as the sociology and anthropology of the sciences and cognitive sciences.

However, we are not concerned with the *what* (which knowledge is produced), nor with the *why* (why knowledge is produced), but only with the *how*. Following anthropological Laboratory Studies (Latour and Woolgar 1979; Knorr Cetina 1981, 2001; Niewöhner and Liburkina 2017), we examine "science in the making", and observe

4 We owe the expression *integrative space* to the reflections of Henrike Rabe, Friedrich Schmidgall and Christian Stein.

5 Additionally, attempts to view "cyber-physical space" or "ubiquitous computing" as a unified networking of material things with virtual spaces exist within the sociology of technology (Schulz-Schaeffer 2013; Schulz-Schaeffer and Meister 2015).

6 Own translation.

scientists in their everyday work. As a result, we are neither interested in studying the history of ideas for the investigation of scientific theories nor in pursuing an institutionalist approach to science research, but, instead, in observing the knowledge practices. We focus on the processual and thus embed ourselves in the discourse of practice theory.

The praxeological approach goes back to the work of Bourdieu and his "Praxeology", among others. It refers to the interest in a structural explanation of the genesis of practical knowledge (Bourdieu 1977). As the sociologist Hans-Peter Müller comments, the dichotomy of structures and actions can be countered by observing practices, processes and routines (cf. Müller 2014). Beyond Bourdieu, practical theory has developed in many directions, including anthropology (Reckwitz 2002; Beck 2015).

Practice theory seems particularly relevant insofar as it positions itself against the dematerialization and intellectualization of science studies (Reckwitz 2002; Schmidt 2012). In particular, two dichotomies are questioned, namely those between mind and body and subject and object. Instead, the analysis focuses on the materiality of the practices, i.e. the practices' (conscious as well as unconscious) physicality and their reification.

In this context, the reflections of the anthropologist Tim Ingold on materiality prove inspiring (Ingold 2013). He asserts that artifacts are not created by imposing an idea on an existing material, but during a creative process of making that resembles one of growth (Ingold 2013). He therefore places the "maker from the outset as a participant in amongst a world of active materials" (Ingold 2013, 27). By questioning the concept of materiality, "Ingold develops a theoretically advanced theory of practices in which material space plays a central role as an integral component of learned, embodied and localized practices"[7] (Niewöhner 2014, 20).

We follow in the footsteps of the Laboratory Studies with this practice-theoretical program, focusing on two specific areas: *Firstly*, the originality of our project lies in the fact that the target group does not consist of natural scientists, but, above all, of researchers from the fields of the humanities, design and architecture. This is a highly understudied topic, and only a few authors have analyzed the work of humanities scholars to date (Frietsch and Rogge 2013; Camic et al. 2011; Keller and Poferl 2018) or that of designers and architects (Farias and Wilkie 2016; Delitz 2009; Yaneva 2009). *Secondly*, we focus on an analysis of the digitality of these practices. Observing science in the making among scholars from the humanities and design disciplines means observing them "at their computers". What kind of technical infrastructure structures their practices? What is the role played by the computer in the production of knowledge? How does digital media condition the production of knowledge?

Here, we intend to carry out a micro-sociological and praxeological analysis of specific scientific working practices, namely analogous and digital practices in the humanities and design disciplines. Our analysis of the manifold activities of scientific work was inspired by communications engineering, particularly by the different ways in which information is treated in terms of the processing, storage and transmission phases. We distinguish between three main scientific practices: *Producing knowledge, distributing knowledge* and *storing knowledge*. Scientists produce knowledge by reading, writing, researching, designing, thinking, etc. They distribute it by communicating, performing and publishing essays and books. They store it by documenting and archiving their findings. This schematic separation is used as a heuristic tool for practice analysis, even if the work phases are not easy to separate. We are particularly interested in the roles played by space, analog and digital tools and artifacts. Additionally, we aim to scrutinize those spaces which unfold as a result of the encounters between the bodies or gestures of the researchers and the media or research artifacts.

3 The Research Gap: The Interrelation of Knowledge Practice and Space

Our study analyzes the effects of space on scientific knowledge practice: What does space do? How does it affect the practices of collaborating, conceptualizing, writing, reading, drawing, researching and storing? How do these practices materialize and unfold spatially? And to what extent can design—both on the part of the designers and the participants—influence them?

7 Own translation.

Despite the growth of so-called Laboratory Studies and Science Studies, the architecture of scientific institutions has been neglected for some time. In Latour's and Woolgar's "Laboratory Life", the architecture of the laboratory is hardly described at all (Latour and Woolgar 1979). Knorr Cetina's concept of "reconfiguration" demonstrates that "the scientific laboratory is not only a place of research, but an instrument that can bring epistemic profit [and· represents a framework within which a large part of scientific practice is not only carried out but formed"[8] (Knorr Cetina 1999, 45). However, in her study she conveys a rather absolutist understanding of space as a container—if not a metaphorical concept of space—and fails to explain the extent to which knowledge is shaped by physical-material space, instead emphasizing social orders and structures of knowledge production (Edinger 2015, 43).

Since the turn of the millennium, some authors have devoted themselves to this topic, examining the architecture of scientific institutions. In this context, the anthropologist Albena Yaneva (Yaneva 2010a) highlights the investigations by Galison and Thompson, on the role of architecture in the shaping of scientific cultures and identities (Galison and Thompson 1999), Gieryn, on the relationship between the quality of space and the quality and identities of science (Gieryn 2002), Bonetta, on the influence of physical environment on scientific creativity (Bonetta 2003), and Livingstone, on the influence of the place on the contents of academic work (Livingstone 2003). In her own contribution, Yaneva uses the case of an atrium to show how an architectural design concept can affect the collaborative practice of researchers (Yaneva 2010a). Additional works of interest include the spatial-sociological investigations by Eva-Christina Edinger on the library as a knowledge space (Edinger 2015) and by Cornelia Thierbach on spatial distribution and power struggles (Thierbach 2016).

All these works address the issue of whether architecture can shape science. However, they refer to the natural sciences, and focus on laboratories. But as Thierbach writes, "the spaces of science differ in their form depending on the scientific discipline and the corresponding objects of research. The spectrum ranges from simple offices and libraries, conference and lecture halls, laboratories, remote jungle regions to space stations"[9] (Thierbach 2016, 372). However, hardly any studies on scientific office spaces exist.

In order to remedy this lack of spatial research in a scientific context, we see an opportunity in linking it with the discourses on the media lab and Studio Studies, on the one hand, and with research on "the workplace" on the other. A number of works from the fields of Studio Studies and media lab discourse influenced our approach, in particular those examining processes in design studios (Yaneva 2009; Emerson et al. 2019; Farias and Wilkie 2016; Ash 2016). Yaneva applies the Actor-Network-Theory to assemblages of creative production in her investigation of the architectural office OMA (Yaneva 2009). However, the main focus of this investigation is placed on the architectural design process and the role of the artifacts, i.e. the multiplicity of models and documents, not on the role of space. In their anthology "Studio Studies" (2016), Farias und Wilkie assembled a set of empirical case studies which explore and examine the studio as a key setting for aesthetic and material production. One of their objectives, especially relevant for us, is to analyze creativity as a socio-materially distributed practice rather than the cognitive privilege of the individual. In one of the contributions, media scientist James Ash examines a video design studio as a spatial assemblage (2016). He develops the concept of the *sphere* to investigate the emergence of atmospheres in video game studios. Using objects such as servers, headphones and screens, he shows how the influence of non-human objects is fundamental to the emergence of spaces.

The discourse surrounding the media lab (Emerson et al. 2019; Plohmann 2012; Butcher and Plohmann 2009) is also relevant to us insofar as it accommodates similar interdisciplinary working constellations at the interface of science and design. Moreover, if we adopt the definition of the research project "What is a Medialab?" (Emerson et al. 2019), namely "places where the production, labor and conceptualization of media occurs", the Experimental Zone actually formed a kind of media lab in and of itself. The authors emphasize the situational nature of research practices in media labs: They speak of the place

8 Own translation.
9 Own translation.

Fig. 1.3–1.5: Experimental Zone between two settings. Photo © Henrike Rabe

as a physical site or as a "place of making and apparatuses" (Parikka 2016) where the practices are enacted. However, they focus chiefly on the institutional character of the media lab as opposed to analyzing the characteristics of the spaces, or examining what it does with the practices. We therefore hope to contribute to this discourse through a systematic empirical investigation emphasizing the role of space.

In addition, we would like to follow up on several fragmented discourses regarding the workplace. Firstly, so-called Workplace Studies have emerged at the interface between the anthropology of work (Suchman 1987) and information and engineering sciences (e.g. HCI[10]), this in connection with the increasing digitalization of the workspace. Researchers within this field are concerned with the qualitative analysis of work with highly developed information and communication technologies, and aspire to make "generalizable statements about the interactive and social organization of cooperative work, which can also be used for the design of technological, 'user-oriented' systems" (Heath et al. 2000, 160). These works are relevant to our investigation insofar as they examine the practices performed within the workplace. However, they primarily demand the coordination of activities, not space (see Knoblauch 1997). Secondly, another study on the subject of the office focuses more strongly on space. The research on office spaces by Space Syntax is of key interest to us in that they have developed a methodology that permits a quantitative examination of the "social logic of space" (Hillier and Hanson 1984), e.g. the influence of architectural factors such as visibility and spatial structure on the interactions in offices (e.g. Sailer and Penn 2009; Penn and Hillier 1992). These studies have also initiated further research in other disciplines, such as studies at the interface of architecture and HCI (Dalton et al. 2016) or an investigation by Backhouse and Drew (1992), who show that qualitative micro-sociological analyses are necessary in order to trace the complex processes in offices. However, a large majority of these empirical studies espouses an absolutist understanding of space: They look at scattered activities "in a space", not taking into account the spaces these activities create. Furthermore, and especially in the field of HCI and architectural research, a normative approach to optimizing working conditions is adopted, which differs from our approach.

Nevertheless, some of these works have proved very inspiring, such as the study on scopic media by Knorr Cetina (2012) for its integration of digital displays in the analysis, or the study on programming practices by Schmidt (2012). In this context, Schmidt developed the concept of the *habitat*, which is central to our study. He writes that the habitat includes "all those artifacts which are present, certain and embodied in the enactment of the practice and that contribute to the accomplishment of the practice"[11] (Schmidt 2008, 1964). Only in the enactment of the practice is the assemblage of human and non-human, analog and digital actors activated into habitats. What we find particularly exciting about the term is that it places the interaction between space and practice precisely at the center.[12] In this context, we examine the extent to which the interdisciplinary habitat can lead to an acculturation of the respective participants, i.e. to a "scientification" of the designers, if you will, or a "designification" of the humanities scholars.

4 Individual and Collaborative Research in an Interdisciplinary Context

The specific context of our investigation follows in this section. Institutionally, the project was part of the Cluster of Excellence *Image Knowledge Gestaltung. An Interdisciplinary Laboratory* of the Humboldt-Universität in Berlin. This background was anything but insignificant: Among other things, it exerted a strong influence on the formats, content and handling of our subject. In addition, our project had a special status in that we investigated the Cluster of Excellence itself—as a meta-analysis. Some explanations are necessary here in consequence.

The Clusters of Excellence are a funding line of the Excellence Initiative of the Federal Government and the Federal States in Germany

10 Human-computer interaction.
11 Own translation.
12 "The arrangement of artifacts is characterized by a fundamental relationship to the programming bodies. This can be seen, for example, in the combination of finely executed and imagined body movements and code or in the choreography of the programming bodies through chair, desk, keyboard and screen. The digital and representational infrastructure is fundamentally dependent and incomplete; it articulates itself in the practices only in the specific relation to the participating bodies" (Schmidt 2008, own translation).

Fig. 1.6: Table frames, inauguration of the Experimental Zone. Photo © Fabian Scholz
Fig. 1.7: Equipment, inauguration of the Experimental Zone. Photo © Fabian Scholz

Fig. 1.8: Furniture stacked between two experimental settings. Photo © Henrike Rabe

(Winnacker 2005). Providing project-related funding for internationally competitive research fields at German universities, they are intended to strengthen the universities in the long term. They are characterized by "their long-term nature, [. . .- their high funding volume and prestige"[13] (Thierbach 2016, 373-374). The Cluster of Excellence examined here—*Image Knowledge Gestaltung. An Interdisciplinary Laboratory* (hereinafter referred to as "*Interdisciplinary Laboratory*") —ran from 2012 to 2018 in Berlin and focused specifically on interdisciplinarity. Interdisciplinarity is one of the key points of the Excellence Initiative, following "a science policy imperative [. . .-, which in view of the observable differentiation of the research areas (cf. Felt et al. 1995, 8) is intended to counteract "fragmentation" through the funding of interdisciplinary research"[14] (Sondermann et al. 2008, 84–85). How was this implemented at the *Interdisciplinary Laboratory*?

The *Interdisciplinary Laboratory* was based on the hypothesis that "complex problems cannot be solved within the boundaries of a single scientific discipline", with the result that the knowledge and skills of researchers from different scientific disciplines are required (Interdisciplinary Laboratory 2019). The understanding of interdisciplinarity was an integrative one[15], as "the individual disciplines are by no means negated in this approach, but are integrated into interdisciplinary work precisely with their partly radically different methods"[16] (Bredekamp and Schäffner 2015, 9). Moreover, for this understanding of interdisciplinarity, it was essential to re-incorporate the knowledge acquired in the interdisciplinary research within one's own discipline.

The particularly exciting feature of the *Interdisciplinary Laboratory* was the attempt to involve the design disciplines—alongside the humanities and natural sciences—as essential actors in

13 Own translation.
14 Own translation.
15 Or, in the words of Horst Bredekamp, the cluster's spokesperson: "The Cluster of Excellence defends an interdisciplinary idea of a university in the broadest sense, which is being increasingly harassed, perhaps even fought against. Our magic formula is not to reduce the specific specialist knowledge, but to want to deepen it in order to guarantee cooperation" (Bredekamp and Schäffner 2018).
16 Own translation.

basic interdisciplinary research. The "differentiation of technical universities, art colleges and universities as a whole in which the humanities are separated from the natural sciences" (Schäffner 2015, 202) led to a polarizing model of four very different knowledge cultures (design disciplines, engineering, humanities and natural sciences). How can an "integrative understanding of science and design" (idem) be promoted in this consolidated context? The *Interdisciplinary Laboratory* "takes the stance that creative processes make a real contribution to research in a technologically advanced knowledge society, and that research on its part should give creative processes due recognition" (Interdisciplinary Laboratory 2019). Or, to put it another way, we suggest an understanding of the scientific in terms of design and the design in terms of science. The idea of "Gestaltung as Synthesis"[17] (Schäffner 2010b) was represented in the *Interdisciplinary Laboratory*, i.e. as its own way of knowledge production: It was not exactly a matter of levelling, but of preserving the disciplinary differences between science and design (cf. Oswalt 2015). How can such an interdisciplinary approach be put into practice?

As mentioned previously, the *Interdisciplinary Laboratory* comprised the priority area "Architectures of Knowledge", which aimed to create reflexivity regarding the research project between science and design, its implementation and realization. The aim was to investigate interdisciplinary research "from within" and "in the making". In this sense, the priority area itself was a response to the demands of scientific policy to obtain increased feedback concerning interdisciplinary research. Our investigation within this priority area posed the specific question of space: What is the impact of space on interdisciplinary research? What are the qualities of space which make it particularly "interdisciplinarity-promoting" or "-impeding"? How can such a space be designed?

We founded the Experimental Zone in order to explore these questions. We redesigned the wing of a building covering an area of 350 m^2, in which forty scientists and designers from different disciplines could work regularly (fig. 1.3–8). Over the course of three years, the space was modified every two months in order to implement different physical, digital and social experimental settings that we designed, built and observed. Participants in the Experimental Zone project were members of the *Interdisciplinary Laboratory*. Participation was voluntary, open to all, and could last from a few hours to several years. Provided that there were free places, it was possible to get a workstation in the Experimental Zone at any time. To become a participant, one had to register with our team. The only requirement was to work within the *Interdisciplinary Laboratory*. There were three modes of participation: As a *regular participant*, as a *flexible participant* and as a *guest*. Those participants who worked in the Experimental Zone for three days or more per week on average were referred to as *regular participants* and assigned a permanent personal workstation. Those who came in less frequently were referred to as *flexible participants* and were able to use one of the flexible desks. The flexible desks were also available for the *guests*, i.e. people who only wanted to work in the Experimental Zone for a short period of time.

Who were the participants in the Experimental Zone? Figure 1.9 shows the ways in which the composition of participants developed between April 2015 and March 2018. The analysis emphasizes the fact that we had a very mobile, changing target group. On average, participants remained in the Experimental Zone for 14.7 months. Twenty participants were involved in the study for a longer period of time (at least 13 experimental settings), sometimes with a few short breaks due to overseas stays or parental leave, for example. These individuals form the core of our target group. The graph clearly shows that the target group underwent three phases of development, namely from April 2015 to February 2016, from March 2016 to October 2016 and from November 2016 onward. The rapid increase in the number of participants in the second phase was due to the fact that many projects were now entering a "hot phase" of implementation, or final spurt. Additionally, the Experimental Zone had established itself as the main base for some projects, often attracting further members. The drop in the number of participants from autumn 2016 onward was related to the end of the two-year duration of many projects—in particular, scientific staff from the humanities left the Experimental Zone, as can be seen in the graph.

17 Own translation.

Experimental Setting	Month, Year	Participants: Total count	Female	Male	Permanent working space	Flexible working space	Design disciplines	Humanities	Natural sciences	Engineering sciences	Scientific staff	Student assistants	Scholarship holders	Other
00 Basic Setting	April 2015	39	21	18	25	14	20	14	4	1	28	9	1	1
01 Activity wall	May 2015	38	20	18	25	13	20	14	3	1	28	9		1
02 Working Topics - Working Methods	June 2015	41	21	20	23	18	20	16	4	1	28	8	2	3
03 Newspaper, Sun & View	July 2015	43	20	23	21	22	20	16	5	1	28	10	2	3
	August 2015	42	20	22	20	22	20	16	6	1	27	10	2	3
04 Navi	September 2015	44	20	24	22	22	20	16	6	2	28	11	2	3
05 Practices	October 2015	40	17	23	23	17	17	16	5	2	27	8	2	3
06 Diary	November 2015	39	18	21	22	17	17	15	5	2	25	9	2	3
07 Work & Play	December 2015	41	19	22	23	18	17	17	5	2	26	10	2	3
	January 2016	43	20	23	24	19	17	19	5	2	28	10	2	3
08 Exchange: Temporal	February 2016	40	19	21	23	17	16	19	4	1	28	9	2	1
	March 2016	45	23	22	27	18	16	23	5	1	28	14	2	1
09 Exchange: Permeable	April 2016	45	22	23	26	22	16	22	5	2	26	14	3	2
	May 2016	48	23	25	25	20	17	24	5	2	28	14	3	3
	June 2016	50	24	26	25	25	19	24	5	3	28	15	4	3
10 Exchange: Hermetic	July 2016	52	26	26	24	28	19	26	5	2	27	17	4	3
	August 2016	52	26	26	23	29	18	25	5	2	26	18	4	3
11 Compartments	September 2016	52	27	25	20	32	19	24	6	3	27	16	3	6
	October 2016	52	27	25	20	32	19	24	6	3	27	17	3	5
12 Strange Objects: Conversation Pieces	November 2016	42	20	22	14	28	17	18	5	3	23	12	3	4
	December 2016	44	22	22	14	30	16	18	6	3	22	13	4	4
13 Tools	January 2017	42	22	20	21	20	18	15	6	4	20	11	4	6
	February 2017	41	22	19	21	21	19	14	6	3	20	13	3	6
	March 2017	42	24	18	21	21	18	16	5	4	20	14	3	5
14 Basic setting II	April 2017	45	27	18	21	23	18	18	5	5	22	14	3	6
	May 2017	44	27	17	21	24	16	18	6	5	22	13	4	5
15 @experimental zone	June 2017	42	23	19	18	24	18	16	4	7	21	13	4	4
	July 2017	43	24	19	19	24	17	16	4	7	22	13	4	4
	August 2017	44	25	19	19	25	17	15	4	7	22	14	4	4
	September 2017	43	24	19	17	26	17	15	5	7	22	14	3	4
16 Clockwork	October 2017	44	25	19	17	27	15	14	5	7	22	14	3	5
	November 2017	43	24	19	16	27	16	14	5	7	21	14	3	5
	December 2017	42	24	18	15	27	16	14	5	7	21	14	3	4
	January 2018	43	24	19	16	27	18	14	5	7	22	14	3	4
	February 2018	43	24	19	17	26	18	15	5	7	22	14	3	4
17 Participatory Setting	March 2018	43	24	19	17	26	18	15	5	7	22	14	3	4

Fig. 1.9: Composition of participants during the 18 settings.

The target group included scientists from the four disciplinary fields previously mentioned: Humanities, natural sciences, engineering sciences and design disciplines. However, the majority of the group consisted of researchers from the humanities and the design disciplines, assuming a relatively balanced relationship to one other. The following disciplines were represented in the Experimental Zone: Architecture, art history, art studies, biology, computer science, cultural studies, design, design theory and research, engineering, English studies, ethnology, forestry and timber industry, game design studies, history, law, life sciences, linguistics, literature, material science, media studies, medicine, philosophy, physics, political science, psychology, science studies, sociology and theatre studies.

The Experimental Zone was used chiefly by scientific staff (the so-called intermediate level, consisting of doctoral and postdoctoral researchers) and student assistants. Although a high number of professors were also involved in the *Interdisciplinary Laboratory*, many retained their jobs at their chairs, attending these on a regular basis. From a gender perspective, the relationship between women and men was relatively balanced. While there were more men than women in the first half of the project, the ratio reversed from September 2016 onward.

Participants in the Experimental Zone worked in many different research projects of the *Interdisciplinary Laboratory*, from "Historical Structural Investigations in the Laboratory", "The Anthropocene Kitchen: A Laboratory Connecting Home and World", and "Image Guidance", "Transdisciplinary Indexing of Cultural-Historical Collections" to "Experiment and Observation" and "gamelab.berlin". Some entered the Experimental Zone as a whole team, others individually. We were interested in exploring how space could foster interdisciplinary research processes in this particular target group. Or, to put it another way: What is the impact of space on such interdisciplinary knowledge practices?

On the one hand, the question of what happens when very different disciplinary cultures meet head on in one place arises. How does interdisciplinary co-presence function? How do the disciplinary working practices react to one other? Can they coexist? On the other, an analysis of interdisciplinarity "in the making" necessitates a focus on the collaborative practices of researchers: How do they work together? What types of interactions can we observe in the Experimental Zone? And how does space affect these? Collaboration in the academic field is subject to structural stresses: The precarious employment structures in force within the field of science ensure a lasting competitive climate (Rogge 2015; Riegraf 2018), in which scientists are obliged to work on their own profiles in order to remain employable and competitive—that is, as soloists following an "ideological individualism", as Bahrdt put it in the 1970s (Bahrdt 1971, 169). At the same time, many research questions require a team effort in order to produce original, innovative scientific results.

Depending on the various phases and practices, researchers need opportunities for retreat and encounter. This process of alternation, in different gradations, proved one of our chief challenges, and led us to formulate the following key questions: What are the characteristics of a collaborative space for soloists? What effect does space have on individual work, but also on collaboration within or among interdisciplinary teams? How do the different research spaces relate to each other, when do they unfold, coexist, dock or merge, when do they interrupt each other? The investigation performed in the Experimental Zone has enabled us to find empirical explanations in response to these questions, which have, in turn, influenced our theoretical positioning.

Part 2

Experimental Design-based Field Research

Each discipline has its own methods and, frequently, a discourse which surrounds them: If the research question is sociological in nature, sociological methods are usually applied. If the focus of the question lies in design[1] research, methods from this field are used. However, what is the best approach to take if the question is located at the interface of social sciences and design? Which methods can be used to examine the question? How can methods from both fields be combined and turned to account when it comes to addressing complex questions between the disciplines? We faced precisely this challenge in our research project, *ArchitecturesExperiments*, as it is impossible to explore the question of the interrelationship between space and knowledge comprehensively using the methods of a single discipline (Baur et al. 2014). How does knowledge impact space, and vice versa? How can the interrelationship between space and knowledge production be understood?

Our aim was to analyze the role played by spatial assemblages in the everyday production of knowledge. In order to investigate these questions, we have developed a new research approach linking sociology and design, which we call "experimental design-based field research". We reconstructed the wing of a building covering 350 m^2, allowing forty scientists from different disciplines to work there regularly. This space was redesigned every two months with the aim of testing its effects on different collaborative and individual working practices. The potential impact was determined by using a set of qualitative and quantitative observation instruments.

This setup created several areas of tension, at the crux of which the project is located: Is the approach an experiment or a field research project? Is it hypothesis-based or explorative? How can insights be gained: Through optimization or irritation? As yet, the interface of design and sociology is largely unexplored and untested, and experiments in qualitative empirical social research are the exception to the rule. On the other hand, empirical observations supported by a methodological discourse are rarely used in design to test the intuitions of designers and architects. To what extent can such qualitative design experiments prove relevant as far as the exploration and design of the spaces of scientific practice is concerned? Which methodological challenges do they entail? And which instruments are best suited to this purpose?

1 We use the term "design" for the translation of the more complex German concept Gestaltung as an overall designation for the disciplines of architecture and design (Mareis 2010; Schäffner 2010b).

Fig. 2.1–3: Building wing before (2.1), during (2.2) and after (2.3) reconstruction for the experiment.
Photo © Julia Blumenthal (2.1), Henrike Rabe (2.2), Fabian Scholz (2.3)

1 Experimentalization of Space

In order to be able to experiment with the design of the space, we developed a research method involving regular design interventions. For this purpose, we created the Experimental Zone, a research area of 350 m^2 designed for the work of forty scientists. To make room for the experiment, we transformed the fourth floor of a wing of a Humboldt-Universität building, demolishing all interior walls and installing a ceiling rail system supplying the space with electricity and lighting (figs. 2.1-3). In this way, we created an open space that allowed maximum flexibility in the arrangement of furniture, partitions and instruments. In addition, flexible furniture was designed and built for the scientists' workstations (fig. 2.4).

The experimentalization process took place in the context of experimental settings, each lasting two to three months, which we designed, built, and observed. Between April 2015 and April 2018, a total of eighteen experimental settings were created (→ see Catalog of the Experimental Settings, page 52). The settings included e.g. physical configurations, instructions and digital interventions. In contrast to commercial design projects, it was by no means our aim to just optimize the conditions, but, instead, to also deliberately create irritations in order to gain insights.

1.1 A Design-based Qualitative Experiment

The interdisciplinary nature of the research project resulted in a new scientific approach characterized by a combination of partly contradictory methods of knowledge creation—experimental and field research. While the concept of field research is relatively unambiguous, involving the collection of empirical data by means of observation and questioning in a "natural" context, the concept of "experiment" requires some explanation. How do we interpret the concept of experiment? A diverse range of interpretations of the term exists in the natural sciences, the humanities and in the design disciplines, and this not only between the disciplines but within the disciplines themselves (Marguin et al. 2019). What sort of experimental culture is our approach based on?

As the literary scholar Gunhild Berg notes, the traditional definition of a scientific experiment still shapes the term today (Berg 2013, 140). "By performing series of measurements under continually varied but accurately known conditions a large volume of quantitative experimental data is obtained, and from these the attempt is then made to discern a regular correlation between the measured values and to represent this correlation by an equation" (Westphal 1968, 1). Referring to the ideal case of a laboratory experiment, the "quality criteria of scientificness [in the sense of reproducibility, standardizability and measurability formulated by Karl Popper"[2] are crucial (Kühl 2009, 535). The experiment primarily serves to test causalities, which can be statistically established as a law through experimental repetitions. For this purpose, variables are isolated and manipulated by the researchers and tested in an artificial, strongly controlled environment.

This scientific understanding of the experiment is found in design, but also in the social sciences: In architecture, it becomes particularly visible in the engineering tradition (Moravánszky and Kirchengast 2011). Variables such as form, construction, material, wind flow and light are tested either in the context of experimental buildings or on the basis of simulations or physical models (idem). In interaction design, it appears in usability studies: Eyetracking[3] is used to find out how visitors explore a website visually, and where their attention falls most frequently (Nielsen and Pernice 2010). In the social sciences, quantitative experimental studies assume this type of scientific character (Kühl 2009). In this context, socio-psychological experiments that investigate social behavior, such as the Milgram experiment (Milgram 1963), are particularly well known.

However, experimental approaches which distance themselves from this traditional scientific understanding can be observed both in the design disciplines and in the social sciences. In architecture and design, the concept of "experimentation" or "experimental" also refers to an artistically influenced approach, to an "exploratory, trying, unusual procedure" (Jäger 1997, 546). In general, no hypothesis is formulated, but the focus is placed on improvisation and the opening up of new worlds (Ishigami 2014; Sailer 2019). In the chiefly qualitative social sciences, the experiment is used as a heuristic device in an exploratory phase of research (Kleining 1986, 724): It is a matter of intervening in a social circumstance in order to explore its structure, e.g. by means of a

2 Own translation.
3 Eye movement recording.

Fig. 2.4: Workstation. Photo © Julia Blumenthal

crisis experiment (Garfinkel 1973). Such a selective disturbance in the field and, in particular, the resulting interactions, are associated more closely with improvisation as opposed to systematic experimentation.

An ambiguous understanding of the concept of experiment prevailed in our research project. How can this interpretative knot be unraveled? Stefan Kühl distinguishes between four types of experiment in social research: Laboratory experiments, quasi-experiments, simulation games, field and crisis experiments, which "do not meet the requirements of reproducibility, standardizability and measurability in the same way"[4] (Kühl 2009, 535). How should our research project be characterized?

In the Experimental Zone, design-based experimentation in the sense of the inventive exploration and design of spatial constellations, was integrated within a systematic empirical investigation. From a socio-scientific point of view, this resulted in an amalgamation of quasi-experiment and field experiment. On the one hand, it resembled a quasi-experiment insofar as we intervened regularly, changing one variable at a time, but many of the disturbing variables were difficult to control. On the other, it could be described as a field experiment insofar as a "natural environment" was created in the space we staged, i.e. converted and furnished. What were the characteristics of our experimental setup?

4 Own translation.

1.
Limited time periods: The experiment began in April 2015 and ended in March 2018. In these three years, eighteen different experimental settings were created over a fixed period of time—four, eight or twelve weeks. This means that we performed many small, time-limited experiments in rapid succession.

2.
Natural environment: With the Experimental Zone, we created a large space in which scientists set up their regular workplaces. This allowed a natural environment to form in which working routines unfolded. For this reason, according to Kühl, it clearly represented a field experiment. However —and this is where the amalgamation begins— we deliberately refurbished a staged object of investigation for this purpose, in which we regularly intervened. What are the different variables of the experiment?

3.
Independent variables: Within the framework of experimental settings, various adjustments were made in order to manipulate the spatial and temporal conditions of the research approach, namely the size of spatial areas (large—small), the distance between workstations (near—far), the connectivity of spatial areas (directly accessible—not directly accessible), the visibility (visible—not visible), the noise level (loud—quiet; also depending on the time of day), the readability of the space (chaotic—ordered), the communication in the space (virtual—face-to-face; professional—private), the spatial arrangement of working methods (individual work—teamwork), the artifacts (enabling—restricting practices), and temporal regulations. The design process of the experimental settings was inspired by Japanese design practices (Geipel 2010), i.e. numerous variants were tested as a model (→ see Collection 3, page 66). The various proposals were tested, photographed and discussed in the so-called "model apparatus" (→ see page 47).

4.
Dependent variables: While we manipulated the independent variables mentioned above as far as the experimental settings were concerned, the dependent variables consisted in the practices of the scientists. In other words, with the help of a set of different observation instruments, we observed the effects of the design-based interventions on the participants of the Experimental Zone, focusing in particular on their collaboration with one another and on the enactment of their practices.

5.
Confounding variables: As stated above, the Experimental Zone resembled a quasi-experiment because we had "very limited possibilities to control all confounding variables"[5] (Kühl 2009, 535). The first confounding variable was caused by our particular target group, whose composition we could not influence. The Experimental Zone was open to all employees within the *Interdisciplinary Laboratory*. The participation was based on a voluntary decision and was coupled with the use of a workplace within the Experimental Zone. Firstly, this meant that we could not control the development of the target group over time, i.e. the precise durations of the participants' involvement in the experiment, their original disciplines and their status, etc. The second confounding variable was the fact that we were unable to control the participants' histories before their time in the Experimental Zone. Some had a common history and knew each other (well) before participating in the experiment. They had studied or worked together, sometimes for several years. This constituted an important confounding variable which had to be taken into account in the analysis of the interactions or collaborations.

6.
Control group: Instead of a control group, we preferred to draw a comparison between the different experimental settings. Our aim—and here the design understanding of the concept of "experiment" comes to the fore—was to test and compare different designs in an explorative manner within a long-term study, according to the "trial and error" logic which characterizes the design practice.

In this respect, our experiment combines a deductive with an inductive approach: Specific design-based hypotheses are formulated, deductively

5 Own translation.

Fig. 2.5–7: Experimental Zone between two settings. Photos © Henrike Rabe

tested and analyzed for each setting, which is based on a hypothesis expressed in the design of the Experimental Zone. The setting 05, "Practices" was based, among other things, on the assumption that a high density of workplaces promotes collaborative working practices and was accordingly designed as a dense arrangement of tables on a minimal footprint, more precisely in five directly adjacent table groups (→ see Collection 1, page 62). However, the observations in the setting provided indications not only of the relationship between physical proximity and collaboration, but also of the growing incompatibility of the design with the scientific practices of the participants. Therefore, following this analysis, we decided to investigate the spatial dimensions of this "co-presence" more specifically. This forms an inductive approach in the sense of grounded theory (Glaser and Strauss 1967), in which the research question is gradually and exploratively developed from the basis of the field work. Following the design theorist Claudia Mareis' characterization of designing with the help of a so-called morphological box, we understand the Experimental Zone as an experimental system in the sense of a "material, open-ended spatiotemporal arrangement [. . .· (Rheinberger 2001, 22), in which creative coincidences and events can be systematically framed and methodically promoted, but not forced. Rather, the ability and intuition, the virtuosity of the experimenter (Rheinberger 2008), as well as the experimental setup itself with its material-medial stubbornness play a significant role in the production of new facts" (Mareis 2019, 323–324).

The interdisciplinary question of the relationship between space and knowledge practices led us to discover a new interdisciplinary experimental format, an experimental field research approach at the interface of social science and design. But how does one structure an inductive-deductive project like this in everyday research, and what are the methodological challenges faced?

1.2 An Interdisciplinary Procedure Model

The unusual and complex approach required a strict framework of implementation—not only to ensure systematics and comparability, but also to coordinate ourselves, an interdisciplinary and non-hierarchical team. The complexity of the procedure consisted particularly in the fact that three experimental settings were treated in parallel: While the previous setting was evaluated, the current setting was created and future settings were designed and planned.

We have therefore developed a procedure model (→ see page 69), which illuminates the cycles of conception, planning, implementation and analysis, as well as the simultaneity of these processes and the precise interleaving of the three disciplines (fig. 2.8). Although our research and design process was thoroughly interdisciplinary, with the sociologist participating in the design discussions and the designers and architects co-developing and using observation and analysis tools, specific disciplines held greater responsibility for certain phases than the others. Design and planning were under the care of the design disciplines, while the social scientists were responsible for observation and analysis. Furthermore, the model embodies the oscillation between the inductive and deductive approaches which characterized our approach.

2 Methodological Challenges of a Science-Ethnographic and "Single-sited" Field Research

In addition to the ambiguous conceptual categorization of the experiment conducted, the experimental arrangement involved further methodological challenges: Firstly, in view of the project's science-ethnographic dimension, secondly, in terms of the limitation of observations to a single location, and thirdly as regards the protection of scientists' personal data.

2.1 The Question of Reflexivity

The Experimental Zone formed a specific field of investigation insofar as the target group consisted of colleagues and members of the research team. This posed a methodological challenge for the study, because investigations in ethnology are usually conducted on other groups and with a view from the outside. How can one investigate one's peers? And how can one investigate oneself?

As already mentioned in Part 1, we locate our research in the field of Laboratory Studies, which explores science "in the making" from an

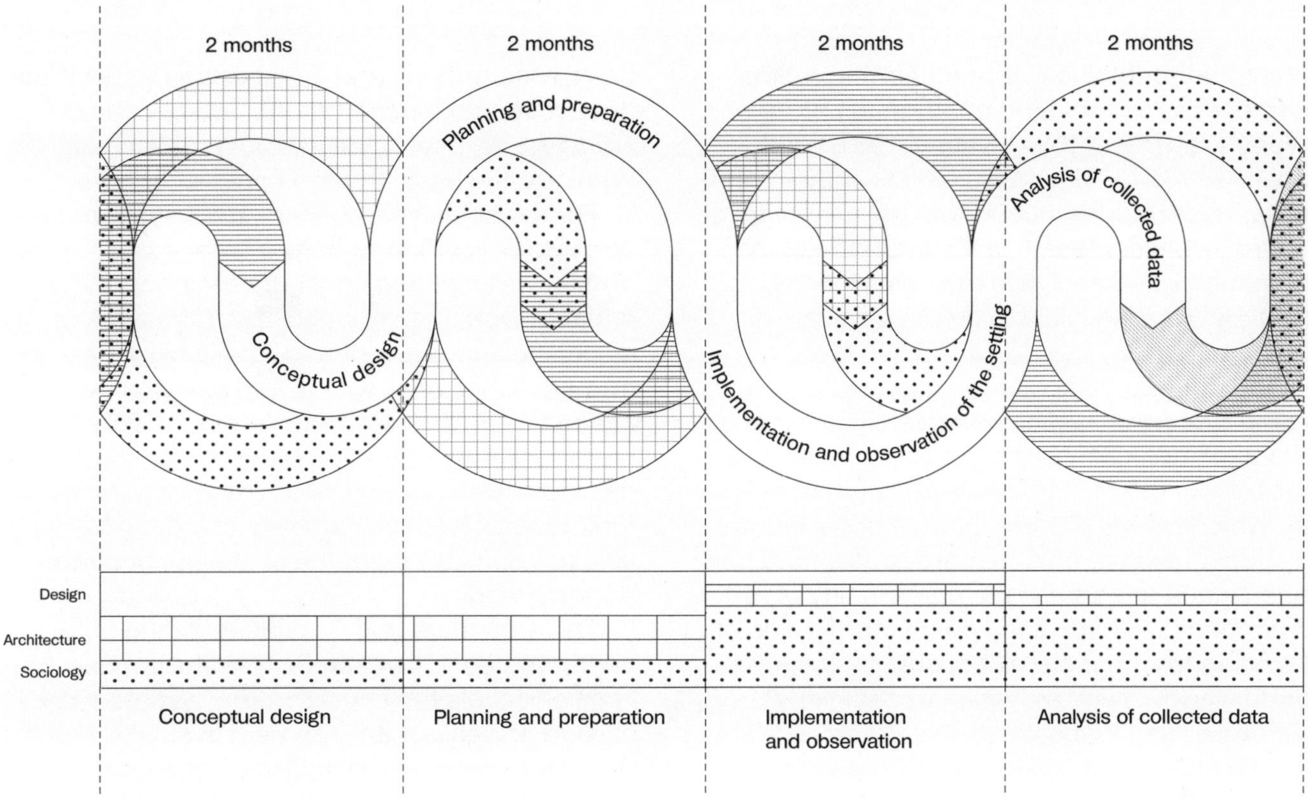

Fig. 2.8: Procedure model of the investigation.

ethnomethodological or practice-theoretical perspective. However, in contrast to Latour and Woolgar (1979) or Knorr Cetina (1981) we do not observe "exotic" natural scientists in their "unfamiliar" laboratories, but concentrate, instead, on interdisciplinary teams at the interface of the humanities and design in our own working context. How is it possible to create a certain distance or "a new view" in such a situation, in which the scientists observed emanate from the same disciplines as the observers (Latour and Woolgar 1979, 24)? In the social sciences, this problem is referred to as the question of reflexivity, which we will discuss in more detail below.

For some time now, numerous attempts have been made to address the positionality of researchers, their influence on the production of knowledge, and their relationship to the group under review, such as "reflexive sociology" (Bourdieu and Wacquant 1992; Bourdieu 2004; Camic et al. 2011), "reflexive anthropology" (Clifford and Marcus 1986), and "reflexive methodology" (Alvesson and Sköldberg 2016; Knoblauch 2018). In our research project, this problem has developed in two main respects: Firstly, we addressed the question of the positionality of researchers and their influence on the field of investigation. "In the course of the spread of the "interpretative paradigm" (Schütz 2004) in social research, the distinction between first order constructions, i.e. everyday ones, and second order constructions, i.e. scientific ones"[6] became common (Knoblauch 2018, 228). Or, phrased differently: What sort of knowledge about knowledge do we produce? How can we reflect and reveal our specific subjective perspective? The reflections found in reflexive methodologies are very helpful here, in that they take the various dimensions of positionality into account: In addition to subjective self-reflexivity, a reflection on the social conditions of one's own scientific habitus as well as on one's own basic theoretical assumptions must be performed.[7]

Our self-reflection focused particularly on the interdisciplinary constellation and the various basic assumptions and questions it raised: What does research mean from the perspective of architecture, interaction design and sociology? What are the basic theoretical assumptions?

For the social researchers, the central question was how different actors span spaces: How do they arrange and configure their own differentiated workspaces within the framework of a specific and given infrastructure? And how do they work in it, on it, with it, and perhaps even against it? Empirical studies are considered important to systematically determine the everyday inventiveness with which researchers design their research space, but also how they, as soloists, spatially meet the challenge of collaborative work.

The architects and designers, on the other hand, wanted to investigate how the spaces, objects and tools they design affect people. How can we design our environment in such a way that it facilitates a variety of activities and uses, e.g. promotes both collaborative and individual ways of working? They want their designs not only to meet people's needs, but also to surprise them, stimulate social change, try radically new things.

This brief comparison shows how different the perspectives and questions of social research and design are. How do we manage not to talk at cross purposes in this context? In our constellation, different understandings of science (What is science?) but also different functions of science (Why science?) collided. Based on these reflections, our approach toward a new form of interdisciplinary spatial research and design has emerged.

Secondly, we have thought a great deal about how to deal with the reflexivity of the participants: Can we be more reflexive in this research context than the group under review? Or, as the social anthropologist Jörg Niewöhner asks, "Will [we· have anything new to add to the natives?" (Niewöhner 2016, 3). From the field of anthropology has come what Dominic Boyer calls "third-generation reflexive anthropology: *Studying sideways, epistemic partnership, para-sitism*" (Boyer

6 Following Bourdieu's statement: "Social research is a social construction of a social construction" (Bourdieu 2004, 88).

7 Within the framework of reflexive methodology, Knoblauch advocates going even further, in the sense that he espouses an "empirical theory of science". In concrete terms, this meant filming our own evaluation sessions and evaluating them afterwards ourselves, for instance, i.e. "absorbing oneself when interpreting and then interpreting one's own interpretation" (own translation of Knoblauch 2018, 229). In our case, we were first observed by Stefan Solleder, a fellow researcher at the Cluster of Excellence, and secondly, we systematically collected all the physical documents associated with our collaboration, such as sketches, and archived them both analogously and digitally.

Fig. 2.9: Co-laborative approach: Participants and research team designing an experimental setting together. Photo © Friedrich Schmidgall

2015). These approaches have further developed the epistemological discourse surrounding the relationship to the group under review and shaped our approach to the question of reflexivity. In principle, all three approaches are about researching not about but together with the participants.

Studying sideways goes back to Ulf Hannerz's research on foreign correspondents, in which he modulated Laura Nader's critical statement on "study up" into a proposal on "study sideways" (1998), providing "a method of reflexive connectivity that takes the intimacy of shared practices and concerns as a baseline for the development of dialogues that help to interilluminate (both critically and affirmatively) the techniques both kinds of practitioners have developed" (Boyer 2015, 17f.). *Epistemic partnership* or para-ethnographic refers to the anthropological knowledge the observed experts possess and use in their exchange with the observers. Both Douglas R. Holmes and George E. Marcus as well as Boyer strongly advocate the integration of such knowledge into the scientific analysis (Marcus 1995; Holmes and Marcus 2008). They developed the method of *para-site*, a series of experimental formats to enable the exchange between the observed experts and the observers (for example in the form of workshops as deliberate *disruptions* in the field research process). This literature inspired us greatly, in that it proposes a new way of dealing with the group under review, characterized by transparency and feedback.

In this context, we follow Niewöhner's approach of *co-laborative research*, which further specifies these relationships between observers and those under investigation. While collaboration refers to an "ethical, political and public mode of anthropological research", co-laboration (with hyphen) is an "epistemic mode of anthropological research" (Niewöhner 2016, 10): It refers to "conducting joint epistemic work, experimenting with formats, without necessary aiming for a shared goal" (idem). How did we use this approach in our research project?

We experimented with different strategies to involve the participants of the Experimental Zone in our investigation as much as possible without affecting their own research:

— Firstly, we communicated regularly with the participants, both via email and via our own Slack workspace, which was used for collective discussions particularly during the final settings. After each experimental setting, we also used a questionnaire to gather feedback from the participants.
— Secondly, we organized regular meetings with the participants: E.g. for the presentation and discussion of our revised research design, or for the introduction of new settings.
— Thirdly, we ensured the constant visualization of our observations on pinboards in the Experimental Zone, naturally in an anonymized form. While setting-related observations were displayed in a comparable format on some pinboards, other pinboards contained overview data or work in progress analyses. In the final months of the project, we digitized these reflections and made them available to the participants on a website.
— Fourthly, we conducted workshops with the participants in which they could reflect on their working practices. In autumn 2017, we designed and realized an experimental setting in a participatory workshop series (fig. 2.9).
— Fifthly, we also worked in the Experimental Zone ourselves. This presence made us approachable and accessible.

Co-laborative research according to Niewöhner has clear methodological implications, especially in the disclosure of the observers' research questions. The moment this was revealed to the participants, their involvement increased. As researchers, we could only benefit from their self-reflection and curiosity and incorporate it into our insights. In this sense, co-laborative research is a plea for collective thinking.

2.2 Single-sited Ethnographic Approach

A second challenge posed by the research project constitutes the limitation of the experiment to the fourth-floor wing of a building. This research design was implemented not only as a result of financial constraints, but also on the grounds of the data protection problem which did not allow us to examine the entire *Interdisciplinary Laboratory* or building. The resulting focus on a specific part of the building meant a double limitation for both a) the design and b) the field research.

a) The **spatial limitations**, meant that our architectural scope was rather restricted. We were able to test different arrangements of walls, mobile partitions and furniture within the outer walls, but could not experiment with the immalleable properties of space such as room height, windows, entrances and technical connections.

b) Within the context of experimental **field research**, we adopted a single-sited ethnographic approach in which we were able to realize an in-depth study over three years. However, such an intense focus on a single locus in today's globalized field of research raises the question of a *multi-site* (Marcus 1995). It goes without saying that our participants' knowledge production not only took place in the Experimental Zone. On some days, they also worked in other places such as the library or the laboratory. In the sense of a multi-sited ethnographic approach, it would have been exciting to follow the movements of ideas, people and artifacts: How is an idea developed through the different stages of emergence, discussion, presentation, etc.? But this was not the subject of our enquiry. We didn't pursue individual ideas, but rather explored the effects of the constellations designed by us on knowledge production, and this is why we opted for a single-sited ethnographic approach. Independently of this, we do not regard the Experimental Zone as a detached entity, but as a place anchored in existing infrastructures, embedded in the *Interdisciplinary Laboratory* itself, in the Berlin university landscape and in the international field of academe (→ see Part One). This anchoring was taken into account in different ways in the analysis, e.g. in the analysis of the target group, but also in the analysis of the equipment.

2.3 Data Protection

Due to data protection laws, it is extremely difficult to conduct field research into one's own colleagues in Germany, particularly as regards collecting personalized data. The development of a comprehensive data protection concept thus required many meetings, hundreds of emails and many preliminary versions, taking over a year to complete.[8] However, this initial concept became obsolete after around a year of observation, when the said methods shifted from purely quantitative to more qualitative in nature.

Both data protection concepts—the first and the second—were based on the fact that use of the Experimental Zone was voluntary, meaning it was not necessary to enter this wing for any activity in the *Interdisciplinary Laboratory* (workplaces, kitchen, rest areas and the library were also outside the Experimental Zone). Furthermore, the success of the concept rested on the fact that the Experimental Zone could only be entered if the participants had been informed of all the details of the observation in advance and had given their prior written consent.

The first data protection concept was aimed at ensuring the protection of personal data with regards to largely quantitative, automated observation methods such as the *Diary* software, RFID tracking and anonymous surveys. From a legal perspective, linking the personal data generated by *Diary* and RFID tracking posed a major challenge. Data protection was achieved by the following measures: Firstly, the data was collected pseudonymously—also here on the basis of explicit consent. For security reasons, the data collected was subsequently collated on a separate server, which was only accessible to those responsible for the project. Access by superiors was explicitly excluded. Information via which identities could theoretically be established was stored separately and locked. De-pseudonymization could only take place temporarily and in the presence of the data protection officer. The concept also included anonymizing the personal data at the end of the project and destroying the list of actual names.

It became necessary to review the data protection concept when qualitative observation methods such as participant observation and interviews were introduced. At the same time, the limitations of the methods *Diary* and RFID tracking in relation to our research questions became obvious. This resulted in the decision not to realize the planned link between the two data sets and to make the data collected by Diary and RFID tracking completely anonymous by destroying the list of actual names. Furthermore, as far as the additional qualitative survey methods (participant observation, interviews, mental maps, autophotography) were concerned, the data protection concept was supplemented by the following measures: Separate written consent was obtained from the participants. The data collected was stored on a separate and locked hard disk which was only accessible to the two sociologists in the team. Access by superiors or other persons was explicitly excluded here too. Personal data was anonymized at the end of the project and the list of actual names was destroyed.

3 Mixed Methods Approach with a Visual Focus

After clarifying the specifics of an experimental field research, in this section the observation instruments will be presented: How can the interrelations between space and knowledge production be investigated? After a presentation of the set of instruments for data collection, we would like to discuss novel instruments for data collection and analysis developed in the project.

3.1 Instruments Used in the Investigation

Our project, which lies at the interface of architecture, interaction design and social science, has a special potential for the advancement of the methods of spatial research: Some noted spatial researchers have recently deemed an “integration of different methodologies and methods of spatial research necessary”[9] (Baur et al. 2014). Our research in the Experimental Zone constitutes a contribution to just this type of integrated interdisciplinary methodology relating to spatial research.[10]

We pursued a mixed methods approach, using qualitative as well as quantitative instruments of spatial and practice research. The interdisciplinary nature of the study resulted in a wide range of instruments, insofar as both traditional methods of social research and of architectural analysis as well as hybrid forms were used. Some methods have not proved their worth in implementation;

8 The data protection concept was developed in cooperation with the data protection expert and Associated Investigator Prof. Jan Roggenkamp and the data protection officer and staff representative of the Humboldt-Universität in Berlin.

9 Own translation.

10 This brand of integrated interdisciplinary methodology relating to spatial research is further developed in the Collaborative Research Center 1265 “Re-Figuration of Spaces” at Technische Universität Berlin (www.sfb1265.de).

nonetheless, they, and their shortcomings, are explained here for purposes of documentation.

In order to explore the interrelations between space and knowledge production on an empirical basis, we focused particularly on three objects of observation: Physical-material spatial arrangements, spatial practice, and research practices. The attempt to analytically integrate this heterogeneous data is one of the central contributions of our spatial research project, insofar as such an integration within spatial research is still largely terra incognita.

Observation Object 1: Physical-material Spatial Arrangements

Different instruments, particularly those drawn from architecture, permitted the documentation of the physical-material spatial arrangements. Firstly, a **mapping of the spatial arrangement** of all immobile and mobile elements in the Experimental Zone was conducted on a weekly basis. The location of each wall and each individual piece of furniture, from the desk to the pinboard to the chair and stool, was drawn in a digital floor plan. This way, the extent to which these physical-material arrangements underwent gradual shifts became observable.

Secondly, a **photographic documentation** of the arrangement of all immobile and mobile elements in the Experimental Zone from 38 fixed angles was created (→ see Collections 2, 16 and 17, pages 64, 166 and 168). The Experimental Zone was photographed twice per setting.

Thirdly, **architectural models** of every experimental setting were built (→ see Collection 1, page 62). The so-called *model apparatus* was available for this purpose, a multi-functional instrument developed by us and used not only for empirical purposes but also for design and visualization (fig. 2.10). The apparatus consisted of a table with a model of the Experimental Zone on a scale of 1:20 and a scaffold suspended from the ceiling, which contained two LED light panels directed at the model, as well as a projector and a camera. The model, built from a durable material, initially contained only the fixed, unchangeable elements of the Experimental Zone, i.e. the outer walls with the windows and entrances, the floor, the columns, the sanitary facilities and the kitchenette. In addition, miniatures of the movable elements of the Experimental Zone were prepared, i.e. tables, chairs, partitions, etc. The model fulfilled the following three functions: Firstly, it was used as a *working model* for designing new experimental settings, with different proposals and variants tested, photographed and discussed. The working model was also used for the participatory design of the seventeenth setting: During a joint workshop, participants were able to improvise using the model, experimenting with their ideas and discussing them with their fellows. Secondly, the model was used as a *visualization model* to make the data collected come alive for the participants in accordance with our *co-laborative* approach. With the help of the integrated projector, floor-plan-related data was projected vertically from above into the model. The positions of the participants, recorded by RFID tracking, and the manually recorded movements and interactions and simulations were visualized and made visible via the model. Thirdly, the model was used as an *analysis model* in order to review and analyze the data collected in three dimensions. In contrast with two-dimensional drawings, this method permitted us to view the movements and interactions within the space in their three-dimensional context, and to relate them to the vertical dimension of space.

Fourthly and finally, the method of **auto-photography** was used (fig. 2.11), in which, the participants take a photo themselves in accordance with the researchers' instructions (Dirksmeier 2009, 2013). We carried out two rounds of auto-photography: The first during the ninth setting, "Exchange: Permeable" with seventeen participants, and the second during the fourteenth setting "Basic Setting II" with twenty-one participants. Eight participants were involved in both rounds, all others took part in only one round. According to the protocol, participants were interviewed individually and given the following verbal instruction: "Could you please take a picture of your workplace?" The results show the spatial arrangements of the respective participants' workplaces. As the participants themselves could choose the angle, the perspective and the width of the area depicted, this method granted us subjective insights into the individual research space.

Fig. 2.10 Model apparatus. Photo © Fabian Scholz

Observation Object 2: Spatial Practice
A second object of observation was the participants' spatial practice. This refers to the manner in which the participants moved and interacted in the space and how they experienced and perceived it. We collected both quantitative and qualitative data in line with our mixed method approach. A combination of several methods was used to observe movements and interactions: A quantitative **tracking** method with RFID[11] tags was combined with the qualitative manual mapping of the movements and interactions in a floor plan and additional simulations.[12] The tracking method, a real-time localization system using RFID tags, captured the location of participants in the room and precisely where and with whom they interacted. RFID tracking proved attractive for our investigation because it had previously enabled other researchers to achieve a systematic analysis of movements and interactions (Mastrandrea et al. 2015; Eberle et al. 2017). However, the localization of this technology proved too imprecise for small premises such as the Experimental Zone (the above-mentioned studies were conducted in much larger facilities such as exhibition halls, where no such precision was needed). Although we optimized the calculation of the positions several times and improved the investigation protocol, we were unable to collect any meaningful data using this technology. The

11 Here, the real-time localization system of the OpenBeacon project was used (www.openbeacon.org).
12 Visibility graph- and agent-based simulation was applied with help of the depthmapX software by Space Syntax (Penn and Turner 2002). In the visibility graph analysis, the number of points visible from any one standpoint in the building is calculated. The findings are shown in the form of a heat map, whereby red stands for a particularly high and blue for a particularly low degree of visibility.In the agent-based analysis software, agents representing the participants are released into the environment. Their movement and choice of the next destination is informed by the visibility analysis.

second collection method, the manual **mapping of movements and interactions**, proved more reliable, albeit point-by-point and thus not end-to-end. The movements and interactions were documented graphically in a floor plan during several weekly time windows (→ see Collections 11 and 12, pages 140 and 142). In addition, we used the architectural method of **simulation according to Space Syntax** for the investigation of the movements, specifically the visibility graph and agent-based simulations (→ see Collections 10 and 13, pages 138 and 144). The architectural researchers at Space Syntax have developed a comprehensive methodology since the 1990s and conducted empirical research in different building types to explore the "social logic of space" (Hillier and Hanson 1984; Penn and Hillier 1992; Sailer and Penn 2009). Specifically, this simulation method can provide indications of what the scientists see, how they move and ultimately how this affects their interactions.

Methodologically speaking, the comparison of the different results is relevant, for example comparing the mapped movements and interactions with the simulation of visibility (→ see Part Four, page 125). We regard the synthesis of such heterogeneous data as a direct contribution to an integrated interdisciplinary methodology of spatial research.

For the investigation of spatial practice, we also used two traditional methods drawn from social research and human geography: Explorative problem-centered interviews and mental map interviews. These methods have enabled us to collect "qualitative spatial data" (Dangschat 2014, 973ff.) for the analysis of "experienced space". **Problem-centered interviews** were conducted at the beginning of the research project in the fifth setting, "Practices", with twenty-one participants, and acted as explorative interviews to investigate the understanding of space and its use in the context of scientific work. In the further course of the research project, we conducted two rounds of **mental map interviews**. Using the geographical method of mental mapping (also known as *cognitive mapping*), spatial perceptions of the subjects are collected on the basis of drawings (Lynch 1960; Shobe and Banis 2010; Smiley 2013; Götz and Holmén 2018). We used an investigation protocol with a white sheet of paper—i.e. without a template such as a floor plan—and various colored pencils. In the first round, which we conducted in the ninth setting, "Exchange: Permeable", with twenty-two participants, we asked participants about the spatialization of their research practices (→ see Collection 9, page 136), but also about the atmosphere in the Experimental Zone (→ see Collection 15, page 164). Our aim was to generate "spatial narratives" (Dangschat 2014, 975) about the working context.

In the second round, which we conducted in the fifteenth setting, "@experimentalzone", with twenty-one participants, we asked respondents about the digital workplace (→ see Collection 6, page 102). We were interested in the perception of virtual scientific spaces—assuming they could even be described as such. This method has proved itself in both cases insofar as it allowed us to glean information about the participants' understanding of space.

Methodologically, it should be noted here that the reinforcement of the dichotomy between physical and virtual space could have strongly influenced our results and ultimately reflected our understanding of space as researchers at the time. Here, we must face the common methodological challenge of an unintentional interference with the results via the research question itself. However, since the group under review largely consisted of individuals who were, simultaneously, experts on the question of mediality and medialization (media scientists, interaction designers, information scientists), our question around "virtual space" was questioned and discussed animatedly during the interviews. The collaborative dimension of our field research is clearly expressed in this informal approach by the participants to our questions and research.

Observation Object 3: Research Practices

Closely related to the question of spatial practice is the third and final object of observation: The participants' research practices. This object of observation is analyzed separately from the others, as we collected a great deal of data regarding research practices which had no direct spatial connection. Here, too, a mixed method approach was adopted.

Firstly, a systematic recording of the participants' software usage was facilitated by the use of the **Diary**[13] software developed in the Cluster of Excellence. *Diary* was installed locally at the participants' computers in order to determine which programs they use, how often and for how long.

Secondly, **participant observation** was carried out in the Experimental Zone between April 2016 and April 2018 in order to collect qualitative data on the knowledge practices and their materiality (→ see Part One, page 23). For this purpose, the observations were first noted by hand, and later recorded using the software *empiric.assemblage*[14]. Here, the main focus was placed on the corporeality of the scientists, the artifacts and the routines. The method served to record the continuity between the settings. By focusing on the routines, an attempt was made to comprehend the implicit rules of the Experimental Zone which have prevailed over the course of the various settings. The participant observation also served as an important addition to the mapping of movements and interactions, in that it enabled us to understand the substance of the same, and relationships associated with them. The method is also an important tool for documenting co-laborative research and the self-reflexiveness of researchers (→ see page 41–42).

Thirdly and lastly, we conducted **interviews-at-the-computer** (→ see Collections 7 and 8, pages 104–107). Our aim was to gain insights into the digital working practices of the participants in the Experimental Zone, since this could not be achieved by participant observation alone. We were interested in how the digital research space unfolds and how participants structure the same. Our research on knowledge production made it essential to learn more about the concrete approach to the computer (or other digital devices). Since the digital workplace is an intimate area, it was necessary to embed research into this within the formal framework of an interview, yet in a manner which would elicit responses from the participants. We filmed the interviews with a camera which recorded the participants' screen and hands. We conducted a total of 23 inteviews-at-the-computer over a longer period, namely between August 2016 and May 2017.

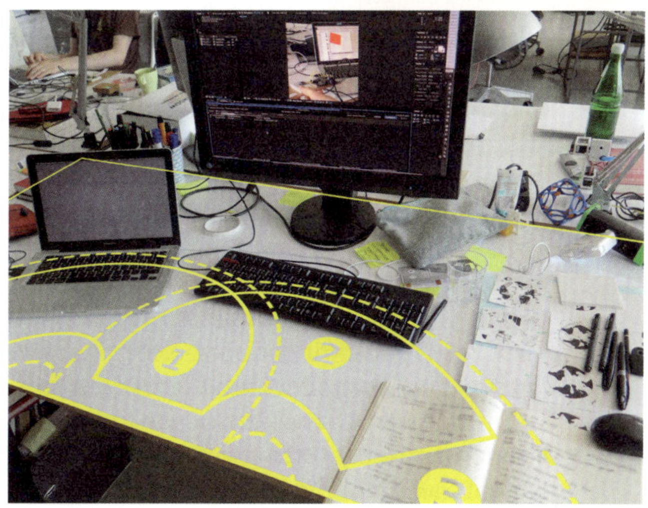

Fig. 2.11: Auto-photography.
Fig. 2.12: Color-coding (blue = digital, orange = analog).
Fig. 2.13: Analysis of space within reach.

13 The Diary software was developed by Sammy David, Friedrich Schmidgall, Christian Stein and Benjamin Thomack.

14 With the empiric.assemblage software developed by Anouk Hoffmeister and Séverine Marguin, observations can be directly recorded digitally and are categorized and searchable (Hoffmeister et al. 2018).

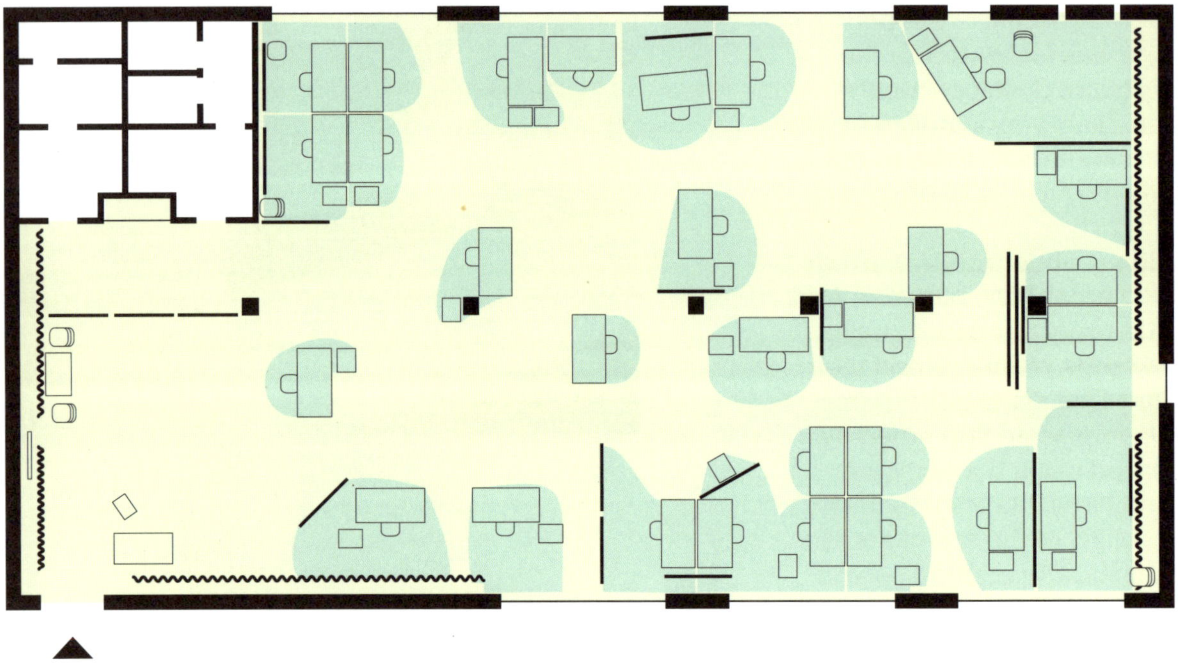

Fig. 2.14: Analysis of spatial appropriation (green = individual territories, yellow = common area). Drawing © Dimitra Megas

This extensive set of observation instruments allowed us to study the three interwoven focal points (physical-material spatial arrangement, spatial practice, research practice). While most collection instruments ran more or less continuously through all settings, interviews and autophotography were rather sporadic for pragmatic reasons, such as the heavy workload of both participants and ourselves. A final retrospective questionnaire was conducted in order to gather the participant's feedback on the comparison of settings. Thirty-three current and former participants took part. The extensive survey included questions regarding how the different physical arrangements were experienced, interactions, the workplace and instruments. Methodologically, the question of retrospective recollection arises. Many participants noted that it was difficult for them to recall previous settings. This was expressed in the results to the extent that many questions were answered with a neutral rating. Here, memorable and striking impressions came to the fore above all.

3.2 Novel Instruments for Data Collection and Analysis

In order to conclude this presentation of our methods, we would like to finish with some comments on the interdisciplinary character of our methodological approach. This reflects the customary formal approaches of our respective professional activities: While, for social researchers, the primary tool is the word, for architects and designers, this takes the form of the visual realm. In social research, data is collected primarily in text form or based on statistics. Visual material, particularly photography and videography, is also included to a certain extent, but is rapidly transposed into a literal description and analysis. In design practice and research, on the other hand, the production of visual material such as drawings, prototypes, physical and virtual models, photos, sketches, renderings or simulations predominates. This formal difference between a textual and a visual approach results in a differentiated handling of concepts on the one hand and a similarly differentiated approach to form, model and image on the other, both of which can, by turns, frustrate or inspire the other.

Bridging this gap between social science and design has led to the "invention" of new hybrid collection and analysis methods in our research project. As far as the collection of data was concerned, for instance, the mapping of movements and interactions was used to observe participants visually and spatially. As regards the analysis of data, we would like to introduce two examples of hybrid methods which have proven themselves helpful and relevant.

Color-coding and Analysis of the Spaces Within Reach

In the analysis of auto-photography (fig. 2.11), we were interested in understanding the arrangements of analog and digital media. Photography is analyzed in terms of content (Dirksmeier 2013; Traue 2013) in the context of traditional social research: "However, the decisive step in data acquisition with photographic methods is the transfer of the visual raw material into the scientific text. This transfer, decoding and interpretation frees photography from its limitation of being a pure illustration or documentation and transforms it into systematic knowledge" (Collier and Collier 1987, 170). However, systematic knowledge can also be produced through visual analysis. For this, graphic methods from (urban) design, e.g. the coloring of image areas (fig. 2.12), or from interaction design and ergonomics, e.g. the marking of the spaces within reach (fig. 2.13), can be used systematically. Here, a visual coding of the images takes place, which reveals shared attributes of and differences between the photos that are otherwise difficult to grasp, particularly with large amounts of data (→ see Collections 4 and 5, pages 98–101).

Analysis of Spatial Appropriation

Using data from participant observation, mapping of movements, auto-photography, systematic photographic documentation and documentation of the spatial arrangements, we have analyzed the participants' spatial appropriation. Based on the architectural and urbanist method of analyzing public, semi-public and private space (Lynch 1960; Venturi at al. 1972), we have attempted to draw individual and group territories as well the common area in the Experimental Zone.

The drawings function as a visual analysis tool insofar as they integrate different data: The floor plan is based on the weekly mapping of the spatial arrangements. The analysis of spatial appropriation is a synthesis we have undertaken on the basis of the other materials: They are based on the observations of the movements—where the participants go and where they don't—and on the auto-photography, providing information about the extent of the workplaces claimed by the participants (fig. 2.14).

Conclusion

Our method, which lies at the interface of architecture, interaction design and social research, represents a special contribution to the establishment of an interdisciplinary method of spatial research: Firstly, because it reveals the potential of an experimental qualitative approach to design; secondly, because it boldly dares to integrate heterogeneous data and thirdly, because it emphasizes the potential of visual research for spatial research. The invention of three visual collection and analysis methods (mapping of movements and interactions; color-coding; analysis of spatial appropriation) demonstrates what such an approach can achieve. Methodologically, much remains to be explained, but we hope that this detailed presentation of our method will encourage others to embark on the path of experimentation.

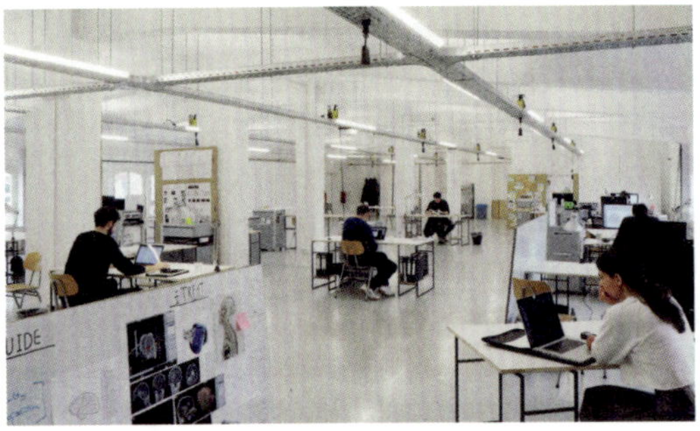

Basic Setting

The Experimental Zone began with the so-called Basic Setting. Imagine a large open space with no requirements or restrictions on how to use it: How do scientists appropriate the space? Which spatial arrangements do they prefer for their work over others? E.g. do they prefer to sit alone or in a group? Do they prefer to be seen or not, etc.? After a shared kick-off breakfast, the participating scientists were invited to set up their workstations in the completely empty Experimental Zone. They were equipped with a starter kit consisting of a table, a chair and a mobile container and could add pinboards as flexible dividers.

View of the Experimental Zone (left) and architectural model (right). Photos © Henrike Rabe (left), Dimitra Megas, Fabian Scholz (right)

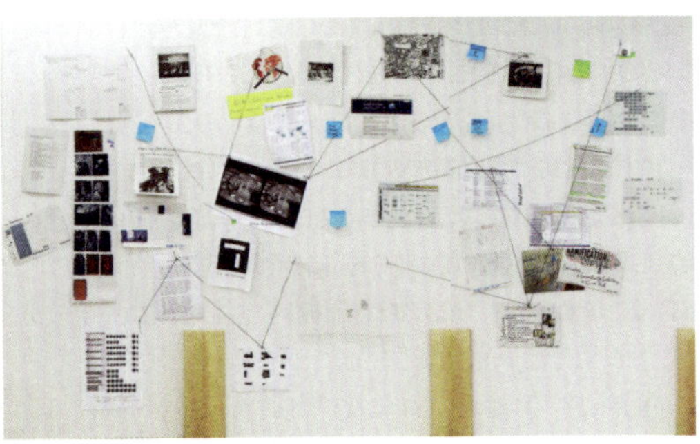

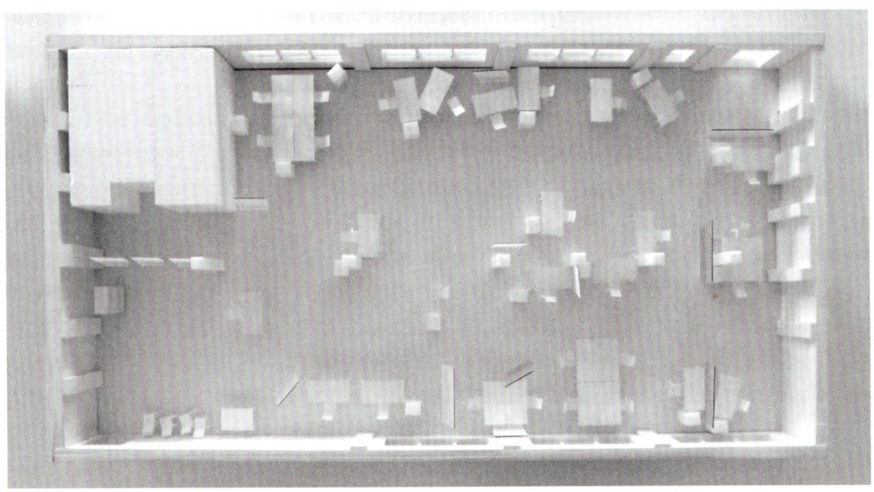

Experimental Setting 01 "Activity Wall"

May 2015

The first experimental setting explored the visualization and entanglement of work themes. The participants were asked to pin an object representing their current work and topics focused on to a so-called Activity Wall installed in the entrance area once a week. This could be a post-it with a theme or a question, a photo, a text, a screenshot or a drawing. Each object required a name and date, and a string was to be used to draw connections to other objects with similar content.

Activity Wall (left) and architectural model of the setting (right). Photos © Friedrich Schmidgall (left), Dimitra Megas, Fabian Scholz (right)

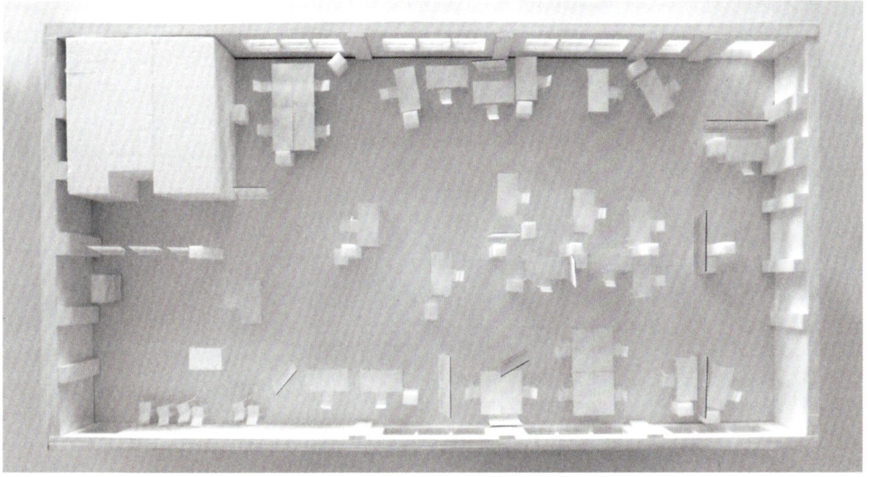

Experimental Setting 02
"Working Topics-Working Methods"

June 2015

The second setting focused on a personal and detailed assessment of one's own work. The aim was to examine which topics were investigated by whom and when, the number of different topics dealt with by participants and the frequency with which they switched between topics. We were also interested in the connection between the topics and the working methods. In order to make the survey as easy as possible, we added a function to the Diary software (→ see page 49). At lunchtime and in the evening, the topics and working methods of the participants were queried using a simple digital form.

Architectural model of setting 02. Photo © Dimitra Megas, Fabian Scholz

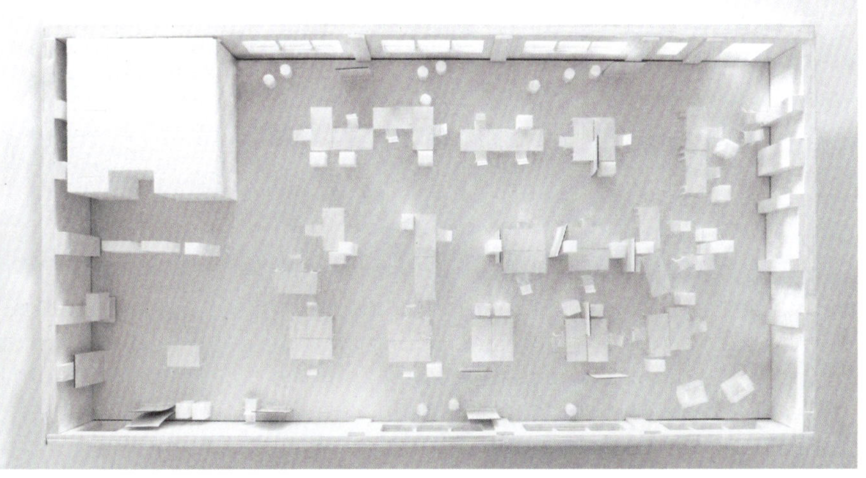

Experimental Setting 03
"Newspaper, Sun & View"

July–August 2015

In the third setting, we tried out a new spatial arrangement of the workstations. In the Basic Setting, a constellation had formed in which the workplaces were positioned predominantly along the edges of the room. Shared spaces, paths and meeting points were primarily created in the "residual areas" in between. We experimentally reversed this allocation of space by creating a workplace-free, informal zone along the windows and outer walls, encouraging the participants to walk around as well as linger, take a break and look out of the window. Additional stools and armchairs and a weekly newspaper were intended to further stimulate these informal activities.

View of the Experimental Zone (left) and architectural model (right). Photos © Fabian Scholz (left), Dimitra Megas, Fabian Scholz (right)

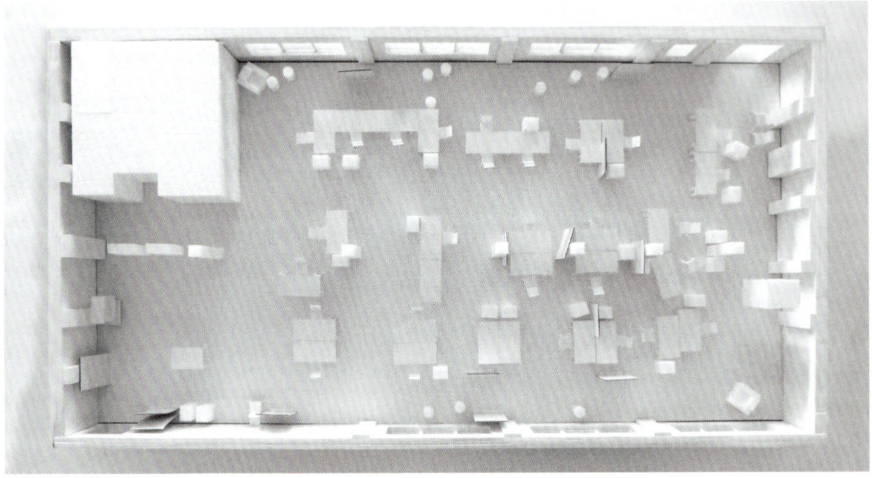

Experimental Setting 04
"Navi"

September 2015

In the fourth setting, the physical space was equipped with a kind of "commenting navigation system". With the help of hanging signs, the participants were able to mark what was happening at that position on the spot. Among other things, the signs could provide answers to the following questions: What does the room do? What is the space like? What is done in and with the room? Which activities take place, which activities cannot take place? Which human expertise is located where? Which spatial, technical and infrastructural possibilities and impossibilities are located where? What concerns me? Which question would I like to ask of the space?

View of the Experimental Zone (left) and architectural model (right). Photos © Fabian Scholz (left), Dimitra Megas, Fabian Scholz (right)

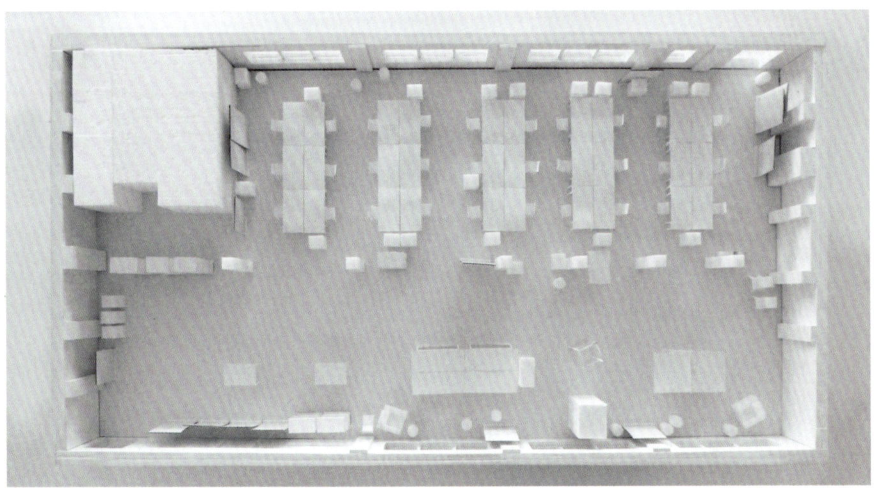

Experimental Setting 05
"Practices"

October 2015

Until this point, the Experimental Zone had offered little opportunity for practices other than desk work. In spaces of knowledge such as laboratories and design studios, however, knowledge is produced in an interplay between desk work and experimental or manual practice. In the fifth setting, we thus wanted to create space for practices such as experimenting, designing, prototyping and building, and also collaborating. Two areas were created for this purpose: On the one hand, the thirty individual workstations were arranged in close proximity in five table groups. On the other, an interdisciplinary trading zone (Galison 1999) was created in form of an open space containing the participants' experimental setups, a work-'shop area and collectively-used furniture.

View of the Experimental Zone (left) and architectural model (right). Photos © Fabian Scholz (left), Dimitra Megas, Fabian Scholz (right)

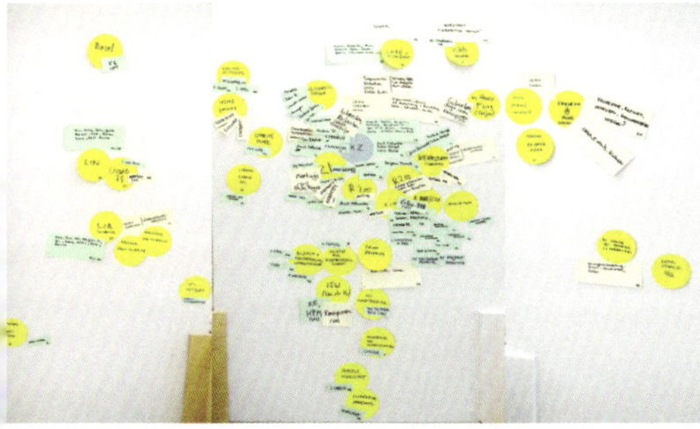

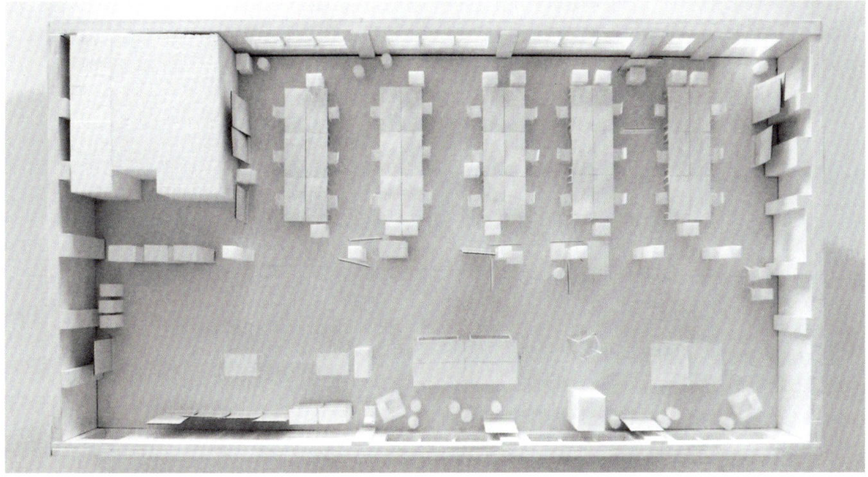

Experimental Setting 06
“Diary”

November 2015

How do the scientists view their work in the cluster? Where does the work take place, which tools and methods are used and what does the scientists’ network look like? We approached these questions in the sixth setting in two steps. Firstly, the participants were asked to keep a simple diary with the following information: What (was done), where (the activity took place), who (was involved) and how (which tools and methods were used). Secondly, we amalgamated and visualized the data collected during a workshop with the participants.

Visualization of the participants’ research locations and activities (left) and architectural model (right). Photos © Fabian Scholz (left), Dimitra Megas, Fabian Scholz (right)

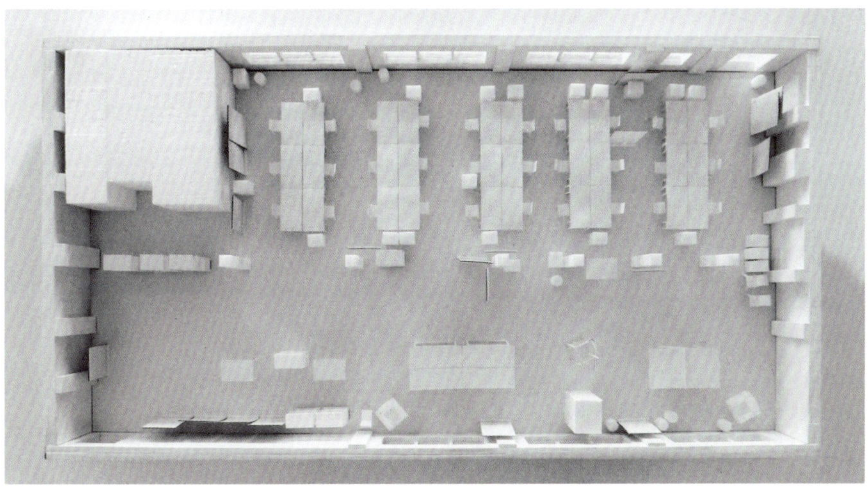

Experimental Setting 07
“Work & Play”

December 2015–January 2016

The seventh setting was dedicated to the experimentalization of social spaces and their temporalities. Based on the assumption that, in addition to individual and collaborative work, social interactions are also an important catalyst of interdisciplinarity, this setting aimed at stimulating such interactions. We defined both regular and special time slots for this purpose: Firstly, a daily sixty-minute slot was introduced for joint activities such as lunch or table tennis matches, which was announced with a gong. Secondly, six special events including a Friday aperitif, a Russian breakfast and a table tennis tournament were organized.

Architectural model of setting 07. Photo © Dimitra Megas, Fabian Scholz

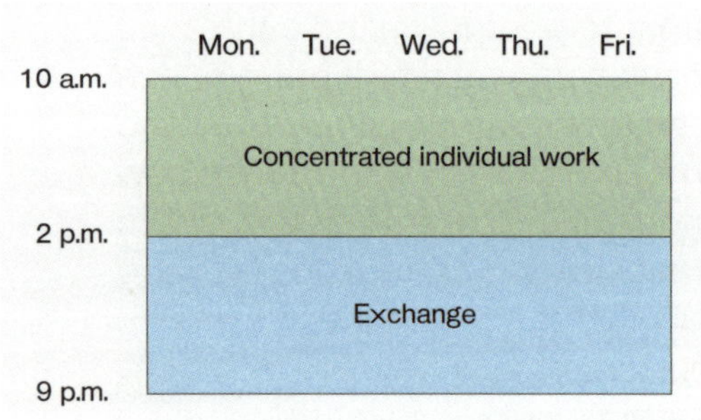

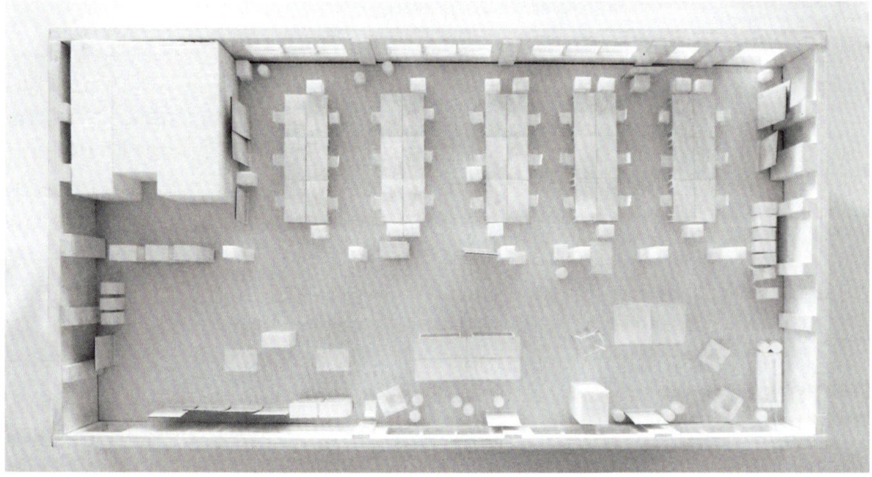

Experimental Setting 08
"Exchange: Temporal"

February–March 2016

In settings 08, 09 and 10, the topic of exchange was examined via three different experimental setups. While exchange, whether formal or informal, plays a central role in interdisciplinary research processes, it does not replace concentrated individual work. How can space facilitate both types of work? In order to examine this question, three different scenarios were tested: "Temporal", "Permeable" and "Hermetic". In "Exchange: Temporal", a temporal negotiation was tested instead of a spatial negotiation between the practices of exchange and concentration: While the first half of the day was reserved for concentrated individual work, the second half was set aside for collaboration.

Time slots for concentrated individual work and exchange (left) and architectural model (right). Photo © Dimitra Megas, Fabian Scholz

Experimental Setting 09
"Exchange: Permeable"

April–May 2016

In the ninth setting, the overarching question of the impact of different arrangements on the exchange between scientists was further investigated and the articulation between the spaces of exchange and individual work redesigned. We approached this by constructing a meeting room in the Experimental Zone which was open to all participants. However, the meeting room was not separated from the open space by a hermetic enclosure, but only by light dividers. The setting thus offered a partial acoustic and visual separation between the spaces of exchange and concentration.

View of the meeting space (left) and architectural model (right). Photos © Fabian Scholz (left), Dimitra Megas, Fabian Scholz (right)

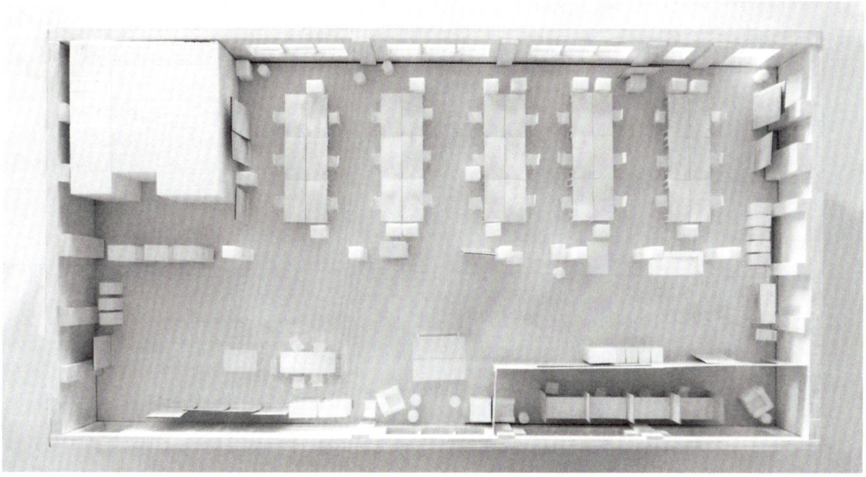

Experimental Setting 10
"Exchange: Hermetic"

June–August 2016

In the tenth setting, the topic of exchange was examined for a third time. We had observed that the participants interacted informally much more often than formally. Since the open space would never offer ideal conditions for concentrated individual work for this reason, we reversed the allocation: We defined the open space as a place of exchange and collaboration, and constructed the Silent Space for concentrated individual work. A more hermetic enclosure, more precisely a drywall with glass doors and a large window, offered a solid acoustic separation between the two spaces. Inside, several working and reading booths with generous amounts of daylight were provided for highly concentrated work.

Silent Space from the outside (left) and architectural model (right). Photos © Friedrich Schmidgall (left), Dimitra Megas, Fabian Scholz (right)

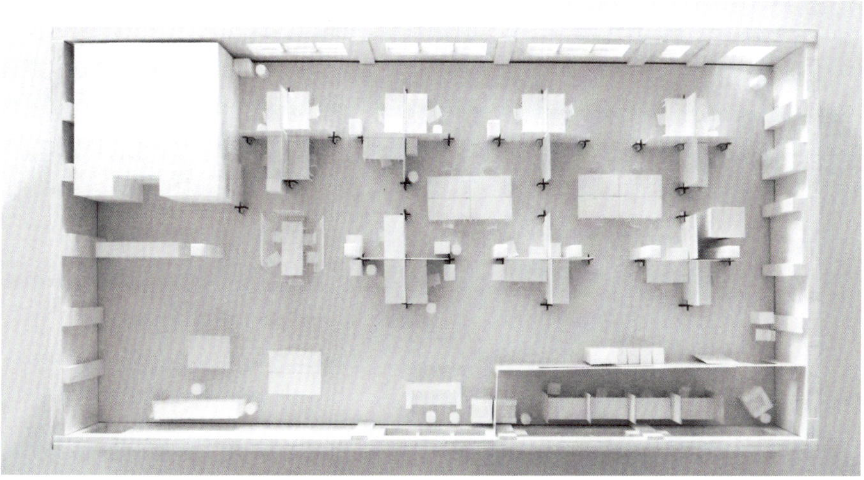

Experimental Setting 11
"Compartments"

September–October 2016

While, in past settings, open spaces had been predominantly tested, a more closed configuration was examined in the 11th setting. What effect do more closed configurations have on us as opposed to open ones? How do they influence our knowledge practices, how do they affect our interactions? In order to explore these questions, we built Compartments for two to four people using office dividers. The compartments could be freely furnished and used for individual or group work. The dividers were made of two materials: The white cardboard honeycomb panels were particularly suitable for pinning, while the translucent multi-skin panels could be written and drawn on.

View of a compartment (left) and architectural model (right). Photos © Dimitra Megas (left), Dimitra Megas, Fabian Scholz (right)

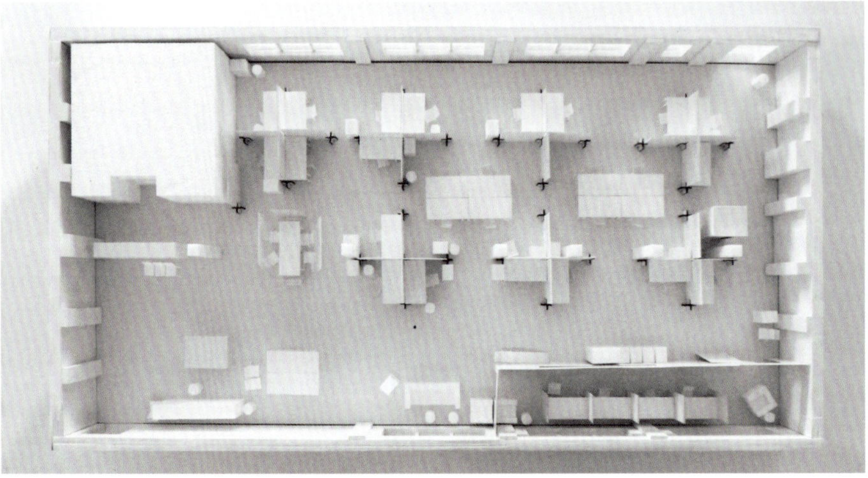

Experimental Setting 12
"Strange Objects: Conversation Pieces"

November–December 2016

In the twelfth setting, we took a closer look at the furniture. What happens when furniture provokes conversations in a different and unusual way? Will it evoke new conversation practices or surprising uses? With these questions in mind, we designed the furniture series Strange Objects in collaboration with the architectural researchers Lars Lerup and Gunnar Hartmann. In an anatomical exercise, classic stacking school chairs were dismantled, reassembled and extended. The resulting pieces each play with the theme of the conversation in their own way, by experimenting with postures, turnarounds and turnaways as well as closeness and distance. The objects were set up for free use within the Experimental Zone.

Strange Object "Freud's lounger" (left) and architectural model (right). Photos © Friedrich Schmidgall (left), Dimitra Megas, Fabian Scholz (right)

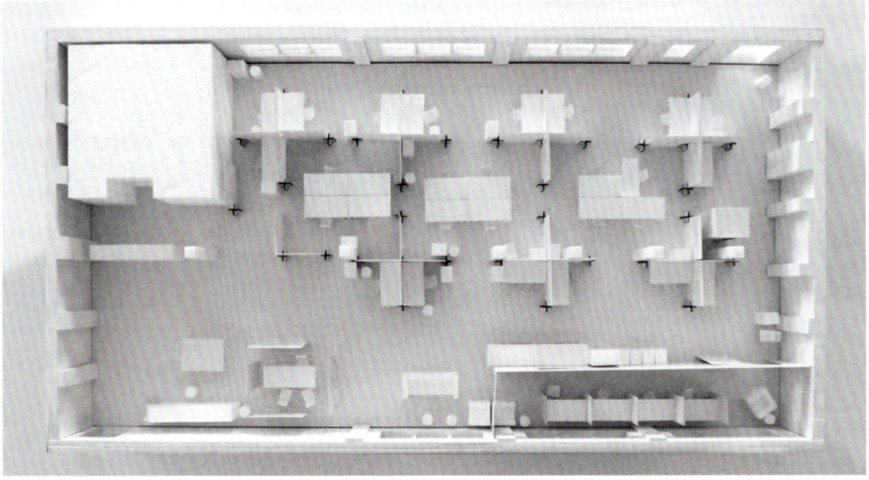

Experimental Setting 13
"Tools"

January–March 2017

In the thirteenth setting, we collaborated with the research project Hybrid Knowledge Interactions focusing on analog and digital tools. How do we appropriate the workplace and the working surface? What role do the analog and digital tools play in our work? And what influence do new, unfamiliar tools have on our knowledge practices? The setting offered participants the opportunity to try out prototypes developed in the cluster and to potentially expand their own knowledge practices.

Architectural model of setting 13. Photo © Dimitra Megas, Fabian Scholz

Experimental Setting 14
"Basic Setting II"

April–May 2017

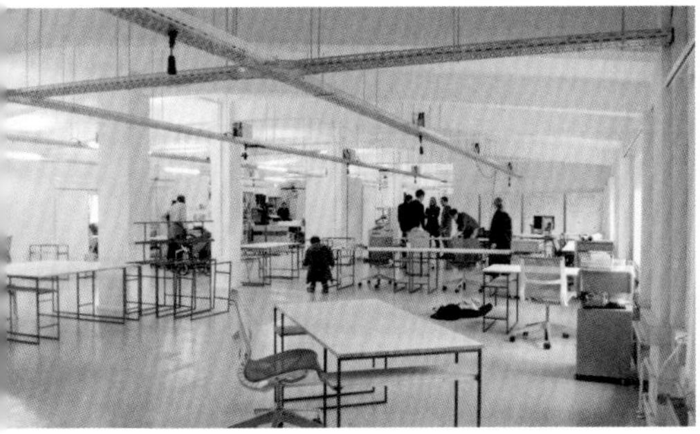

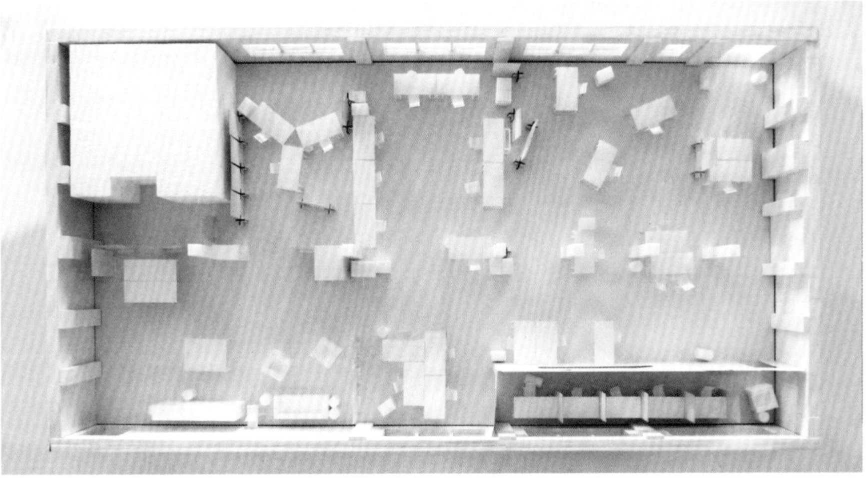

In the fourteenth setting, we focused once again on the free appropriation of space. What happens when the scientists have the entire Experimental Zone at their disposal? How do they appropriate the space, and how do their "personal spaces" materialize? In order to examine these questions, we repeated the Basic Setting (April 2015). However, it was not an exact replication of the experiment: Firstly, the participants' composition had changed. Secondly, they had gained experience of the space and familiarized themselves with different physical configurations. Thirdly, this time the Experimental Zone featured a new collective area as well as the Silent Space described above.

View of the Experimental Zone (left) and architectural model (right). Photos © Henrike Rabe (left), Dimitra Megas, Fabian Scholz (right)

Experimental Setting 15
"@experimental zone"

June–September 2017

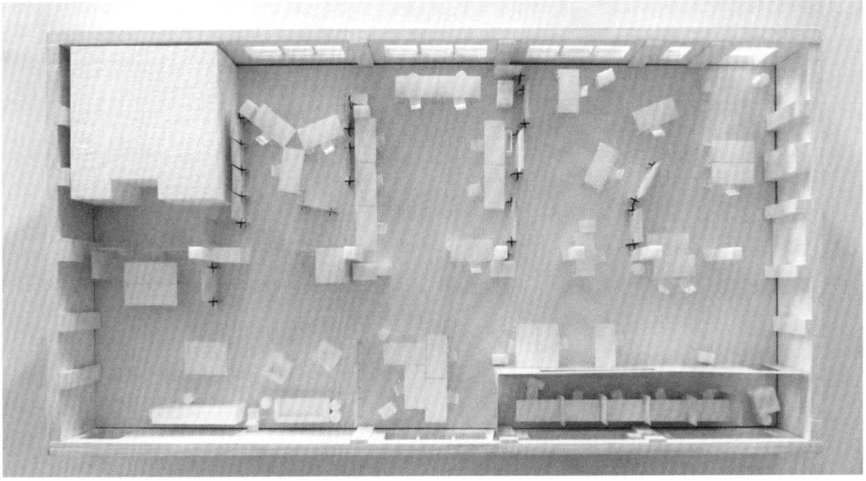

In line with our increasing focus on digital working practices, the fifteenth setting was an attempt to experimentalize the digital aspects of space too. The introduction of a collective communication tool, Slack, enabled participants to chat, discuss, document and share. The digital exchange was visualized at a central location in the Experimental Zone: The activities were displayed live on a large screen in the kitchen area.

Architectural model of setting 15. Photo © Dimitra Megas, Fabian Scholz

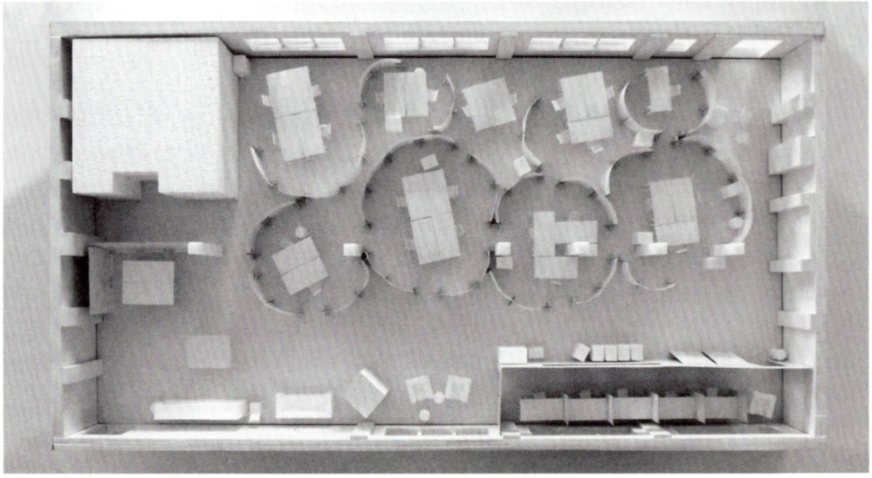

Experimental Setting 16
"Clockwork"

October 2017–February 2018

In the sixteenth setting, we examined a strongly subdivided space combined with high visibility. The design translated the interaction and close interlocking of the teams into a new physical architecture, a clockwork: With the help of curved and translucent dividers, so-called "gears" were created, in each of which one to four scientists could work. In order to achieve high visibility in the Experimental Zone and simultaneously offer privacy, the partition modules were half-high, standing at 1.42 meters.

View of the Experimental Zone (left) and architectural model (right). Photos © Henrike Rabe (left), Dimitra Megas, Fabian Scholz (right)

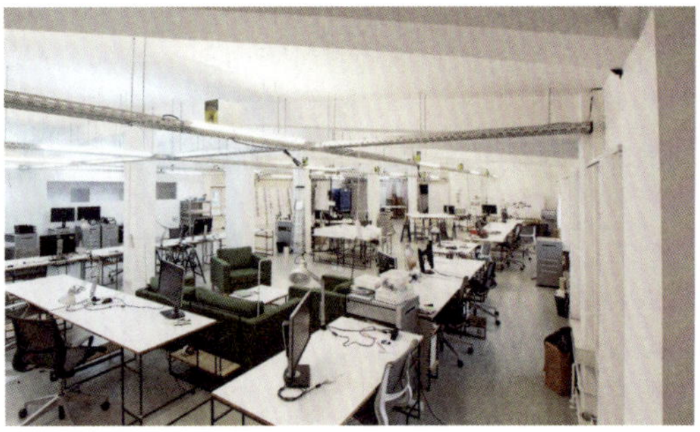

Experimental Setting 17
"Participatory Setting"

March–April 2018

In line with the co-laborative approach (→ see page 43), the seventeenth setting was designed by the participants themselves, and was aimed at transferring their experiences with interdisciplinary working spaces into the design of a setting. During participative workshops, the hypothesis was proposed that making practices visible is fundamental to interdisciplinary research. The concept thus envisaged a trading zone (Galison 1999) as a collective area in the center, surrounded by individual workplaces. The aim of the arrangement was to make both the individual as well as collaborative practices more visible. The trading zone itself contained both a workshop area and a relaxation area.

View of the Experimental Zone (left) and architectural model (right). Photos © Susanne Friedl (left), Theodora Georgopoulou, Fabian Scholz (right)

Experimental Settings

00
01

02
03

04
05

06
07

08
09

10
11

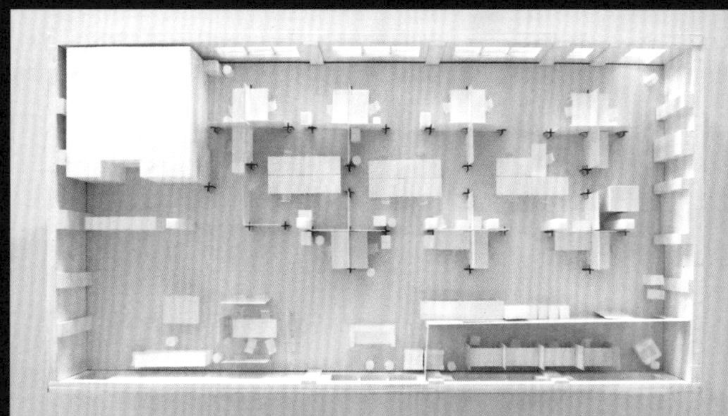

12
13

14
15

16
17

Architectural models of the experimental settings, based on the weekly mapping of the spatial arrangements (→ See Part Two, page 46). Photos © Theodora Georgopoulou, Dimitra Megas, Fabian Scholz

Experimental setting 00 "Basic Setting"
Experimental setting 01 "Activity Wall"
Experimental setting 02 "Working Topics – Working Methods"
Experimental setting 03 "Newspaper, Sun & View"
Experimental setting 04 "Navi"
Experimental setting 05 "Practices"
Experimental setting 06 "Diary"
Experimental setting 07 "Work & Play"
Experimental setting 08 "Exchange: Temporal"
Experimental setting 09 "Exchange: Permeable"
Experimental setting 10 "Exchange: Hermetic"
Experimental setting 11 "Compartments"
Experimental setting 12 "Strange Objects"
Experimental setting 13 "Tools"
Experimental setting 14 "Basic Setting II"
Experimental setting 15 "@experimental zone"
Experimental setting 16 "Clockwork"
Experimental setting 17 "Participatory Setting"

View into the Experimental Zone

05
06

07
08

09
10

11
13

14
15

16
17

View from the entrance of the Experimental Zone per setting. Photographic documentation from 38 fixed angles was introduced in October 2015, therefore only the settings 05 to 17 are documented (→ See Part Two, page 46). Photos © Susanne Friedl, Patryk Kujawa, Benjamin Meurer, Dimitra Megas, Fabian Scholz

Experimental setting 05 “Practices”
Experimental setting 06 “Diary”
Experimental setting 07 “Work & Play”
Experimental setting 08 “Exchange: Temporal”
Experimental setting 09 “Exchange: Permeable”
Experimental setting 10 “Exchange: Hermetic”
Experimental setting 11 “Compartments”
Experimental setting 13 “Tools”
Experimental setting 14 “Basic Setting II”
Experimental setting 15 “@experimental zone”
Experimental setting 16 “Clockwork”
Experimental setting 17 “Participatory Setting”

Design Process

01
02

03
04

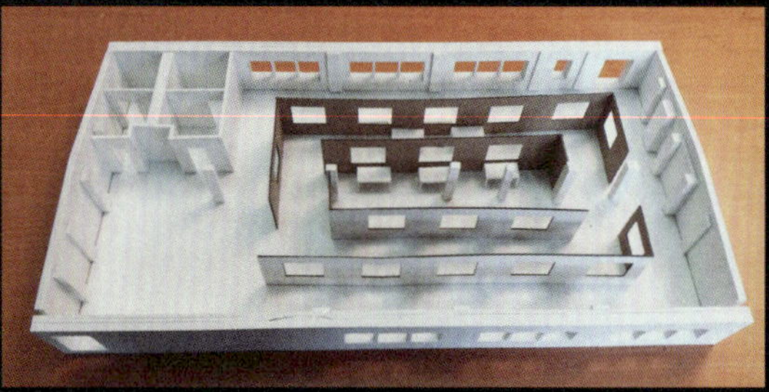 

05
06

07
08

09
10

11
12

13
14

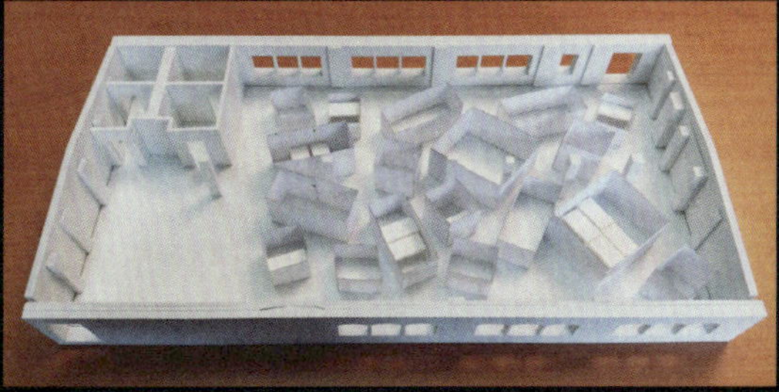

15
16

17
18

19
20

21
22

Selected photos from the design process.
The design options presented here led to the design of experimental settings 11 "Compartments" and 16 "Clockwork" (→ See Part Two, page 38). Photos © Patryk Kujawa, Dimitra Megas

01/02	Pockets 1
03/04	Layered spaces
05/06	Wrapped up space
07/08	Flowing space 1
09/10	Compartments
11/12	Cells 1

Guest Contribution

Finn Geipel,
Fabian Scholz,
Christian Stein [1]

Settings in the Canon, Sprints as Rhythm: Development of an Interdisciplinary Procedure Model for the Experimental Zone

1 The procedure model was developed by Finn Geipel, Peter Koval, Bernd Mahr, Séverine Marguin, Henrike Rabe, Wolfgang Schäffner, Christine Schmid, Friedrich Schmidgall, Fabian Scholz, Stefan Solleder and Christian Stein.

Interdisciplinarity is not only accorded high priority in research at the Cluster of Excellence *Image Knowledge Gestaltung. An Interdisciplinary Laboratory* but is currently called for and initiated at many universities around the world. The non-uniformity of the disciplines and their different approaches are an essential condition and a strength as opposed to a weakness of the sciences. It follows that interdisciplinary research projects present the participants with great challenges: "Inevitably misunderstandings will arise, tensions will build, and egos will be bruised" (Shanken 2010, 26). How can the discipline-specific strengths within a research project complement each other in an interdisciplinary and innovative way? In a sense, the various disciplines speak different languages (Galison 1999). One approach to mediation is to negotiate the existing differences in a common framework: "... the trading partners can hammer out a local coordination despite vast global differences ... cultures in interaction frequently establish contact languages, systems of discourse" (idem, 138). In addition to the demand for a common language and shared boundary objects (Shanken 2010), a "scheme for project coordination and management" is called for elsewhere (Shanken 2005, 417), and the question of the feasible integration of methods from industry within interdisciplinary science arises.

The development process of the procedure model for the interdisciplinary research project Experimental Zone is described in the following and serves as an example for the conception of such a framework.

This project is an investigation with some special features. As explained in Part 2 of this book, it is not an experimental setup in the conventional sense, but rather an explorative device which continuously recalibrates and further develops its structure and inquiry depending on the knowledge and research results obtained at regular intervals. In addition, the process of designing the spaces as well as the execution of the study itself becomes the subject of a superordinate observation. Moreover, the theoretical superstructure was not fixed in advance, but was instead subject to continual development in line with the knowledge gained in the experimental space.

The project was initiated in the spring of 2014, when the idea of experimenting with the design of physical-virtual space emerged in the *Interdisciplinary Laboratory*. The scientists involved—architects, designers, computer scientists, cultural and social scientists—planned to design, test and observe different physical and virtual spatial configurations within the framework of experimental settings. So far, the team was in agreement. However, all other aspects remained undecided. How does an interdisciplinary research team organize itself when so much is open to debate and the task at hand is to design an interdisciplinary experiment, including its theoretical basis, a coherent methodological approach and the physical space required, including furnishings? In discipline-specific projects, it is possible to fall back on established procedures and methods. However, an interdisciplinary team, with its various different perspectives on a challenging project, inevitably breaks new ground.

It quickly became clear that a specific, interdisciplinary approach was necessary, which would require further development during the course of the project and adapt to the experiences gained via its application (fig. 1). A model of this nature was designed at the outset, and developed iteratively over a period of two years. In retrospect, the procedure model was an essential framework condition for interdisciplinary cooperation within the project *ArchitecturesExperiments*.

Discipline-specific Procedure Models

Various procedure models from the fields of architecture, the social sciences, design and computer science could have served as potential frameworks for the project. However, during an initial survey it transpired that none of these options were appropriate.

Architectural practice is characterized by a linear approach, as it usually has a clearly defined goal: The timely construction of a building. In Germany, the design and planning phases that lead to this goal are described in the HOAI, the schedule of services and fees for architects and engineers (HOAI 2019). The sequence of the phases and milestones of the construction process is presented in Gantt diagrams.[2] The HOAI phases are thus a typical waterfall model that does not foresee a return. In reality, of course, the design process is not strictly linear. In keeping with its name, HOAI is, in practice, particularly important for billing and contracts. For the Experimental Zone, however, this aspect was of secondary importance. Neither did the study have a defined goal, the achievement of which could have been outlined with milestones. The HOAI's waterfall model was thus only relevant for the conversion of the Experimental Zone premises and the necessary coordination with the construction department of the Humboldt University of Berlin (fig. 2).

In the social sciences, procedures exist that are described by circular models. Today, for instance, the Grounded Theory method developed by Barney G. Glaser and Anselm L. Strauss in 1960s Chicago represents a central methodology in ethnology and anthropology and forms a basis for qualitative social research (Glaser, Strauss 1967). Data is collected systematically in the field, evaluated, compared and, on the basis of the knowledge gained, the focus is sharpened for further fieldwork. The theory is developed via multiple repetitions until "theoretical saturation" is reached and the study can be completed. Grounded Theory, however, is primarily a subject-specific method of data collection and theory building in social research. It therefore offers few concrete points of reference for collaborative organization within an interdisciplinary team.

In the field of design, too, the working process is generally understood as a sequence of iterative loops in which a concept is developed, a product is designed, prototypes are built, tested, discarded and the design undergoes further development until the product is ready for the market (e.g. Brown 2009). ISO 9241-210:2010[3] can be cited as an example of a formalization of this process, which describes the development of products in the sense of human-centered design in iterative loops for interaction design. This is a supplement to other design frameworks: "The approach to human-centered design described in DIN EN ISO 9241-210 complements existing design concepts. It can be integrated into such different approaches as object-oriented, waterfall and agile development of applications" (Beuth 2011). The organization of the procedure in loops was conceivable for the Experimental Zone project, but this model provides no indications relating to the organization of a team's work processes.

Until the turn of the millennium, the approach to the development of procedure models in computer science was dominated by linear approaches such as the waterfall model, familiar from the field of architecture, and the V-model.[4] In the 2000s, however, a new model appeared in software development which, like the design models or methods adopted by the social sciences, is based on an iterative approach. Thanks to some special features, the so-called Scrum model (fig. 3) proved to be particularly relevant for our project. Ken Schwaber, who wrote the first conference paper on Scrum in 1995, summarizes the findings of decades of work and problems experienced with linear approaches on which Scrum is based on: "Scrum accepts that the development process cannot be foreseen. The product is the best possible software taking into account costs, functionality, time and quality" (Gloger 2011, 19). Scrum is thus a so-called agile method which seeks to react to the changing requirements and goals of projects without losing structure. It allows initial ambiguities, which outweigh all other factors, to be clarified step by step via concrete intermediate results. In this sense, Scrum is empirical, incremental and iterative. It allows long-term future planning to be dispensed

2 Bar charts named after Henry L. Gantt (1861–1915).
3 ISO 9241-210:2010 - Ergonomics of human-system interaction -- Part 210: Human-centered design for interactive systems.
4 As a software development-specific extension of the waterfall model, the V-model assigns corresponding test phases to all linear developmentphases in order to ensure functionality and integration.

Fig. 1: Early sketches for the procedure model. Photo © Friedrich Schmidgall

	Phase	Duration (weeks)	W 20	21	22	23	24	25	26	27	28	29	30	31	32	33
Determining the procedure and the time frame																
Construction documents	LPH 5															
Preparation of the bidding	LPH 6	1														
Preparation of offers		1														
Bidding		1														
Construction administration	LPH 7	3														
Final inspection	LPH 8	1														
Moving in		1														
	TOTAL	12														
Meetings				20.5.				17.6.								

Fig. 2: Schedule for the construction works in the Experimental Zone. Graphic © ArchitecturesExperiments

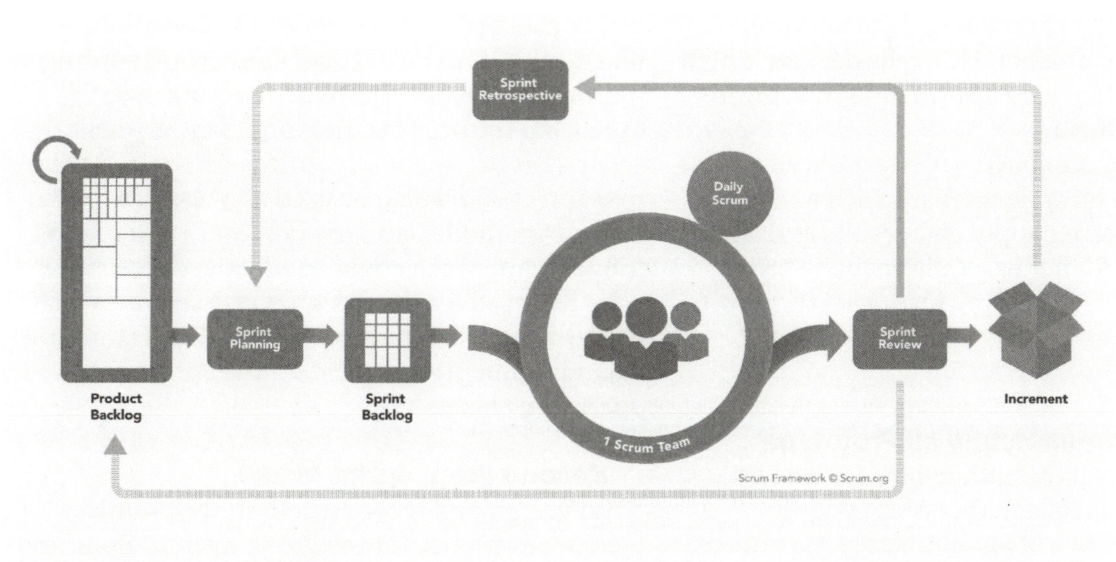

Fig. 3: Scrum Framework. Graphic © https://www.scrum.org/resources/scrum-framework-poster

with and ensures that plans are only put into concrete terms if this is immediately necessary and predictable.

Intermediate results, in turn, are repeatedly analyzed in detail and checked for compliance with requirements and future plans adjusted accordingly. This is intended to create criteria essential for quality assurance and process control: Transparency, review and adaptation. The looser long-term planning must therefore be replaced by more closely meshed short-term planning. The implementation of intermediate goals is realized in so-called "sprints", which feature a predetermined and usually identical duration and remain manageable in terms of time and content. Once the sprint is completed, the process and its result are critically reviewed and evaluated, and the next sprint is planned.

The work is divided into three main roles: The Scrum Master, the Development Team and the Product Owner. The Scrum Master is the person who assumes responsibility for the process, moderates and explains it, reviews its success and removes obstacles. It is his or her job to identify problems, to name them and to find solutions. He or she is on an equal hierarchical footing with the team and must protect it from external disturbances such as tasks outside the scope of the project. The development team is responsible for the implementation of the defined functionalities and their quality. It operates autonomously in relation to both the Scrum Master and the Product Owner. Finally, the Product Owner is responsible for the usage context and attempts to maximize the success of the product. He or she decides which functions are included in a sprint and thus prioritizes the requirements.

An increasing number of software development studios now rely on agile methods such as Scrum, as these deliver better applicable results and adapt more flexibly to changing requirements. Scrum has also established itself in areas other than software development and has developed various permutations.

First Step: Scrum Hybrid as Prototype

The examination of discipline-specific models resulted in the conclusion that only an agile procedure model would be suitable for the project. While the entire project process is defined in advance in linear models, agile models permit the convenient handling of a project's many imponderables. It follows that the initial version of the procedure model was developed on the basis of Scrum (fig. 3). While the Scrum model offered important clues and techniques, in some respects it required hybridization, or adaptation, to the interdisciplinary scientific context and the process of experimentalization between design and science.

The first version of the procedure model consisted of continuously repeating loops with a fixed sequence of repeating steps. At first glance, it made sense to synchronize the loops and the planned experimental settings. However, the Scrum model was modified as follows: Firstly, the distribution of roles and personnel time contingents proved problematic, as those involved participated in other activities in addition to the project. The classic roles of Scrum, i.e. the full-time team as well as the roles of Product Owner and Scrum Master, which are separate from the team, had to be adapted for the procedure accordingly, but this did not happen until a later stage. Secondly, despite the necessary agility, the project required a time frame with fixed deadlines, because a redesign of the space was necessary before the experimental settings could be implemented. This conversion naturally had to be preceded by a design phase. In contrast to the conversion itself, however, this was not tied to external deadlines and the team was able to determine its own working methods. As a result, it made sense to initially implement the design phase as an agile sprint, before proceeding to organize the construction phase with its external dependencies according to the waterfall model from architecture, finally executing the organization of the experimental settings as Scrum model sprints. In this way, the first sprint could also be used as a test run for the new sprint model, and the processes and roles of the agile approach could be practiced. Four weeks were reserved for the design phase sprint, which initially proved to be a successful time frame, and was subsequently adopted for the sprint-based operating phase.

Second Step: Sprint Model

After design and reconstruction, the premises were ready for use for the Experimental Zone and the procedure model had already proven itself in

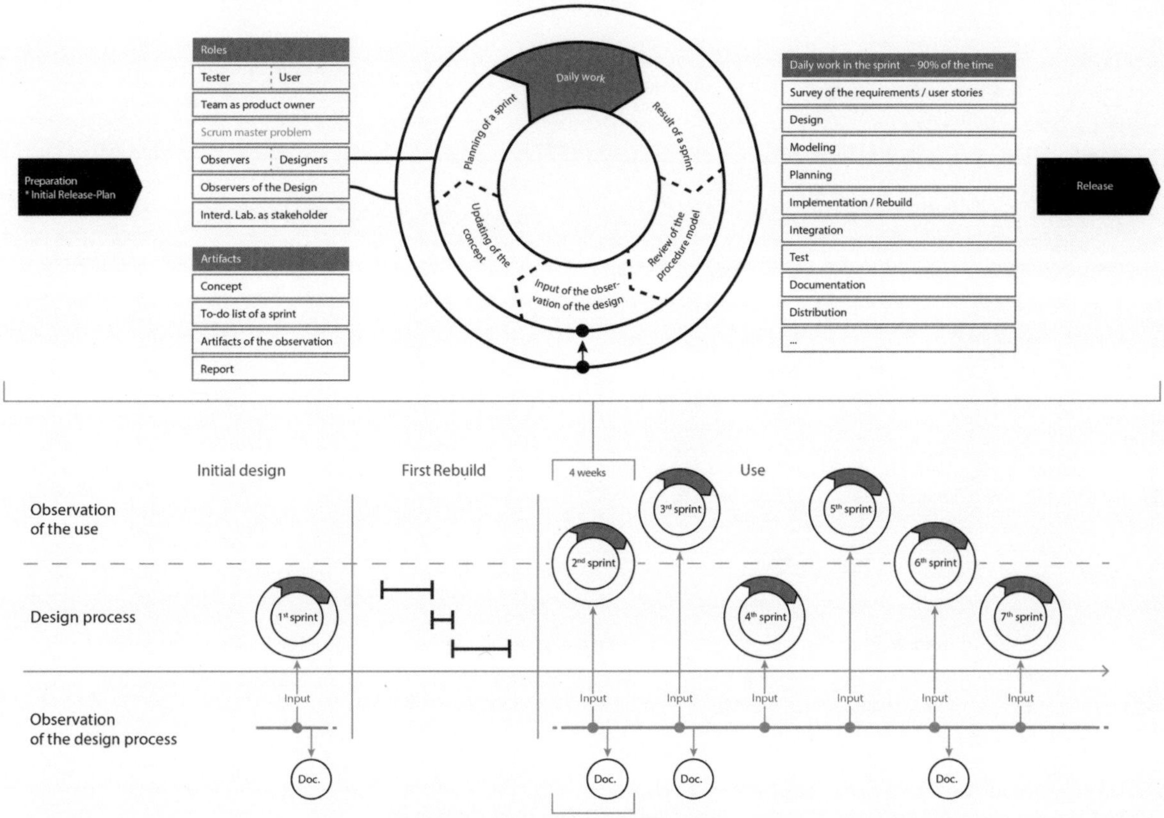

Fig. 4: Second procedure model “sprint model”. Graphic © Friedrich Schmidgall

an initial test phase. But, as expected, there was also a need for revision. While the first version of the procedure model described the initial phase of the study predominantly by means of a diagram and some sketches, the next version went a step further and formalized the procedure in the so-called Sprint model (fig. 4). This second version of the procedure model included the initial phases of design and rebuild, but referred primarily to the operation of the Experimental Zone with its continuous sequence of sprints. By definition, the Experimental Zone must be available for the execution of spatial experimental scenarios and enable the observation of the use, i.e. the work in this area of the interdisciplinary laboratory.

Another field of interest was the observation of the design process itself. According to these activities, roles were defined for the procedure model, which were termed design, observation and observation of the design, whereby the roles of observation and design could also be carried out by one person at the same time. The design role comprised the design and realization of the experimental settings. The observation role included all technical and non-technical as well as all continuous and temporary observation activities in the Experimental Zone (→ see Part Two). The output included sketches, audio recordings, models, prototypes, photos, interviews, questionnaires, diagrams and simulations. The observation and design roles

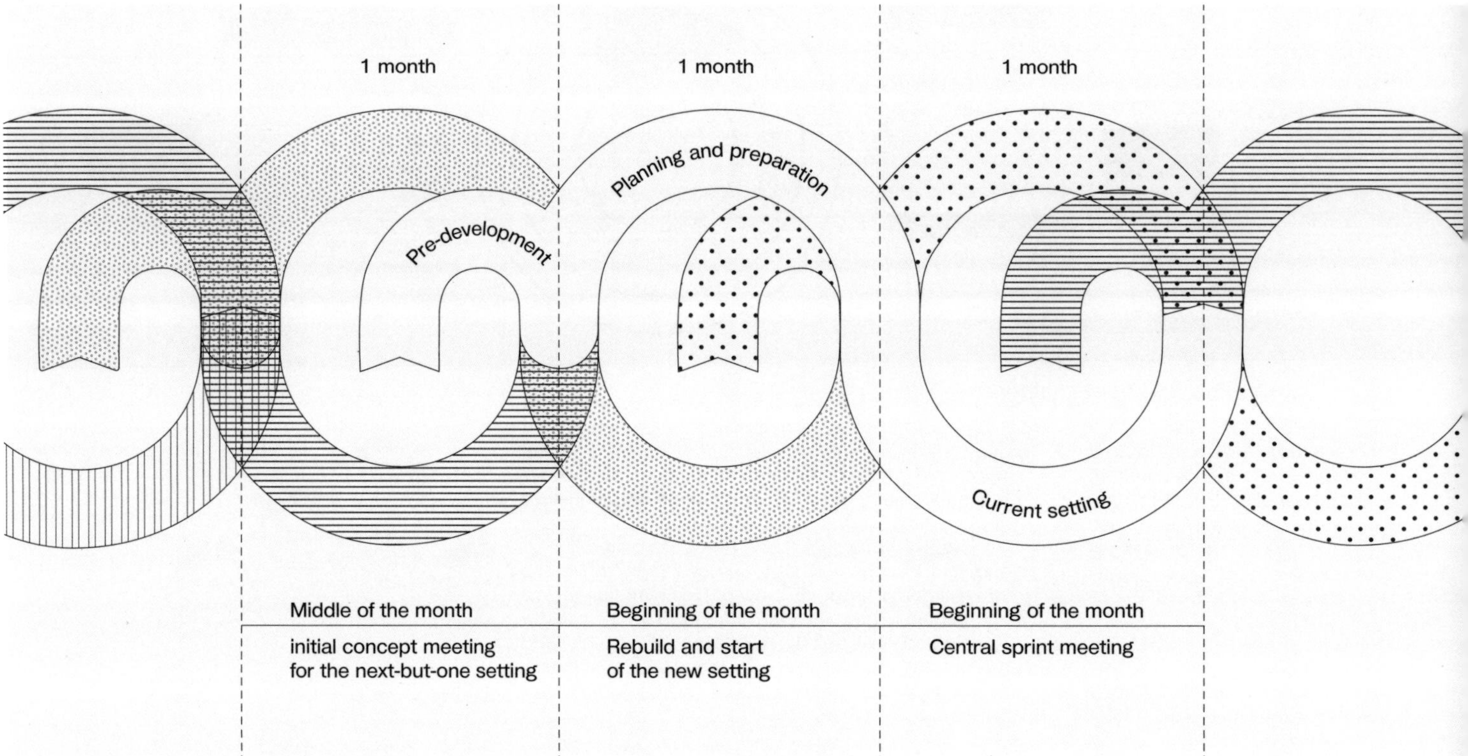

Fig. 5: Third procedure model with sprints and settings. Graphic © Friedrich Schmidgall

were interlinked to the extent that the experimental settings designed were observed and the findings from the observation of the settings were, in turn, integrated within the design of new experimental settings. Given the small size of the team and the desire for the closest possible interdisciplinary cooperation, a strict separation of the personal assignment of roles seemed counterproductive.

However, the role of observing the design, performed by two research assistants from the field of European ethnology, was detached from the other two roles in order to permit an examination of the entire design and research process which was as independent as possible. It took place parallel to the design and observation of the Experimental Zone and thus became a form of second level observation. Employees in this role participated selectively in observation and documentation activities and were able to ask questions at any time. The resulting observations were then presented to the team and discussed together, as the objective of the role of design observation was to perform independent monitoring, relaying the observations to the team and flagging problems or potential for optimization to its members.

The employees undertaking the roles of the design and observation of the settings worked together as a team and, as such, performed sprints together. They all collaborated on the sprint-related tasks, regardless of their discipline-specific roles. Sprint planning was carried out collaboratively, and the sprint's to-do list was also a collective one, with the designers performing observation tasks and vice versa. At this point, the role of the Scrum Master was yet to be clarified. By definition, he or she must not be part of the team or hierarchically superior to it. This made the assignment of this role challenging in terms of procedure. However, dispensing with the role completely would have left an important responsibility undetermined. Ultimately, it was decided to rotate the role within the team depending on availability. Similarly, the role of Product Owner was not assigned to personnel. Instead of specifying an individual, the entire organizational unit associated with the research project *ArchitecturesExperiments* was defined as the Product Owner. However, the personnel-related assignment of the roles of Product Owner and Scrum Master are an elementary component of the Scrum model. In this respect, one could no longer refer to a Scrum model after this development state of the procedure model, which explains the name change to "Sprint model". At that time, the sprint approach was the procedure's key element, comprising a four-week period which encompassed a review of the preceding sprint, the planning of the pending sprint, the input of the design's observation, a concept meeting and several design meetings, as well as two weekly sprint meetings. The trajectory of a sprint was thus precisely defined. Each sprint was also intended to improve the assessment of the actual feasible workloads. At the sprint meetings, the team convened for fifteen minutes to check the status of the to-do list and maintain a close exchange. In the "development" and "design meetings", future experimental settings were conceived and designed. At the end of the sprint, the review of the past sprint, input of the design observation and new sprint planning were combined in a "general sprint meeting" in which those responsible for design, observation and observation of the design as well as the Principal Investigators congregated. Once completed, the sprint was also subject to critical analysis. Each problem addressed was evaluated as a valuable contribution in the sense of potential optimization, and strategies for improvement or solutions were incorporated into the plans for the upcoming sprint. Subsequently, an evaluation of whether or not the sprint targets had been fully met or not took place, and the sprint was deemed a success or failure. In line with the learning effect, the sprints regularly failed because even the smallest unfinished task condemned them to failure. This in no way meant that the work was poor, as the sprints continually delivered valuable results. Immediately thereafter, the design's observation provided input. The concept was updated and reprioritized on the basis of the experience gained and the evaluation of the project's current status. This completed the sprint run and a new sprint could begin. The procedure was recorded in documents accessible to the general public.

Work in Progress: Settings

The sprint model structured the procedure in a sequence of thematic sprints that were designed to run successively. A sprint could either focus on the design or observation of experimental settings, or both. Typically, a design sprint was followed by an observation sprint, which ideally documented and analyzed the effects of the redesign process, allowing the results to flow back into the concept. It is clear that the project duration of approximately two years limits the number of possible configurations which can be executed in the Experimental Zone. However, the definition of the "amalgamated sprint" of observation and design was in itself imprecise: no setup could be designed, observed and evaluated seriously within the brief time frame of a sprint.

The procedure model thus required revision and partial reorientation. The sprint's organizational principle had proven useful, and it was decided to retain this as a result. However, the focus of the procedure shifted from sprints to so-called experimental settings, i.e. physical-virtual, spatial configurations of the Experimental Zone associated with a specific question for the duration of a sprint. In a broader sense, a setting also included the activities associated with the preparation and follow-up of a setting, in which deductive findings from previous settings were inductively incorporated into the succeeding ones. Accordingly, the processing of an experimental setting extended over several sprints. Diagrams were used to examine ways in which several settings could be worked on simultaneously. While one setting was being carried out and observed, the pending settings required development and preparation, and past settings evaluation. From now on, the sprint's fixed meetings and decisions to be made addressed several different settings which were being developed in parallel to one another.

Third Step: Sprints and Settings

The second version of the Sprint model summarized the reflections on the settings' parallel processing in an updated framework. The roles had proved their worth and were retained, and the observation of the design as a second level observation remained a feature of the processes. New aspects included, above all, the continuous flow of the procedure for the systematic and parallel development, planning and implementation of experimental settings. The revised procedure model consisted of two complementary parts. The "Overarching Procedure model" continued to regulate the monthly processes of teamwork with a few adjustments, while the "Concrete Procedure model" (fig. 5) executed the settings' time-shifted processing along a time line adjusted to the rhythm of the sprints. In this version, a setting's processing consisted of the three successive development, planning and implementation phases. These three different activities associated with an experimental setting took place in consecutive sprints. Carrying out a setting took about three months, with a sprint duration of one month. As the experimental settings began at different times, three settings were now being processed simultaneously within a single sprint: The next-but-one setting, viewed from the perspective of the current sprint, was pre-developed, the implementation of the upcoming setting was planned and prepared, and the setting referred to as "current" was the actual configuration of the Experimental Zone at that time. However, this procedure accumulated a large number of observations, the analysis of which was not taken into account in this version of the procedure model. In response to this problem, the team worked on their evaluation for some time in parallel with the specifications of the procedure model, i.e. "informally". In the next development stage, however, this activity was integrated within the procedure model and formalized as quickly as possible.

Final Update: Settings in Canon, Sprints as Rhythm

In the third version of the procedure model (fig. 2.8, page 41), which remained valid until the end of the study, the manner in which the observations' evaluation was integrated within a setting, represented in the form of a snake, was extended by a further loop. This evaluation loop took up half of the sprint following the setting's implementation. A second important revision concerned the discipline-specific division of labor (sociology, architecture and design). While the procedure previously envisaged all activities being carried out together, practice showed that certain activities were best dealt with by the respective specialized discipline. This previously informally practiced discipline-specific division of labor was made explicit in the new procedure model. With the new distribution of roles, it also became clear that the procedure's phases were of different labor intensities for the individual disciplines respectively: The design-related development and planning phases were particularly challenging for the designers and architects, for instance, while the social scientists were concerned predominantly with the observation of the implementation and the subsequent evaluation. It is crucial to note that all important meetings, such as the central sprint meeting, as well as development, design and evaluation meetings, were interdisciplinary in nature, and that all decisions were taken jointly by all in attendance.

The Sprint model with the defined meetings forming the basic structure of the procedure remained valid. However, the duration of each sprint was increased to two months, because the previous, faster rhythm precluded an in-depth evaluation of the data. In some cases, the questions and evaluations had become more complex, requiring more time. Last but not least, the daily users of the Experimental Zone expressed their desire for more tranquillity and fewer rapid changes. Thus, at this point, the practical outcomes had a concrete influence on the procedure model, as planned. The development, planning, implementation and evaluation of an experimental setting now extended over four sprints or six months, and the settings always started with an offset of one sprint. This procedure is reminiscent of a canon in which verses are sung at fixed, rhythmically offset intervals. This procedure led to a stream of parallel settings which continuously provided insights and results. In each sprint, four experimental settings were active in different phases, namely development, planning, implementation and evaluation.

Resume

From the authors' perspective, structuring the processes within a working group is an essential component of successful, interdisciplinary cooperation. Questions arise with regard to the numerous design and observation tasks, particularly in an interdisciplinary, non-hierarchical team: Who does what, when and how? How do we proceed? The answers to these questions could only be found in the procedure model itself and via its refinement. In line with the initial reflections, the procedure model should continue to evolve on the basis of the experiences and insights gained in practice. The initial Scrum-based version which was forced to relinquish the roles of Product Owner and Scrum Master eventually evolved into a Sprint-based procedure model, which remained committed to the principles of agile development even in subsequent conceptual stages. With the introduction of the experimental settings, the Sprint model receded slightly into the background, but continued to provide the daily work with a structured rhythm. The specifications associated with the continuous feedback of the results obtained, the formulation of the questions and the revision of the process itself ensured that the procedure model functioned as a mediator between the study's deductive and inductive aspects. Finally, the adjustments made in the course of the study serve as examples of the evolutive conception of the interdisciplinary procedure model. In the final version, a discipline-specific division of labor was introduced, on the basis of which the social sciences performed a greater amount of observation and evaluation activities, while the design disciplines were involved more closely in design, planning and restructuring. However, this should not be misunderstood as a separation. In the end, it was the procedure model that, with its fixed meetings and decision-making points, impelled the team to make all decisions jointly and in an interdisciplinary manner, without having to renounce the strengths of the discipline-specific backgrounds in its daily work. With regard to the question presented at the beginning, the procedure model can be viewed as a prototype for the organization of interdisciplinary research projects. By scheduling interdisciplinary interfaces in the form of regular meetings, it provided the Experimental Zone and the disciplines involved in the investigation with a productive, interdisciplinary common ground.

References

Beuth. 2011. "DIN EN ISO 9241-210: 2011-01." Accessed January 15, 2018: https://www.beuth.de/de/norm/din-en-iso-9241-210/135399380 01/15/2018 10:55.

Brown, Tim. 2009. *Change by Design. How Design Thinking Transforms Organizations and Inspires Innovation.* New York: Harper Collins Publishers.

Galison, Peter. 1999. "Trading Zone: Coordinating Action and Belief (1997, abridged 1998)." In *The Science Studies Reader*, edited by Mario Biagioli, pp. 137–60. London; New York: Routledge.

Glaser, Barney G., and Anselm L. Strauss. 1967. *The Discovery of Grounded Theory. Strategies for Qualitative Research.* Chicago: Aldine.

Gloger, Boris. 2011. *Scrum. Produkte zuverlässig und schnell Entwickeln.* 3rd edition. München: Hanser Verlag.

HOAI. 2013. "Honorarordnung für Architekten und Ingenieure." 2019. Accessed April 8, 2019: www.hoai.de/online/HOAI_2013/HOAI_2013.php.

Shanken, Edward A. 2005. "Artists in Industry and the Academy. Collaborative Research, Interdisciplinary Scholarship and Creation and Interpretation of Hybrid Forms." *Leonardo* 38 (5): pp. 415–18.

———. 2010. "The History and Future of the Lab: Collaborative Research at the Intersections of Art, Science, and Technology." In *The Future of the Lab*, edited by Angela Plohmann and Clare Butcher, pp. 16–29. Eindhoven: Baltan Laboratories.

Part 3

Individual Research Spaces

In this chapter, we aim to define the characteristics of the individual research space as a dynamic habitat. In recent decades, research practices have become increasingly digitized (Frietsch and Rogge 2013; Terras et al. 2013; Burghardt and Wolff 2014), performed at the computer or with the help of other digital media such as tablets or digital cameras. Accordingly, the analysis of the effects of space cannot be limited to the physical-material space alone. But how can virtual space be understood? And how can it be empirically investigated? Various concepts of the virtual space exist (→ see Part One, page 21). During our empirical observations, however, it became increasingly clear that these concepts, which reference the dichotomy between the physical and the virtual, are not particularly helpful when it comes to an analysis of researchers' physical-virtual workspaces.

We first reproduced this dichotomy in our research design, initially exploring the question of the physical workspace by means of mental maps and of auto-photography, and subsequently examining the "digital workspace" used by the same interviewees. This approach predominantly reflected our own understanding of space. However, the target group examined consisted to a large extent of experts in the field of mediality and mediatization (media scientists, interaction designers, information scientists), who called our investigation of the "virtual space" into question, *co-laboratively* (→ see Part Two, page 43) developing the concept of a *physical-virtual* space with us (→ see Part One, page 22).

It follows that, with Beck's practice theory 3.0 as its basis, our empirical investigation emphasizes the fact that the researcher's practices form assemblages of human and non-human elements at the interface of the digital and the analog (Beck 2015) (→ see Part One, page 22). These assemblages open up physical-virtual research spaces which transcend the boundaries of the classical dichotomy between the physical and the virtual. The investigation shows that these spaces unfold dynamically according to the specific practice (reading, writing, designing, etc.), but also that they refer to fixed, routine arrangements which clearly challenge the post-modern image of an inspired, highly flexible producer of knowledge.

1 A Digitalized Research Practice

In order to understand the transformation of the individual research space in the course of the digitalization process, we first examined the physical-material composition of the individual workspace: What are the coordinates of this invisible space? Where are its boundaries? And what are the tools for carrying out scientific activities? In a second step, we studied how the participants perceive this space at the interface of the analog and the digital.

1.1 The Digitalized Workspace

The scientists' workspaces featured identical equipment: Most scientists had already been provided with a laptop and a mobile pedestal by the *Interdisciplinary Laboratory* before joining the Experimental Zone. Building on this, we also ensured that each scientist was equipped with their own work table[1], chair, mobile pedestal, table lamp, optional mobile pinboards and an

1 We designed and built the work tables as part of the Experimental Zone project. Extremely flexible and lightweight tables were required so that the participants could move them easily. The module size of 0.80 x 1.60 meters allowed them to arrange the tables in larger groups. It was possible to equip the table frames with additional boards to store folders and other items under the table.

Fig. 3.1: Color-coding of the auto-photography (orange = analog media, blue = digital media, green = clothing and bags, yellow = lamp, purple = bottles and food containers, pink = headphones, grey = work surfaces i.e. table and pinboard)

Fig. 3.3: Spaces within reach superimposed onto the auto-photograph

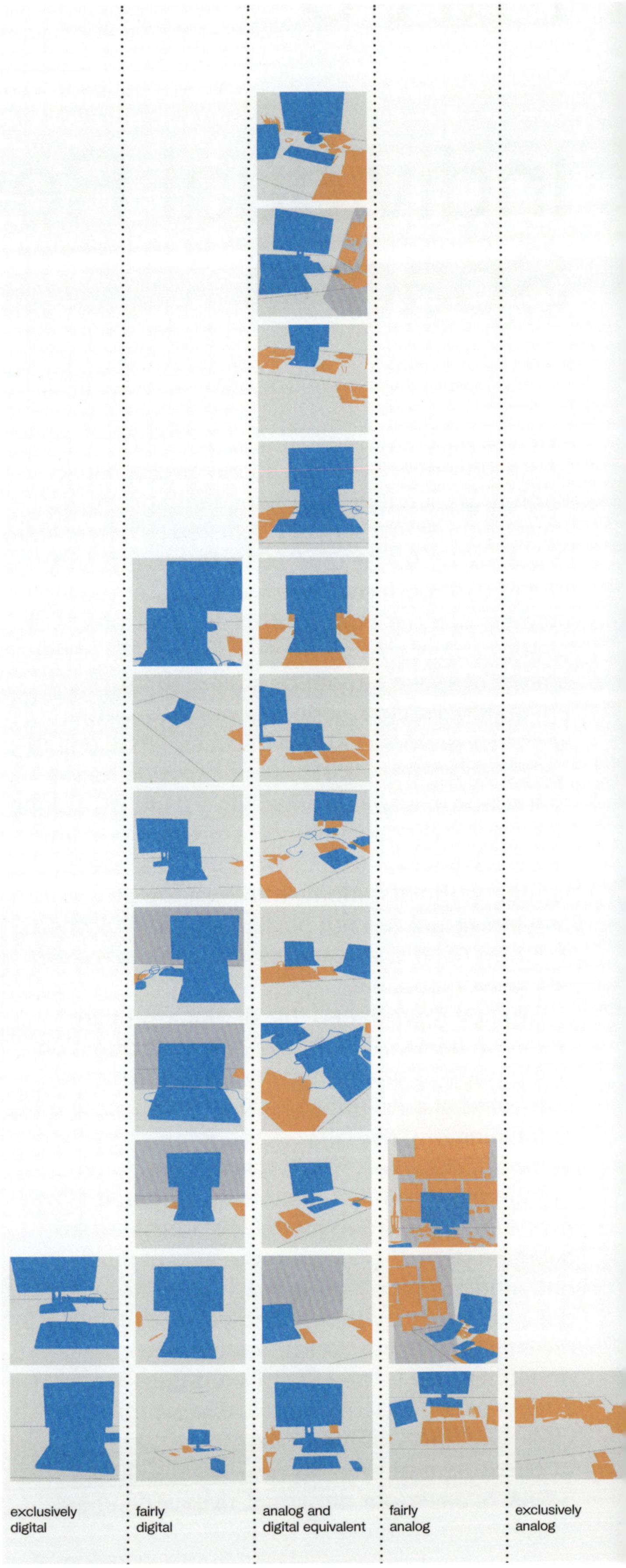

Fig. 3.2: Types of workspaces on a scale from a purely digital (blue) to a purely analog (orange) setup

optional additional display (fig. 2.4, page 37). Despite this identical basic equipment, different arrangements of the workspaces could be observed. The dimensions, general equipment and, in particular, the digitalization of the workspaces were examined with the aid of auto-photography (→ see Part Two, page 46). The auto-photographs were analyzed in two ways: Firstly, all artifacts in the photo were color-coded according to categories, with the categories "analog" or "digital" graphically isolated (fig. 3.1) (→ See Collection 4, page 98). Secondly, the arrangement of objects on the desks was examined as regards their relation to the researcher's body by superimposing the outlines of the *spaces within reach* onto the auto-photographs (fig. 3.3) (→ See Collection 5, page 100).

The analysis of the digital and analog media at the participants' workstations demonstrates the varying gradations of workspaces, ranging from those featuring purely digital or analog media to a host of intermediate types, which can be arranged in five steps on a scale (fig. 3.2): 1. exclusively digital, 2. fairly digital, 3. analog and digital equivalent, 4. fairly analog and 5. exclusively analog.

As anticipated, digital media predominate as far as the workspace equipment is concerned. In most cases, the computer is located centrally and the other media are positioned around it; vertically on the one hand, and horizontally on the other. Vertically, the screens are arranged above each other in many cases. Here, the individual research space extends upwards. And horizontally, analog media serve to expand the space to the left and right of the keyboard.

What is striking about the workspaces that are equally digital and analog (fig. 3.2, middle column) is the entanglement of digital and analog media. The topology of the analog-digital arrangement [2] is usually concentric, in that analog media (such as books, sheets of paper, etc.) surround the digital input devices. Some cases in which the analog media form a wall beside or behind the desk, functioning as a visual boundary for the individual workspace, also deserve a passing mention.

How are the media and artifacts arranged in relation to the body of the researcher? Observing the body at work allowed us to understand how individual research spaces are activated in action (Schmidt 2008). We examined the relationship between the body (in particular the hands and the sitting body) and the objects on the desk. For this purpose, an analysis instrument inspired by ergonomics was used—without, however, pursuing the optimizing idea of an ergonomic approach.[3] By plotting the *spaces within reach* on the auto-photographs, the relevance of the objects on the worktable could be assessed (Lange and Windel 2013) (fig. 3.3) (→ See Collection 5, page 100). The spaces within reach describe those spaces on the table which can be reached by a sitting office worker. They consist of the *work center* (1), the *extended work center* (2) and the *one-handed zone* (3) [4] (Lange and Windel 2013). The *work center* is located directly in front of the office worker and contains the objects used by both hands simultaneously (keyboard, pen and paper). Objects that can be reached easily by both hands are located in the *extended work center*, while those objects that can be reached with only one hand are sited in the *one-hand zone*.

The analysis of the spaces within reach of the participants shows how the bodies moved when sitting at the desk: Where the hands reached, how the body leaned forward, where the elbows rested or where the gaze was directed. Based on these movements we have drawn the invisible perimeters of the individual research space. In some of the cases, the space forms a central channel between head and screen, with very few oscillations to the left or right, while in others, the arrangement of the working tools suggests a certain rotation of the body.

2 A methodological reflection on the color-coding method: How can the units be adapted to each other? A color-coded image could suggest that the practice is equally analogous and digital, or that the computer is the same as a sheet of paper. This would of course be misleading. It cannot be a question of quantification, but rather of highlighting an entanglement of analog and digital media.

3 "Ergonomic instructions for action and ergonomically designed work equipment are similar to sports training methods and training equipment in this respect. They claim to contribute to the continuous improvement of the workers in the sense of the mentioned goals. Ergonomic work makes people healthier, more efficient and more successful—in this futuristic orientation, ergonomics promises a realm of work beyond exhaustion, fatigue, strain, wear and tear" (Own translation of Schmidt 2012, 135).

4 Own translation of Lange and Windel (2013).

The analysis of the participants' perception of the individual research space based on the autophotography highlights another noteworthy aspect: What exactly did they include in their own images of their workstations? Some focused solely on the desk or even on the screen, while others also photographed the chair, the pinboard, or even the window. The scope of the photograph can be interpreted as an indication of the extent of the individual research space.

In a second step, we synthesized these three analytical standpoints regarding the artifacts, the body and the size of the workplace. Two typical arrangements can thus be recognized, each opening up a differently shaped space for individual research (figs. 3.4 and 3.5): The first type is shaped like a *trapezoid prism* (a prism based on a trapezoid), stretching from the upper body and elbows to the outlines of the computer screen. It is therefore rather small, vertically oriented, and relatively rigid, since the body operates only within these dimensions, and the boundaries of the research space remain within the work surface. This arrangement is common among participants with a predominantly digital workspace, highlighting a link between a more digital working style and a verticality of the workspace.

The second type of space is shaped like an *oblate spheroid* (a sphere compressed along its poles), encompassing the whole body, the desk with all its artifacts, and possibly further equipment next to and under to the desk. It is therefore rather large, horizontally oriented and highly flexible, because the body rotates around itself, drawing a circle around the chair, desk, etc. Due to its size, it provides a space of immersion for the participant. This arrangement is common among participants with an equally analog and digital workspace, and reveals a link between the entanglement of analog and digital media and a horizontality of the workspace.

1.2 Understandings of Space: A Balancing Act Between Physicality and Virtuality?

How do the participants imagine their workspace, in both its physicality and virtuality? Or, to phrase it in the terms of Martina Löw, how does "synthesis" take place with regards to the physical and virtual research space (Löw 2001)? In order to explore this question and to elaborate the qualities of this physical and "virtual space" (Löw 2001; Arch+ 1992), we used the methods of mental mapping and interview-at-the-computer (→ See Chapter Two, pages 48–49).

Spatial Understanding

In the first round of mental mapping, we questioned the participants' (physical) spatialization of their knowledge practices. We selected the indeterminate term "spatialization" deliberately in order to address both the places where they conduct their research and the spaces created as a result of their practices. The drawings reveal two different ways in which space is understood: *Topological* and *multiscalar*, each of which indicates a different form of relationality.

The mental maps of participants with a *topological* understanding of space show different places positioned in relation to each other, as on a map or a floor plan of a building (figs. 3.6 and 3.7).

Contrary to expectations, the question led not only to such topological representations, but to a wider understanding that could be described as *multiscalar*. It is characterized by the inclusion of drawings of different scales in one mental map which serve to zoom in on the workspace (figs. 3.8, 3.12) and which, in some cases, form through their arrangement a three-dimensional space. According to this understanding, spaces are "nested" into one another in ever decreasing sizes, rather like a Russian doll: The desk forms a space, with the notebook on the desk forming a smaller space, and the picture in the notebook forming an even smaller space.

Both representations point to the dynamic nature of the research space, either in terms of switching between different places in the building or in the city—such as office, laboratory, workshop or home—or alternating between different scales such as room, desk or book.

In the second round of mental mapping, we asked the participants about their digital workspace. As stated previously, many of the interviewees denied the concept of „virtual space" entirely. They did not find it an appropriate term to describe the digital workspace. However, the majority of participants used linguistic and sketched spatial metaphors to characterize this area. Here,

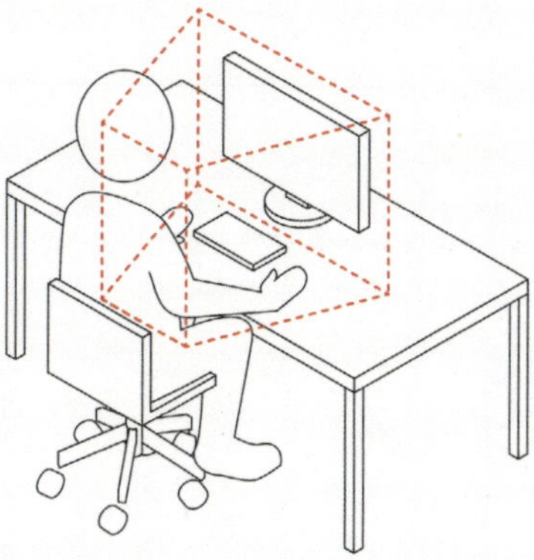

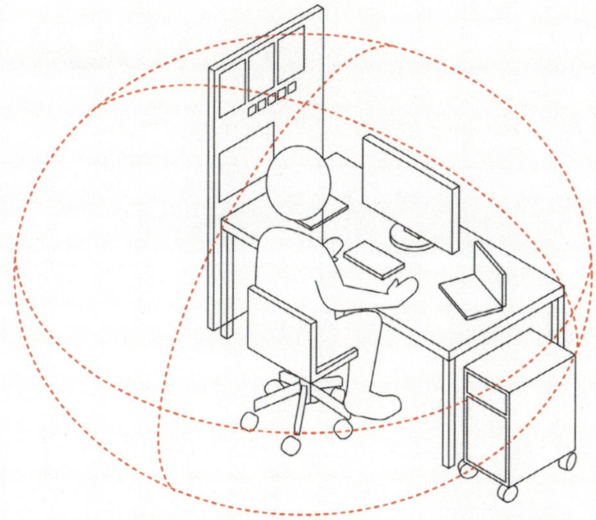

3.4 Trapezoid prism shape
3.5 Oblate spheroid shape

the interviewees can once more be divided into two groups: Those who think and represent the digital workspace as two dimensions, i.e. as a surface (spatial metaphor: Windows, paths, racetrack, etc.) (fig. 3.9) and those who think of and represent it three-dimensionally, i.e. as a space (spatial metaphor: World, river, sea, apartment/chamber) (fig. 3.10).

How do the ways in which the physical and digital spaces are understood relate to each other? Do they coincide? For some interviewees, the topological understanding of the physical workspace corresponds to the *two-dimensional* understanding of the digital workspace, and the *multiscalar* understanding of physical workspace to the *three-dimensional* understanding of the digital workspace—but not for all. This parallel evaluation of mental maps has not revealed any solid correlation. It was particularly unsatisfactory insofar as the separate evaluation showed little about the way these spaces are connected, or their relationships to one another.

Desktop and Worktable

A further attempt to compare both spatial interpretations was made by comparing the computer desktops of the participants with their worktops. Would we recognize a similar design of both dimensions (digital and analog) of the workspace? In order to explore this question, we combined each participant‘s auto-photography data with their interview-at-the-computer (→ See Chapter Two, pages 46 and 49).

As regards the analysis of the computer desktop, it is important to underscore the fact that the concept of the "desktop" is a construct created by its developers. In order to make an abstract start or navigation interface more relatable, they have used a spatial metaphor which "treats the computer screen as if it is the top of the user's desk, upon which objects such as documents and folders of documents can be placed" (Wikipedia contributors 2019). However, our empirical research shows that the desktop is subject to a variety of uses and appropriations: It is messy for some, tidy for others. Some people put a picture on it, others do not. It contains shortcuts to files, programs or websites. Most interviewees share a joint trait: They close neither programs nor their computer. The consequence is that the desktop is rarely used as a start interface or navigation interface. In the interviews-at-the-computer, three different functions could be discerned, which point to three discrete spatial conceptions (fig. 3.11):

— It is used by some as a *surface* that serves as a temporary source of storage for the things they are currently working on. The participants say that they "put things on it" (Maximilian[5], Humanities) or that it works "like a table that is

5 The names of participants in the Experimental Zone were replaced by pseudonyms throughout the publication on the grounds of data protection.

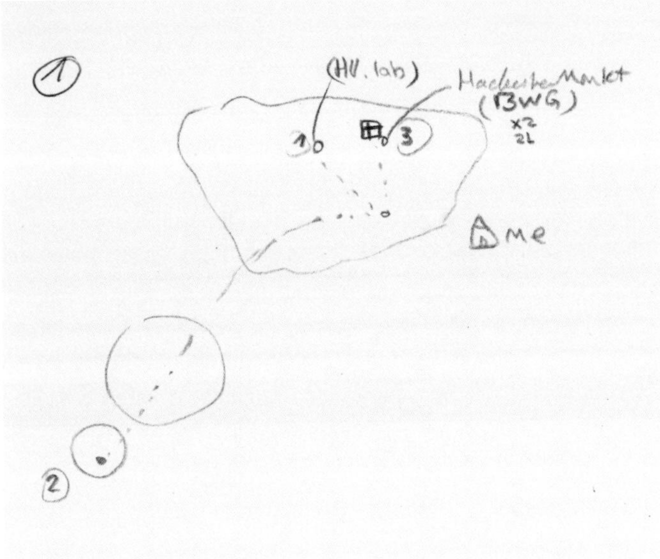

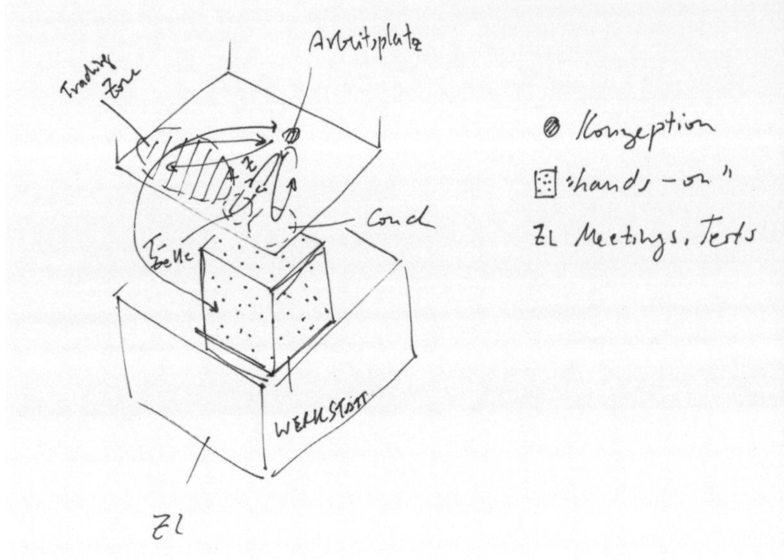

Figs. 3.6–7: Mental maps indicating a topological understanding of space (Arian, Engineering Sciences; Alexander, Design disciplines)

immediate” (Alexander, Design disciplines). Subject to a continual process of tidying up, it is thus dynamic and changeable. In this context, the desktop is conceived of as two-dimensional and limited.

— It is used by others as a *window*, in the sense that it contains nothing at all and opens the view onto the horizon. It is cultivated deliberately as a “pure and empty space” (Arianna, Humanities) that seems endless. The participants insist on the calm atmosphere that they seek as a result. In this context, the desktop is conceived of as an opening to a three-dimensional, unlimited space.

— It is used by still others as a *trash can*, i.e. as a source of storage for temporary files that are not thrown away but stored there and can still be found by using the search function. An analysis of the auxiliary verbs or pronouns appearing in the mental map interviews is particularly interesting inasmuch as it indicates a pit-like depth: “That ends up on the desktop […- The most recent files are on top [of the other files-” (Martin, Design disciplines); “I'll chuck it in here” (Paolo, Natural Sciences). It is as if the space extends “downwards”, rather like a garbage dump.

The evaluation shows the manifold ways in which the desktop can be understood in a spatial sense. With the exception of the first group, where the desktop is a surface, no other analogy can be drawn between physical and virtual space. The question of “analogy” was misleading, in that it simultaneously suggests the separation and comparability of the digital and analog desktop. In the course of the investigation, we realized that we were primarily interested in the interface of the two and their relationship to each other. The biggest shortcoming of this first analysis was that we approached the question of virtuality solely by means of representations, i.e. the participants' depictions of their digital workspace in the mental maps. However, as we had, as yet, failed to create a link with the physicality of the digital media, it was therefore extremely difficult to identify the relationship between physicality and virtuality.

Seamlessness

The integrative analysis of the empirical data belonging to Hannah, a designer, reveals flowing transitions between the so-called physical and virtual spaces (figs. 3.12–14). The analysis of her two mental maps shows how her research space is formed as an assemblage of different artifacts and digital and analog media, as well as on different scales. Several artifacts are depicted on both the “physical” and the “digital” mental

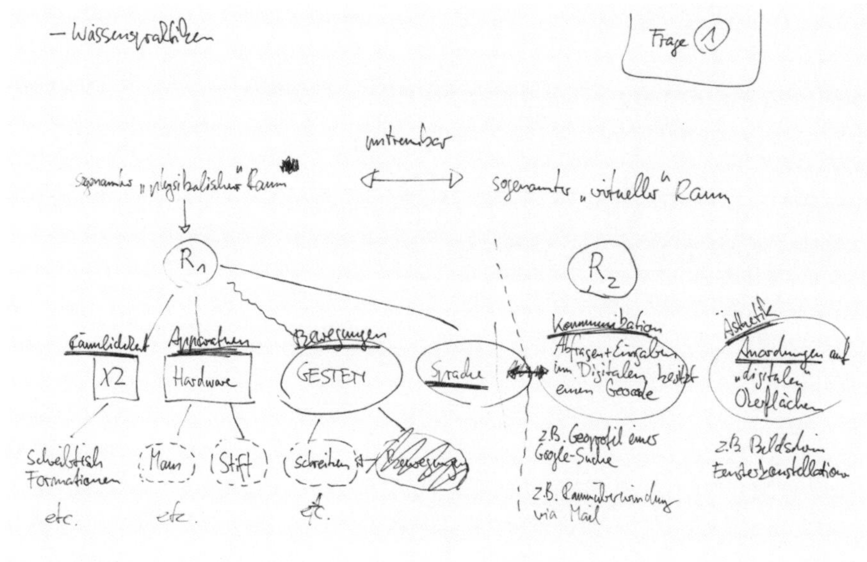

Fig. 3.8: Mental map indicating a multiscalar understanding of space (Fabian, Humanities)

map, including the computer in a central location. This indicates that Hannah's physical and virtual research research spaces do not exist independently, but instead form an integrative continuum. Hannah's auto-photography clearly demonstrates the way in which such a continuous space is created during the working process. She commented that she was in the process of "building icons for a presentation": A sheet of paper with initial sketches lies on the desk and connects almost seamlessly to the first screen, where an image editing program is opened and in which the icons are drawn digitally, and is then extended to the second screen, where a presentation program is in use showing the icons in their final context. This exemplary sequence underscores the seamless nature of analog and digital working steps, and therefore the unity of the observed space.

How can we investigate this seamlessness of physical-virtual dimensions or the integration of both (physical-virtual) dimensions of the individual research space further?

2 Dynamic Enfolding of the Physical-Virtual Workspace by Practice

We continued the evaluation by taking a differentiated look at the practices of the participants. We used a combination of participant observation and auto-photography to explore how space in its physical-virtual dimensions unfolds via the different practices. Our original goal of a typification of workspaces by individual proved to be less productive than an analysis by practice. Which dynamic characteristics do the individual research spaces exhibit as a result of the researchers' diverse activities?

2.1 Interdisciplinary Practice Model

In order to analyze the individual research spaces by practice, a number of key practices needed to be selected. However, our multidisciplinary group, featuring researchers from the humanities, design disciplines, engineering and natural sciences, exhibited a wide variety of practices. Our participants conducted all those practices at the Experimental Zone that were feasible in an office environment and did not require the specific equipment of a laboratory, workshop or computer center, such as reading, writing, designing, thinking, conceiving, researching, drawing, sketching, collecting, analyzing, building models, mapping, programming, and computing.

Our analysis showed that while some practices were common to all researchers, such as reading, writing and sketching, some were specific to certain disciplines, such as drawing, programming or prototyping. For the purpose

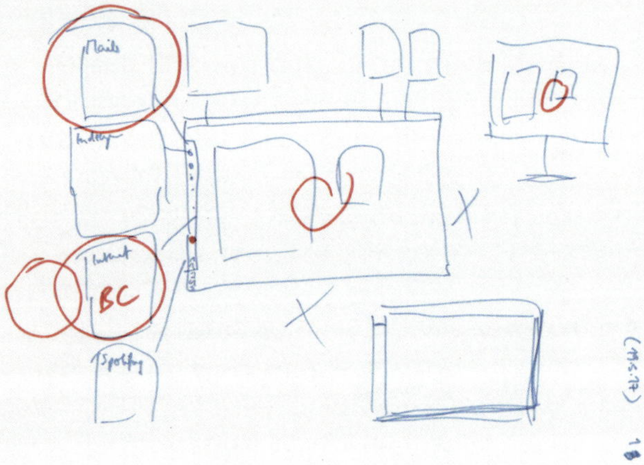

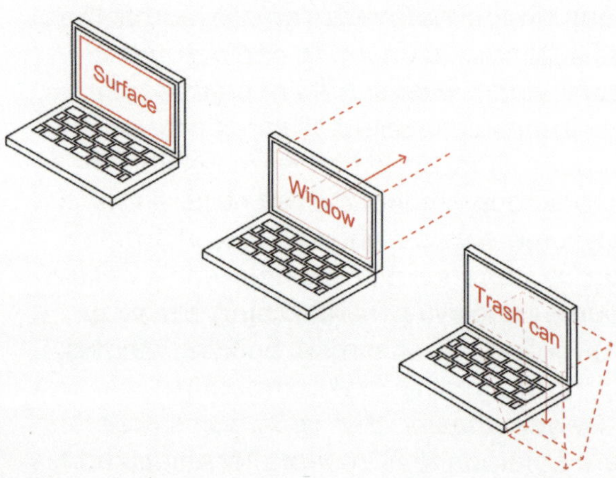

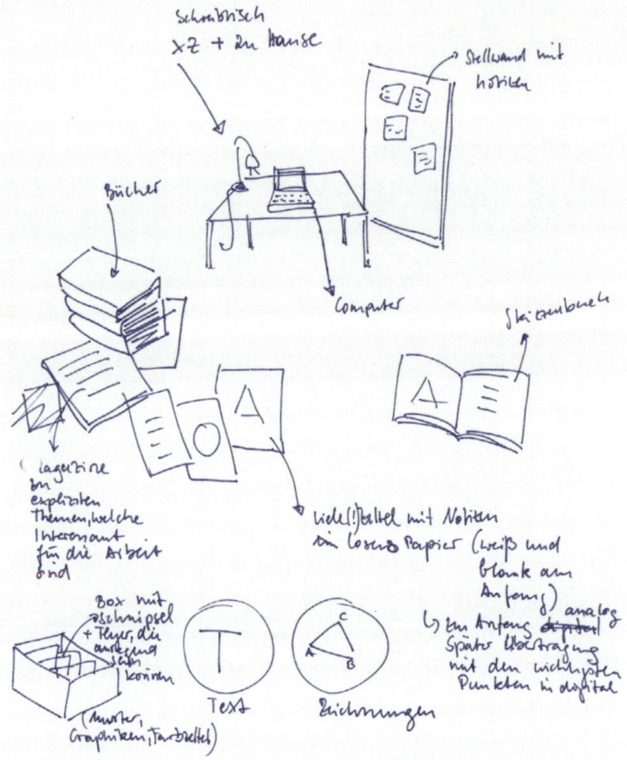

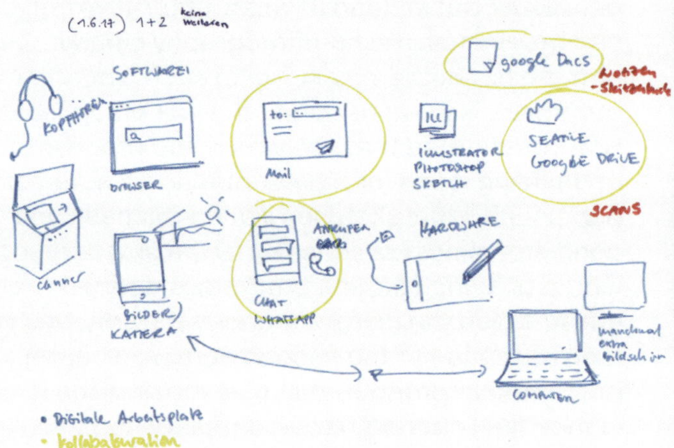

Fig. 3.9 (top left): Two-dimensional understanding of the digital workspace (Laura, Design disciplines)
Fig. 3.10 (middle left): Three-dimensional understanding of the digital workspace (Arianna, Humanities)
Fig. 3.11 (bottom left): Desktop as a surface, window and trash can
Figs. 3.12–14 (right): Mental Map, digital mental map, auto-photography (Hannah, Design disciplines)

of creating comparability between the practices despite the disciplinary-related differences, we developed an interdisciplinary practice model (fig. 3.15) in which the practices from different fields are subsumed within four categories. On the one hand, the practice model is based on our participant observation and, on the other, on the interviews-at-the-computer, during which the participants described their practices. The four categories of practices are defined as follows:

1.
The category **researching-investigating** comprises all practices aiming to collect data, sources, materials and information.

2.
The category **reading-receiving** describes all practices aiming to acquire new specialist knowledge.

3.
The category **conceptualizing-developing ideas** includes all practices aiming to elaborate new thoughts, to create initial contexts or initial sketches.

4.
Finally, the category **formalizing-evaluating** concerns writing, modelling, analyzing and also programming.

It is important to note that this schematic representation fails to do justice to the constant overlapping of the phases. Many of these practices are intertwined in their execution: The researchers sometimes switch from one category to the other within a few minutes, and sometimes practices in different categories occur in parallel or symbiotically. We regard this categorical separation as a heuristic means to make the different phases of scientific practice comparable.

In Chapter One, we distinguished between three central activities of scientific work: Knowledge production, knowledge distribution and knowledge storage (→ See Chapter One, page 23). In the following analyses, we will focus on individual practices of knowledge production such as reading, but also include activities related to storing and making notes that have proven to

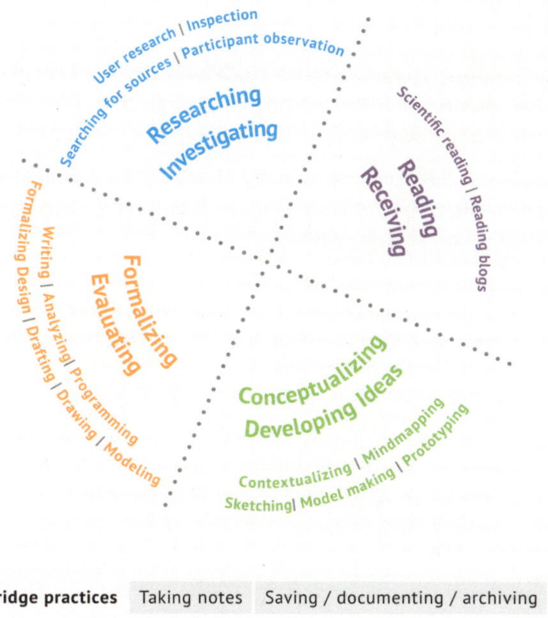

Fig. 3.15: Interdisciplinary Practice Model

be "bridge practices", as they are always active in the background of knowledge production.

2.2 Spaces of Producing and Storing

Our empirical analysis shows that the design of the workspace is not static, but dynamic: The participants rearranged the order of their workspace differently depending on the specific working practice, for example by adding additional elements to the current assemblage (e.g. A3 sheets for sketching) or by assuming different body postures (leaning in the armchair or standing at the workbench). We would like to subject the practice categories entitled conceptualizing, reading, and researching to closer examination. For the practice category "formalizing" we chose the two practices writing and drawing as a result of our interdisciplinary target group. Finally, we examine the bridge practice of storing. The investigation reveals a paradoxical phenomenon: The spaces' dynamic unfolding according to each practice and, at the same time, the marked constancy of the arrangements required for the same.

Conceptualizing

We began by taking a close look at the practice of *conceptualizing*. On the basis of interviews with the participants, conceptualizing is defined as the development of new thoughts or coherency. This practice occurs when researchers attempt to create an initial overview of a problem, order thoughts and establish relationships. All participants, regardless of their disciplinary backgrounds, provided a homogeneous image of what conceptualizing signifies:

> "This is the kind of freedom that paper gives you. [...] You cannot do this at the computer (he shows his notes). [...] Like, this is from yesterday. I don't know, you're thinking, things come up, you categorize them. You see one, two, or different methods you should use, you can draw stuff and show it to people."
> Arian, Natural Sciences, interview-at-the-computer

Several aspects are highlighted by the quotation above. The practice is characterized by a certain speed or a quick production, as if one wants to grasp and hold the thoughts rapidly. It takes place analogously, on paper and usually in visual form (fig. 3.16). The participants described the result as "mind maps", "scribbles", "drawings" or "sketches". The knowledge carriers are thus exclusively analog and image-based media. The *affordance*[6] of the analog medium paper consists in its unstructured or unlimited nature. The hand was attributed a quintessential role: Many participants commented that they "think with their hands" and that only by moving the pen on the paper could they give form to their thoughts. This provides empirical confirmation of the practice theoretical assumption that the dichotomy between mental and physical activities is misleading, and that the bodies of the scientists cannot be ignored when investigating knowledge processes. The computer moves to the edge of the desk, remaining open as a possible display without being used directly. However, as a next step, the scribbles and sketches are often digitized—either scanned or transferred into a digital format. Some participants thematized the next step of the "transfer... [as] a qualitative leap of one's own, [in which] one sorts and precisely defines, [...] and also simply structures everything, and brings things systematically into a sequence, specifies them. So that always goes from the rough to the granular, to the fine" (Isabelle, Design disciplines, interview-at-the-computer). Here, however, the grey zone between conceptualizing and formalizing has already been entered.

The practice of conceptualizing is characterized by its low-key specifications. The simple combination of paper and pen is described as a prerequisite, as is the necessary free space for the execution of the practice. The assemblage thus consists of the following elements: Sheets of paper or a notebook, a pen, a person, a table, a chair and the open computer in the background.

To summarize, the properties of the space of conceptualizing are as follows: In the eyes of the participants, the space should be spacious or infinite. It spreads out horizontally, e.g. on the desktop, the workbench or over many notebook pages. It is permeable to the environment and can become collaborative since, as some participants remarked, conceptualizing is also often practiced during meetings.

Writing

The second practice we subjected to analysis was that of *writing*. Here, we focus on the creation of contents in text form (not notes), i.e. on the writing of essays, lectures, books, reports, blog entries, etc. This form of writing played a central role for all participants. Although the *Interdisciplinary Laboratory* has been open to other output formats (Germer 2019), classical text output has remained central.

As in the practice of conceptualizing, the participants painted a homogeneous picture of the practice of writing, regardless of their disciplinary background. This practice requires a solid framework for its execution. The participants each used a specific writing software, but with some disciplinary differences: Most humanities scholars and designers preferred a word processor such as Office Word, where the user formats the text independently, while engineers and scientists favored a document preparation system like LaTeX, where the user writes a plain text and provides it with formatting commands in order to produce an output format for subsequent printing. What all participants reported, however, is the increasing use of collaborative features: The writing takes place individually, with researchers typing alone on their keyboards and formulating the sentences in silence—but a collaborative asynchronous dimension of the practice is becoming more prevalent:

6 Affordance is a concept developed by the psychologist James J. Gibson, who defines it as the "latent set of possible actions that environment and objects enable" (McDonnell 2010, 1806).

"Because we write a lot collectively, we do it more and more with Google Docs or with other share functions like iCloud, but in the end it's best with Google Drive, even if we'd rather use the university's own solution. But it's still too weak compared to Google. The way you can track changes, comment on them and so on. That's integrated with email and stuff like that."
Fabian, Humanities, interview-at-the-computer

Despite not actually writing "face to face", the participants wrote collectively, yet asynchronously and in a digitally mediated manner. It follows that the knowledge carriers of writing were exclusively digital and text-based media. Only in a few cases was the text converted into an analog form during editing, i.e. printed out. Interestingly, the participants did not thematize the body at all. Unlike other practices (such as conceptualizing, but also reading, drawing, etc.), the practice of writing was reduced to its mental dimension.

Two types of assemblages occurred repeatedly: The first type of assemblage occurs in workspaces that are equipped and furnished to a higher degree, and consists of the following elements: Computer, word processor, PDF viewer (to view literature), potentially previous own texts, online dictionaries, person, table, chair. In addition, other people (whether co-authors or reviewers) feature in the word processing program itself. The interviews point to one of many shared, specific arrangements that stretch across the screens: The text is opened in the main screen while the other sources are displayed in the other screens (fig. 3.17).

The second type of assemblage is rather minimalistic and is used in alternation with the first type: It consists solely of a computer with a spartan display (full-screen mode), a person, a chair, and a table. It was described as a "white sheet" by several participants and, as a reduced version of the assemblage, it should allow the full focus to be placed on the activity and thus facilitate the practice's execution.

To summarize, the properties of the space of writing are as follows: The space is frequently vertically oriented and sequentially structured, i.e. texts are read one after another. It is relatively impermeable to the environment. It has a collaborative dimension, but only asynchronously.

Fig. 3.16: Workspace while conceptualizing, auto-photography (Isabelle, Design disciplines)

Reading

The third practice we analyzed was that of *reading*. By reading, we mean the reception of specialist and scientific texts, which, like the practice of writing, assumes a position of central importance among all participants. It is understood as the appropriation of new ideas through text markings, excerpts and notes. In contrast to the practices of conceptualizing and writing, the participants did not exhibit a single, homogeneous reading practice. An essential difference lied in the analog or digital dimension, splitting the target group between those who prefer the printed text and those who read digitally. The former preferred the materiality of the paper in order to capture complex content. However, digital media were present in the assemblages and served primarily as extraction tools - whether simultaneously or directly afterwards. The participants complained about the difficulties of reading analogously and wanting to extract digitally and developed different strategies in this respect: They "rescanned the manually annotated pdf" (Martin, Design disciplines, interview-at-the-computer) or "transferred individual comments into a word document" (Arianna, Humanities, interview-at-the-computer). To make it easier to switch between media, one participant used speech recognition software to digitally dictate individual passages of the analog text, allowing her to avoid a distraction of the gaze and, accordingly, of her attention. Other participants preferred to read exclusively digitally.

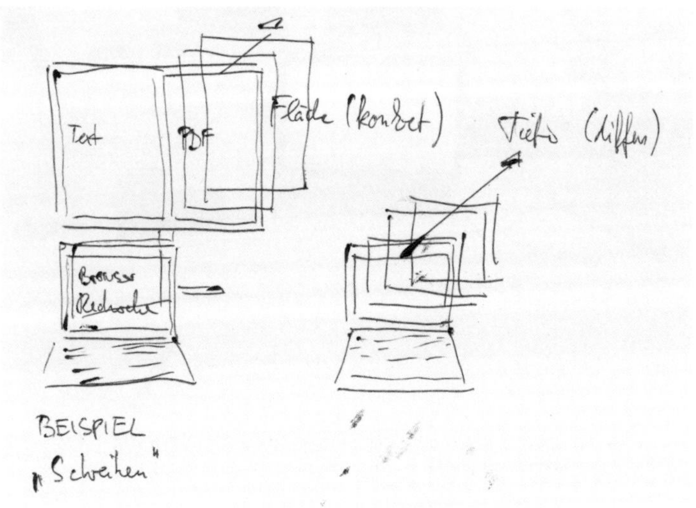

Fig. 3.17: Space of writing, mental map (Fabian, Humanities)

Interestingly, most of them commented that they refrain from using their computer for this purpose, instead employing a different device such as a tablet, an e-book reader or sometimes even a phone.

It is noteworthy that both digital and analog readers assigned a central role to the body: The reception of content requires a certain degree of relaxation—therefore some liked to read in an armchair—but, at the same time, it necessitates active appropriation, which takes place by underlining text passages through hand movements, whether digitally or analogously. Two types of assemblages existed in this context:

The first type consists of a tablet or an e-book reader, a pdf viewer with annotation function, an armchair, and a person.

The second type features an analog version of the text, a pen, a computer, a digital dictionary, a word processing program, a desk, a chair, and a person. To summarize, the properties of the space of reading are as follows: The space is usually vertically oriented and sequentially structured, i.e. texts are read one after another. It is impermeable to the physical-virtual environment, i.e. the boundaries are highly non-porous. It usually has no collaborative dimension.

Drawing

The fourth practice analyzed was that of *drawing*. By drawing, we refer to the creation of content in visual form, i.e. the production of pictorial knowledge. This practice was observed predominantly among the designers in the context of their design activities.

As with the practice of reading, a certain digitalization is indicated here, which, however, nonetheless contains many analog moments. While manual drawing has a conceptual character, as explained above, the digital drawing is viewed more as a finished product. Digital drawing takes place in the context of a fixed or non-mobile assemblage, the central element of which is, ideally, a screen with high resolution. As regards the analog drawing, the participants emphasized its haptic dimension, and—similar to the practice of conceptualizing—the role of the hand: "Drawing by hand somehow contains an intelligence that you don't have at the computer" (Frieda, Design disciplines, interview-at-the-computer).

For most of the participants, the practice of drawing takes place at the interface of the digital and the analog:

> "There is this technique in architecture, to draw something by hand first, then to draw it again on the computer, then to print it out and to lay tracing paper over it—there is this typical transparent paper that you put over it—and then to draw in corrections. And this is then transferred back into the computer."
> Frieda, Design disciplines, interview-at-the-computer

A number of intriguing practices were noted during participant observation, which are characterized by an overlapping of analog and digital media:

> "Alexander [a designer] draws a prototype on a computer in a 3D drawing program. Next, he takes transparent paper and places it on the screen and draws the contours of the digital drawing analogously. Then he continues to draw analogously, he seems to try something out. He continues scribbling. Then he turns toward his screen again and completes the digital drawing based on his analog drawing."
> Field notes, Experimental Zone

The assemblage common among all participants consists of the following elements: A screen, a mouse or a pad, a sheet of paper with the manual drawing, a pen, a computer, a chair, a table, and a person.

To summarize, the properties of the space of drawing are as follows: The space is frequently horizontally oriented and structured in a diffused manner, i.e. contents are processed side by side and in parallel. It is impermeable to the physical-virtual environment, i.e. the boundaries are relatively non-porous. It usually lacks a collaborative dimension.

Researching

The fifth practice we analyzed was that of *researching*, which is an essential activity for all participants. According to the participants, researching signifies the collection of information, sources and, above all, literature. In the Experimental Zone, research took place in an exclusively digital manner on the Internet. The participants described fixed paths via which they always carry out their research: Existing infrastructures, usually large databases, such as Google Scholar or Web of Science, provided them with legitimate knowledge. In contrast to other practices, the body was not addressed by the interviewees at all. What unites the participants was a degree of concern regarding their ability to develop an appropriate manner in which to handle the abundance and over-availability of information. They were all extremely preoccupied with various possibilities of carrying out their research, and tried out different systems to manage the research results. A level of dissatisfaction with the existing software solutions existed, which create a specific dependency and exhibit a lack of long-term stability or compatibility from project to project. The most common assemblage consists of the following elements: A computer, a browser, a database, a form of administration software, a chair, a table, and a person.

To summarize, the properties of the space of researching are as follows: It seems endless and deep, but is actually relatively structured and determined by the existing database infrastructure. It is very permeable to its environment and can be set up collaboratively.

In addition to the main practices, we were able to observe "bridge practices" in the context of our investigation, such as storing, documenting, archiving and noting. These occur in all four work phases and often form transitions between them. As an example, we would like to examine the space of storing.

Storing—a Bridge Practice

Securing search results, initial thoughts and formulated outcomes constituted an important and constant "work-in-progress" which numbers among the participants' everyday practices. Our investigation has provided an original insight into the structuring of the participants' knowledge. The participants' practices of storing were all based on the infrastructure provided by the *Interdisciplinary Laboratory*, such as storage space on the university server or external hard disks.

All data was stored using a combination of analog and digital media, depending on the materiality of the artifacts with which the participants work. In many cases, however, the working documents were completely digitized for storage purposes. This means that the digital structuring was more formative and central. What is noteworthy is the collective dimension of storing, a result of the work on research topics in teams, which, in many cases, led to the phenomenon of storage duplication (once individually, once collectively) despite attempts at synchronization. The common assemblage thus consists of the following elements: A computer, a digital folder structure, the university server, a file storage service (such as Google Drive, Dropbox), a chair, a table, and a person.

In addition to these common characteristics, three ways of structuring knowledge were observed among the participants. These are closely related to the relationship between body and technique. Participants described the practice of storing as a technology-based securing of knowledge that supports the cognitive capacity of their memories. They described different relationships with their memories, which in turn strongly condition their use of technologies. Here, three types of participants were observed, which, however, cannot be hermetically separated from one another and should be understood as a continuum:

1.

Firstly, there were those who trust their memories. These participants did not have the urge to store everything, but trust that they will somehow remember their key thoughts: "If I don't remember

Figs. 3.18-20: Video still from the interviews-at-the-computer
(Martin, Design disciplines; Martina, Design disciplines; Ada, Humanities)

it, it's gone, but. . it's absorbed inside the work somehow. So I'm. . I'm also not obsessed with remembering, you know. . It's like it's there. It somehow comes in circles. . I remember who wrote about what. That's. . that's for sure" (Dana, Humanities, interview-at-the-computer). Their structuring of knowledge was minimal. In some cases, they did not have a folder structure, but loosely stored the current documents and remembered their location on the computer (fig. 3.18).

2.
Secondly, there were those who remember the path leading to the file. This target group was the largest among the participants. They had a folder structure, often by project and topic, in which they stored their documents. This structuring was based on the fact that they remember their personal logic and can thus locate the file time and again (fig. 3.19). They only selected and stored certain documents.

3.
Thirdly and finally, there were those who leave storage completely to technology and do not trust their own memories. These participants used either the download folder or the desktop as a means of storage where everything was deposited. They had a folder structure that functioned only partially and was not subject to further maintenance. Instead, they used the search function to locate their files (fig. 3.20).

To summarize, the properties of the space of storing are as follows: The space is deep as well as relatively structured, and determined externally by the existing server and cloud infrastructure. It is very permeable to its environment and can be designed collaboratively.

Our analysis has focused on the six main research practices in the Experimental Zone. The main emerging characteristics of the respective individual research spaces have been described for each practice (fig. 3.21). While the spaces of conceptualizing and drawing are more likely to be horizontal and flat and the spaces of writing and reading, in turn, vertical and sequentially structured, the spaces of researching and storing are frequently characterized by their depth. Accordingly, the borders of these spaces are either porous (e.g. in the case of conceptualizing, researching or archiving) or non-porous (e.g. writing or reading). The spaces of conceptualizing, writing and storing may also be arranged collaboratively. However, when and how is an assemblage activated as a space, and when is it deactivated? Which points of departure does this reveal, and which questions does it raise within the context of the design of the spaces which feature within interdisciplinary research?

2.3 (De-)activation of the Individual Research Spaces

In Part One, three main characteristics of the activation of space (→ see Part One, page 22), were described, which we are now able to define more precisely on the basis of our empirical findings. Our analyses have revealed three dimensions of this form of activation: Topologically (the spatial relationship between human and non-human, digital and analog elements), bodily (the physical postures and gestures via which space takes shape), and embedded (the nesting of the assemblages within assemblages).

As regards the question of the *topology* of the assemblage, the study has shown that the participants prefer relatively fixed repeated positions. This positioning is more or less determined by the infrastructure to which the researchers have to adapt. Whether fully equipped or minimalist, such topologies permit the retrieval of the appropriate space in everyday routines. This occurs when the researcher enters into a *bodily* interaction with the familiar assemblage, performing the practice by adopting a certain body posture and by means of certain gestures. It is almost as if the hand in the arrangement recognizes what needs to be done. These findings contradict the image of a highly flexible producer of knowledge, whose creativity can unfold anywhere and even feeds on constant changes. On the contrary, our investigation reveals that, despite the dynamic unfolding of the research spaces, a routinized and familiar assemblage lowers the inhibition threshold for the execution of a practice. The challenge for design would therefore be to create environments which promote the development of such routinized assemblages.

Conceptualizing	Porous	Horizontal / flat	Collaborative
Writing	Unporous	Vertical / sequential	Collaborative
Reading	Unporous	Vertical / sequential	Individual
Drawing	Unporous	Horizontal / flat	Individual
Researching	Porous	Deep	Individual
Storing	Porous	Deep	Collaborative

Fig. 3.21: Characteristics of the individual spaces of researching according to practice

Indeed, the third dimension of *embedding* is central insofar as it thematizes the environment as a potential disruptive factor. Depending on the practice in question, the individual research spaces demonstrate varying degrees of (im)permeability. Here, the environment is interpreted as a larger assemblage in which an assemblage is embedded, e.g. several individual and collaborative research spaces form a larger assemblage.

We are interested in the question of how such an assemblage of assemblages can be designed in order to enable the parallel enactment of the highly diverse practices of our target group. Imagine this scenario: Isabelle reads concentratedly at her desk and absorbs new knowledge. Next to her, Fabian and Alexander begin to conceptualize loudly together using a sheet of paper and their computers. At the next table, Eden researches literature and listens with interest to her colleagues' exchange.

How would a spatial structure which permits the coexistence of individual spaces and concomitantly promotes collaboration, e.g. as a new space within a space or as a fusion of individual spaces, look? What effects can collaboration have on this? The interdisciplinary constellation of our target group, located at the interface of design and the humanities, posed a specific challenge as far as the coexistence of certain practices was concerned, but also revealed interesting acculturation processes between the groups. Certain assemblages were imitated, and thereby helped to spread previously rare practices among the respective groups. We were able to observe the learning processes undergone by designers (both architects and designers) when dealing with (scientific) reading and writing and, conversely, those of humanities scholars in terms of drawing and visual documentation. Subsequent parts will include a deeper analysis of these aspects.

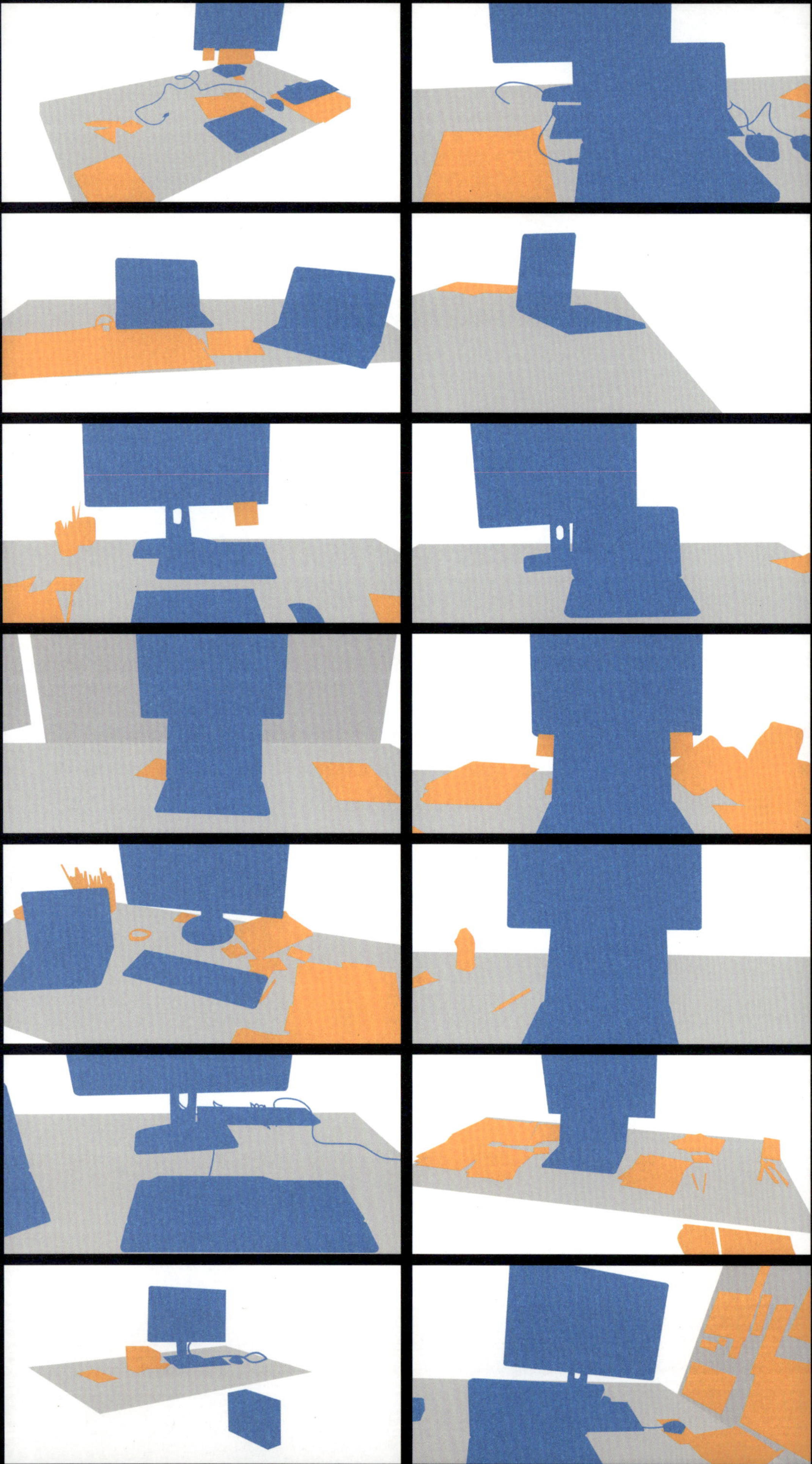

01
02
03
04
05
06
07
08
09
10
11
12
13
14

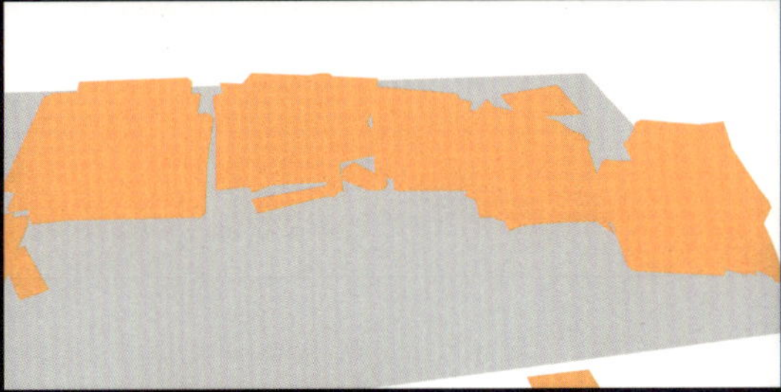
15
16

17
18

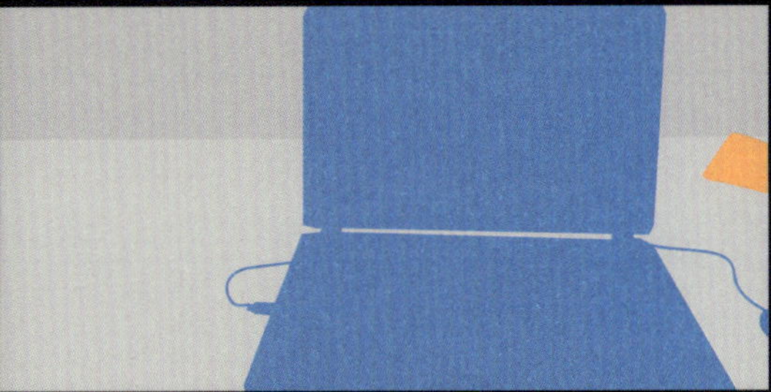

19
20

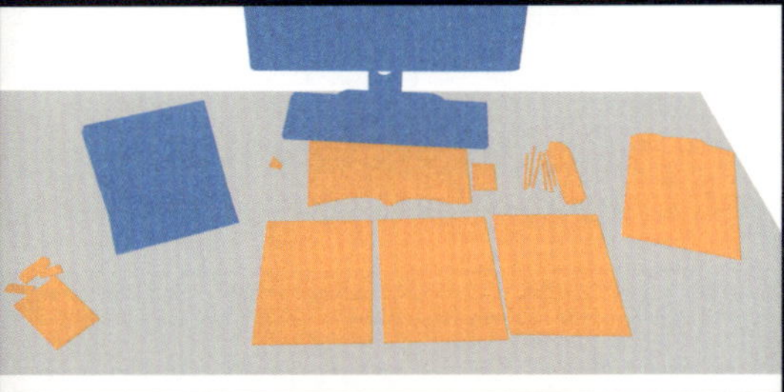

21
22

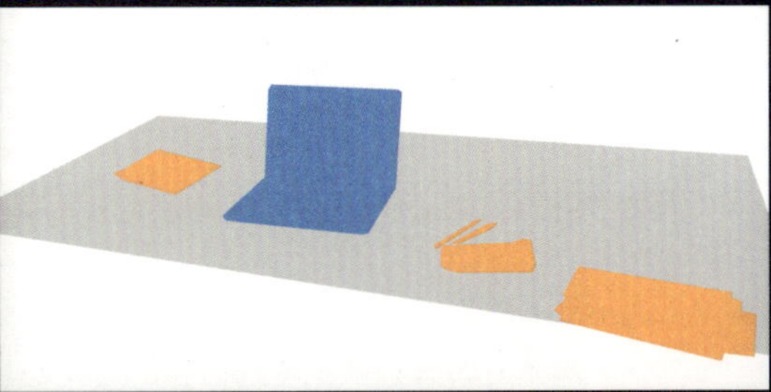

23
24

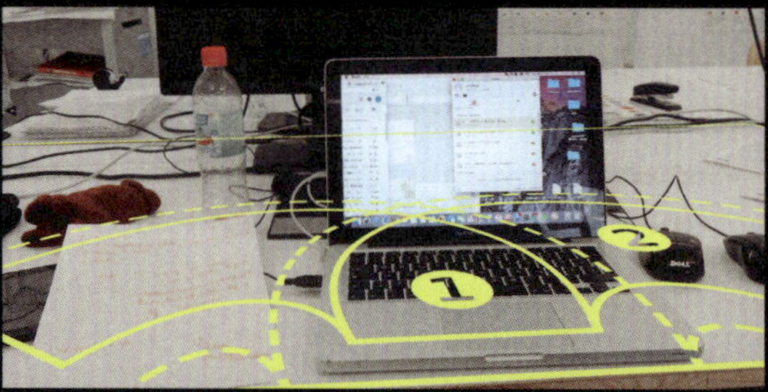

01
02

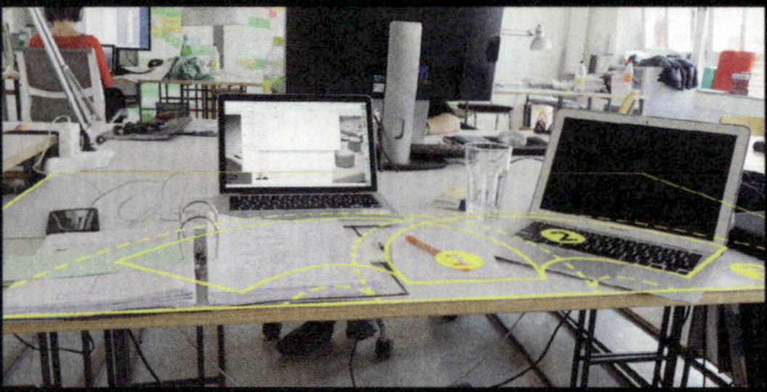

03
04

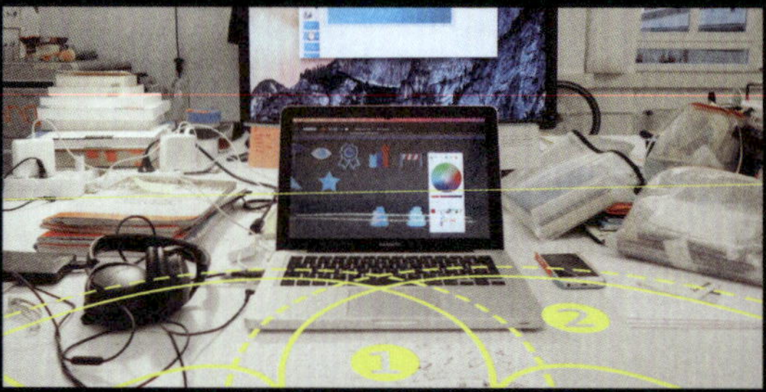

05
06

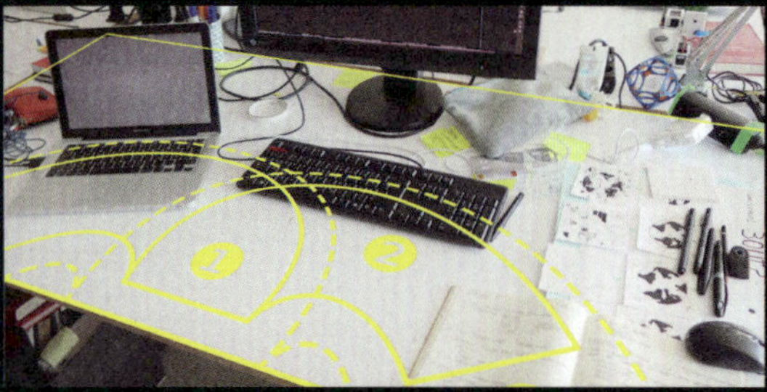
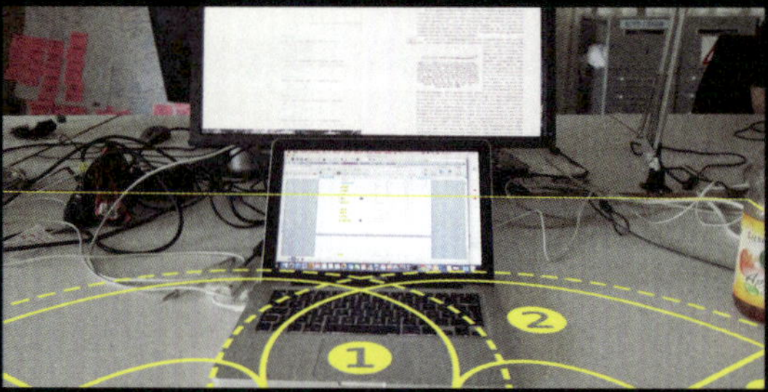

07
08

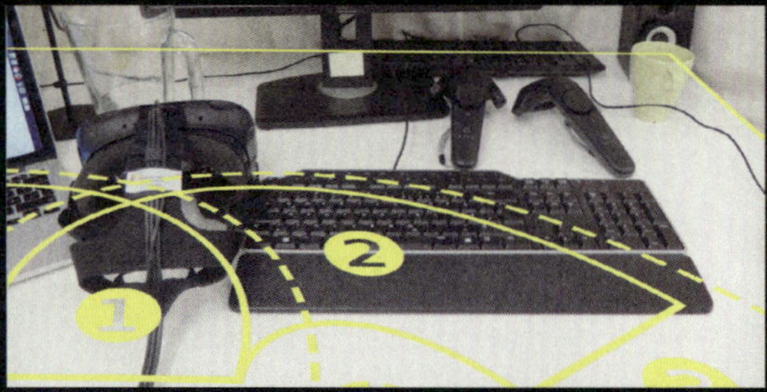

09
10

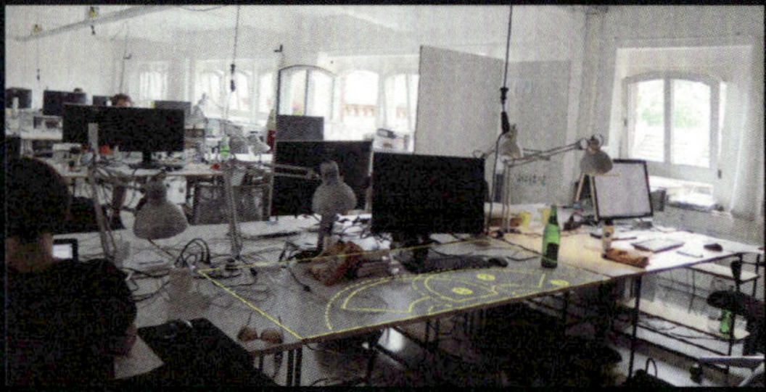
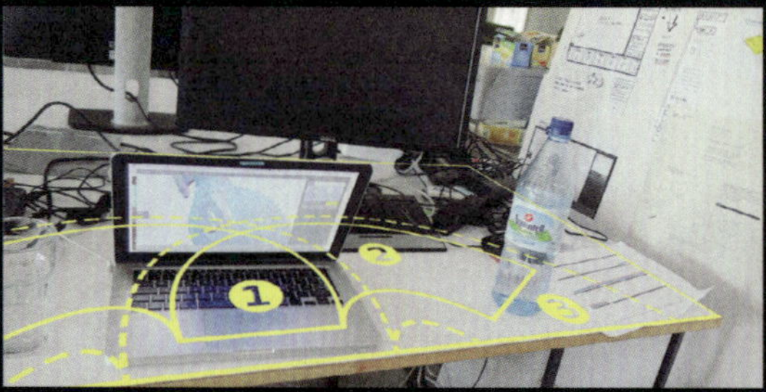

11
12

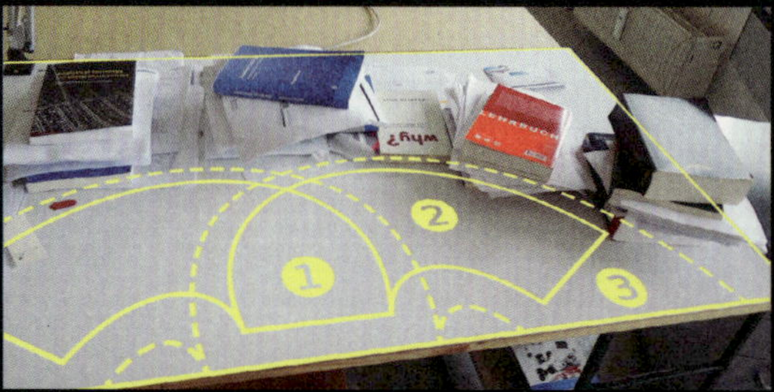

13
14

15
16
17
18
19
20
21
22
23
24

Analysis of the spaces within reach. The analysis is based on the auto-photography, in the process of which the participants photographed their own workspace. By superimposing the outlines of the spaces within reach onto the auto-photographs, the arrangement of objects on the desks was examined as regards their relation to the researcher's body (→ See Part Three, page 51).

01 Alexander, design disciplines
02 Anna, design disciplines
03 Antonia, humanities
04 Arian, natural sciences
05 Arianna, humanities
06 Fabian, engineering sciences
07 Federico, natural sciences
08 Hannah, design disciplines
09 Isabelle, design disciplines
10 Julian, humanities
11 Lars, natural sciences

13 Leona, humanities
14 Lukas, engineering sciences
15 Mara, humanities
16 Mark, humanities
17 Martin, design disciplines
18 Miriam, design disciplines
19 Niko, engineering sciences;
20 Oliver, humanities
21 Ralf, humanities
22 Sibylle, humanities
23 Stefanie, humanities

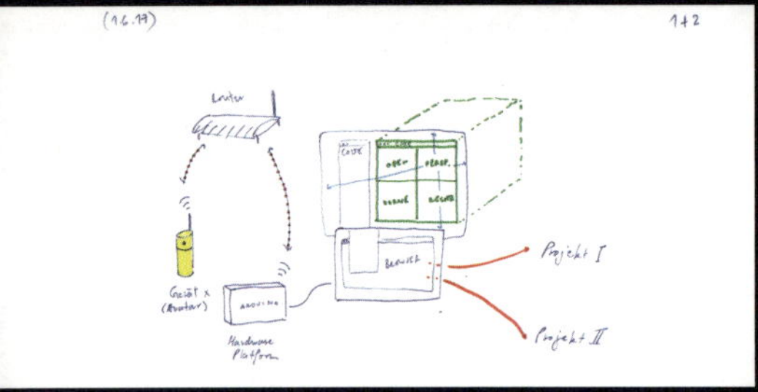

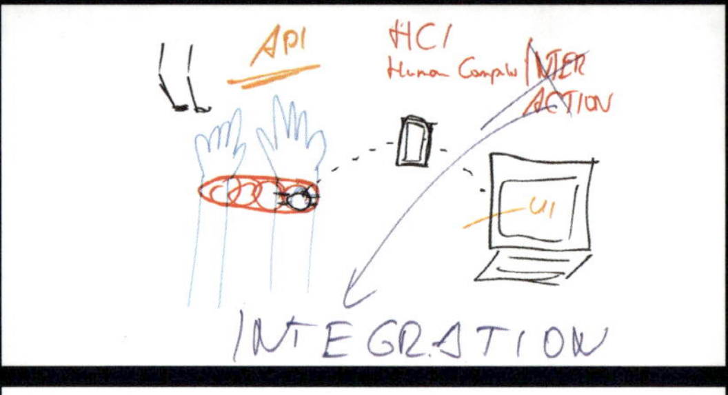

01
02

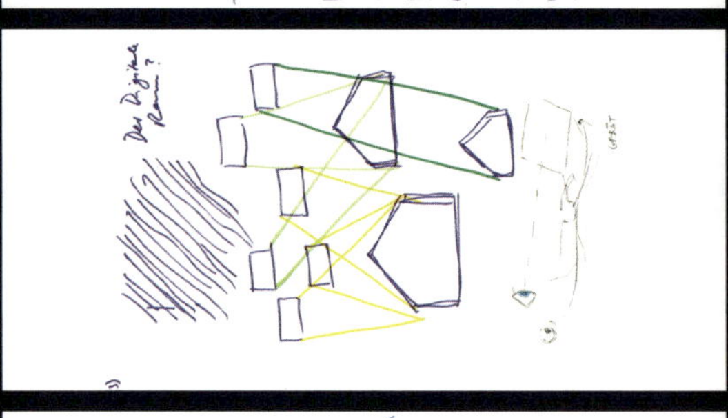

03
04

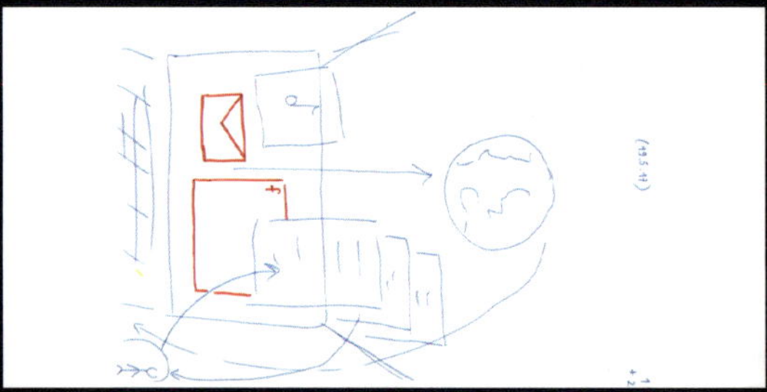

05
06

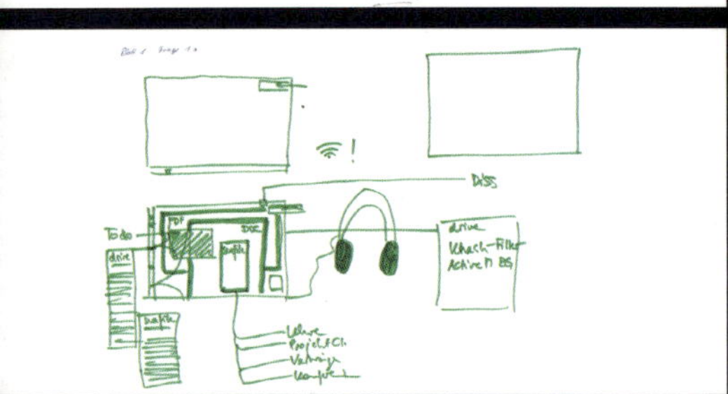

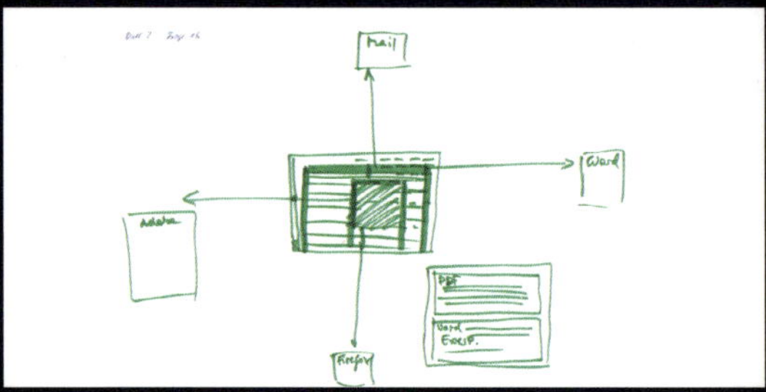

07
08

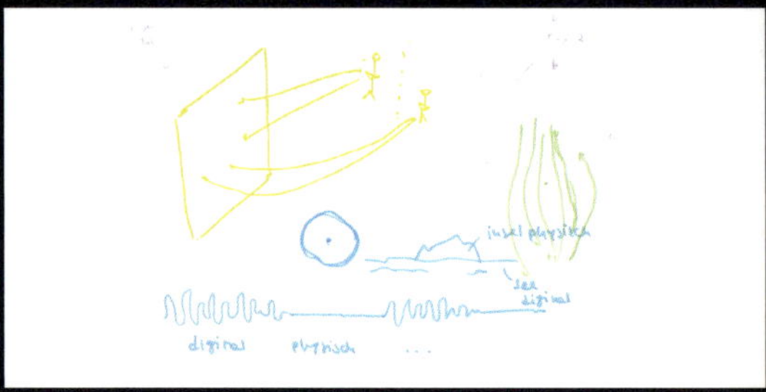

09
10

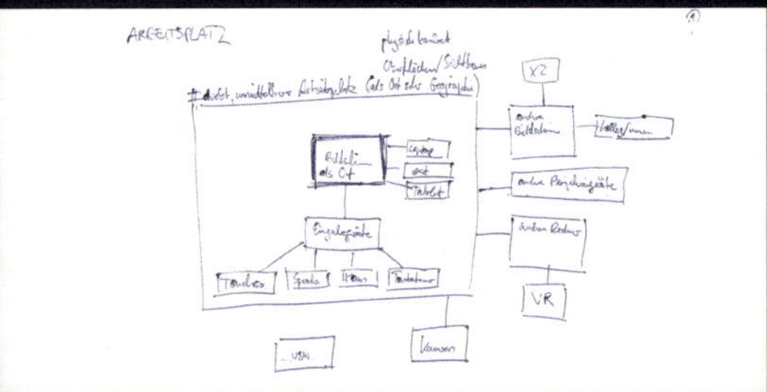

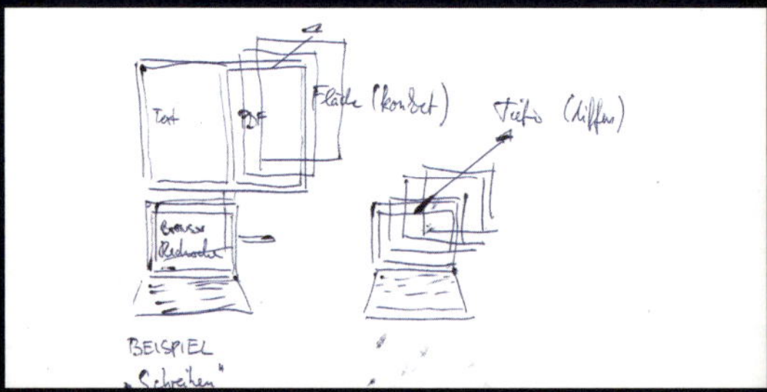

11
12

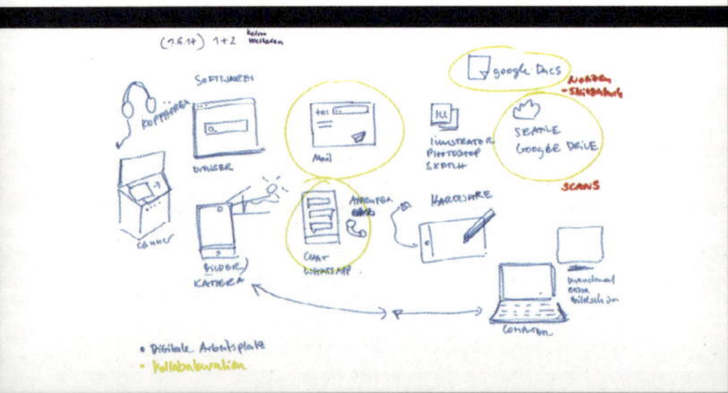

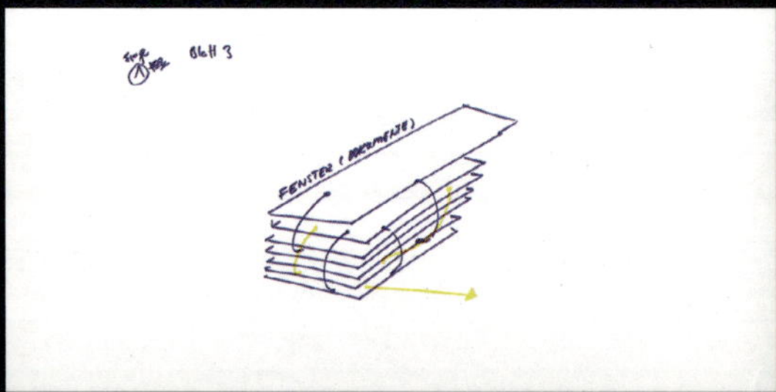

13
14

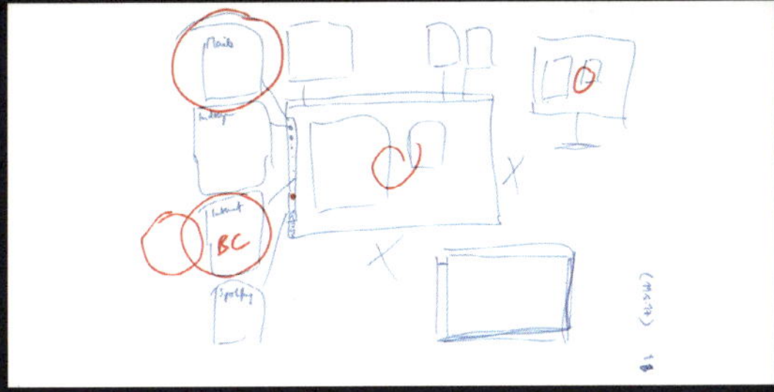

15
16

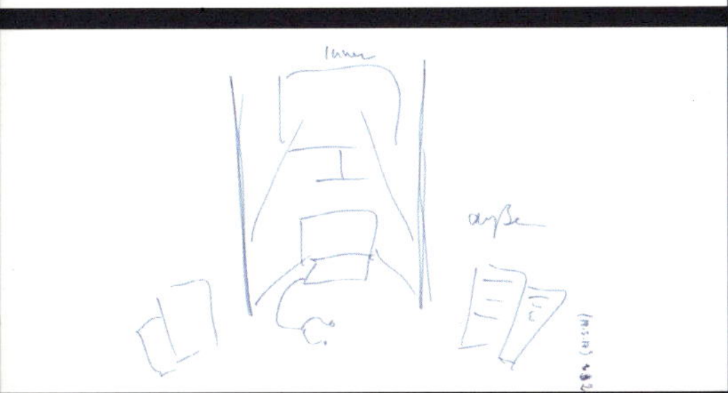

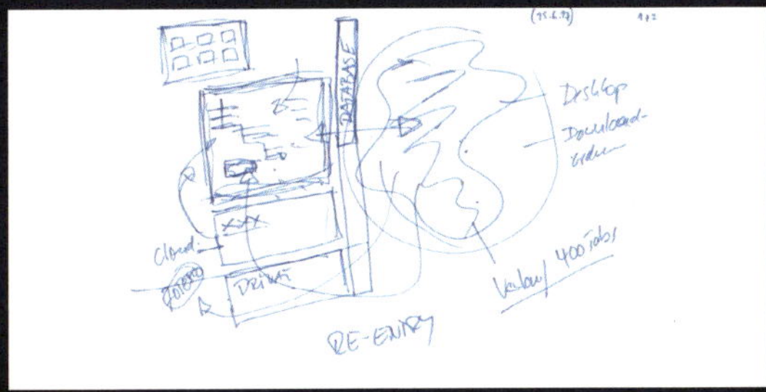

17
18

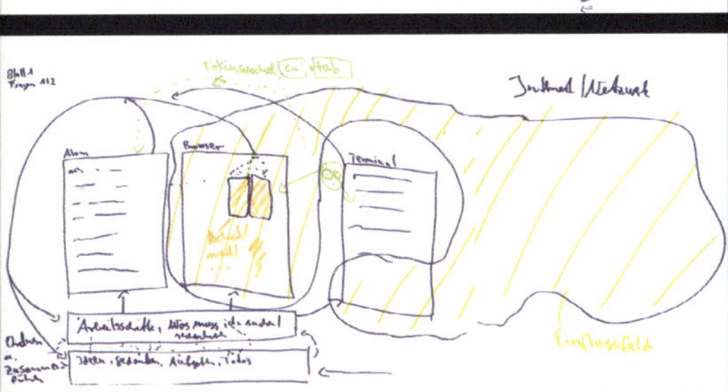

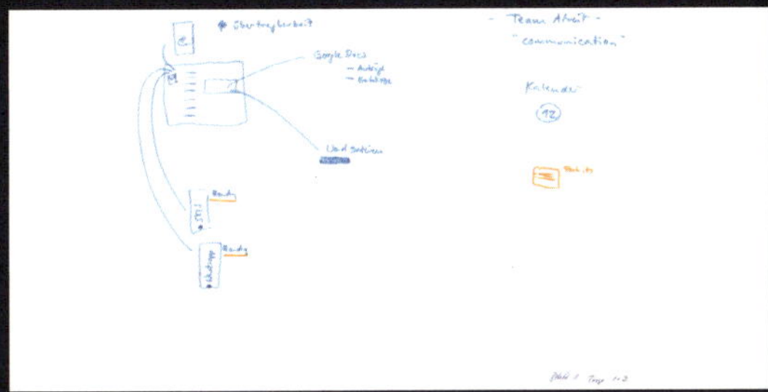

19
20

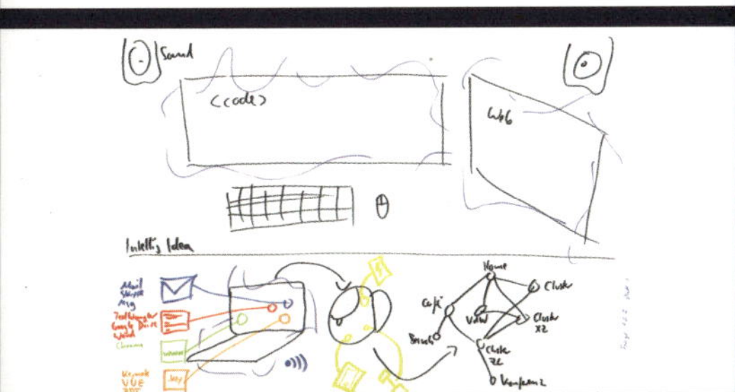

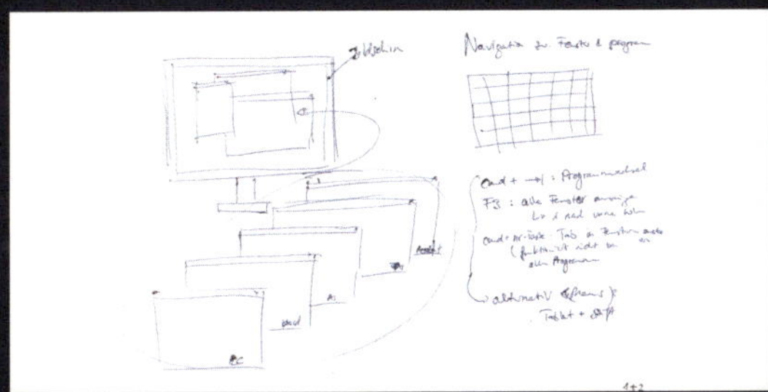

21
22

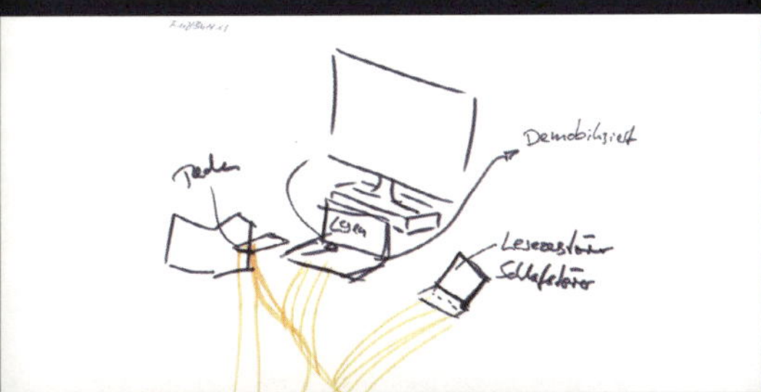

23
24

Mental maps of the digitalized workspace. The method of mental map is used in order to collect spatial perceptions of the subjects on the basis of drawings. Here, the participants were asked to draw their digitalized workspace (→ See Part Two, page 48).

01 Alexander, design disciplines
02 Angelika, engineering sciences
03 Anna, design disciplines, page 1
04 Anna, design disciplines, page 2
05 Arian, natural sciences
06 Arianna, humanities
07 Christine, humanities, page 1
08 Christine, humanities, page 2
09 Dana, humanities
10 Elani, design disciplines
11 Fabian, humanities, page 1
12 Fabian, humanities, page 2
13 Hannah, design disciplines
14 Isabelle, design disciplines, page 1
15 Isabelle, design disciplines, page 2
16 Laura, design disciplines, page 1
17 Laura, design disciplines, page 2
18 Lukas, engineering sciences
19 Martin, design disciplines
20 Martina, design disciplines
21 Maximilian, humanities
22 Miriam, design disciplines
23 Robert, humanities
24 Steffan, engineering sciences

01
02

03
04

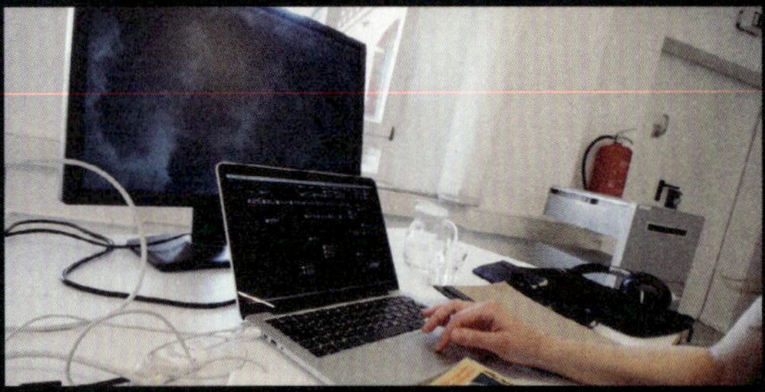
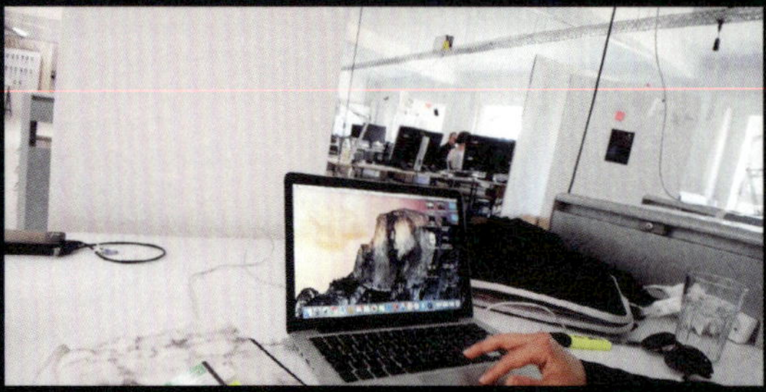

05
06

07
08

09
10

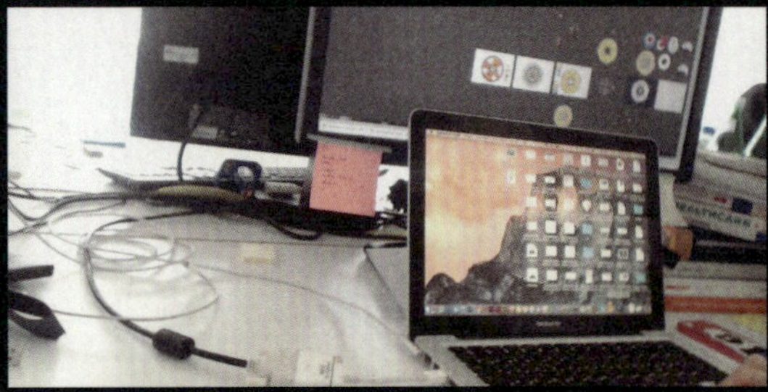

11
12

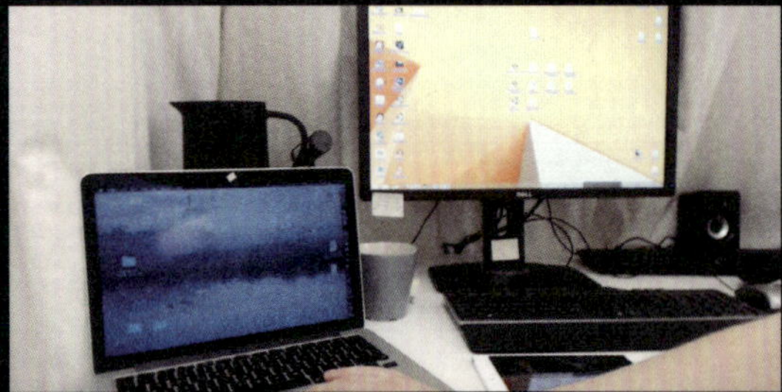
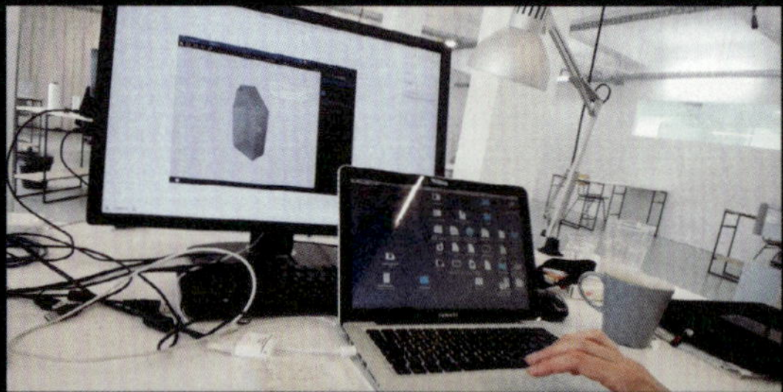

13
14

15
16

17
18

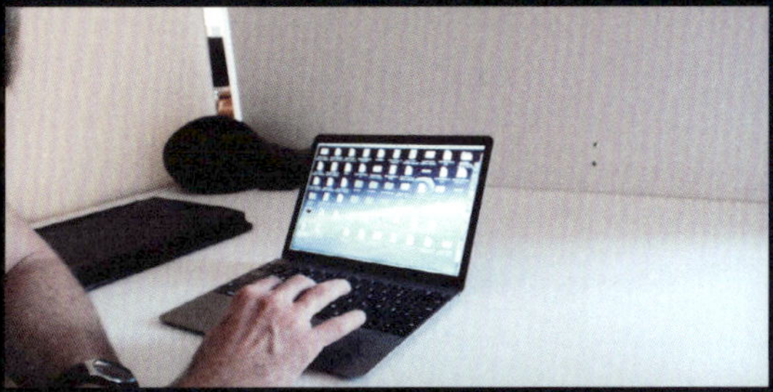

19
20

21

Video stills from the filmed Interviews-at-the-Computer, in which the participants gave us a tour of their computer and explained their practices. Here the different uses of the desktop are shown (→ See Part Two, page 49).

01 Alexander, design disciplines
02 Angelika, engineering sciences;
03 Arian, natural sciences
04 Arianna, humanities
05 Christine, humanities
06 Dana, humanities
07 Elani, design disciplines
08 Fabian, humanities
09 Ferdinand, design disciplines
10 Frieda, design disciplines
11 Hannah, design disciplines
12 Isabelle, design disciplines
13 Lars, Natural sciences
14 Lukas, engineering sciences
15 Martin, design disciplines
16 Martina, design disciplines
17 Maximilian, humanities
18 Paolo, natural sciences
19 Robert, humanities
20 Stefanie, humanities
21 Veronika, natural sciences

01
02

03
04

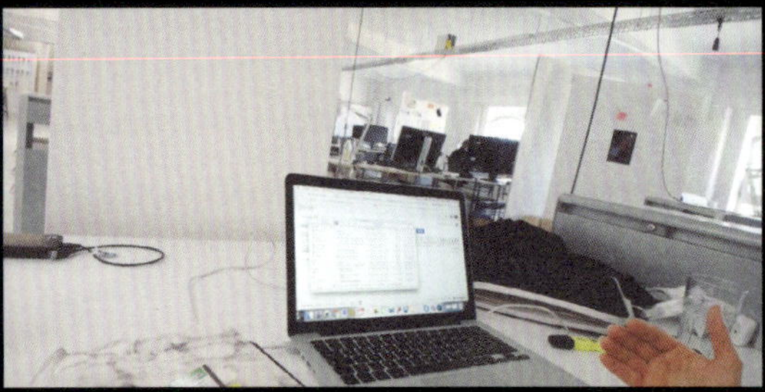

05
06

07
08

09
10

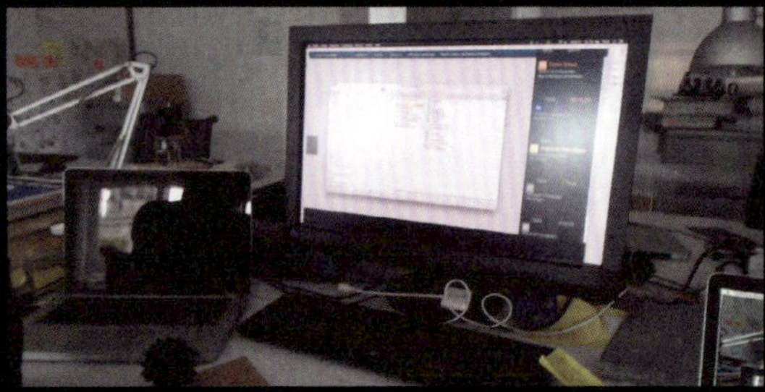

11
12

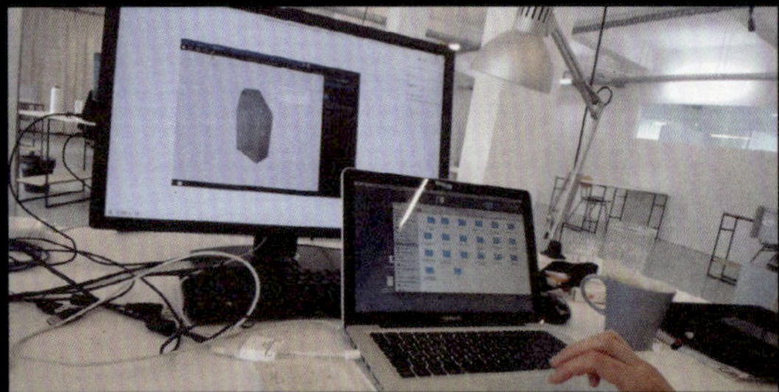

13
14

15
16

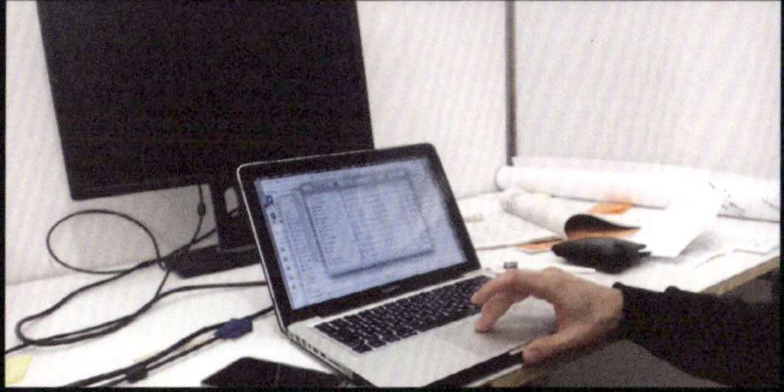

17
18

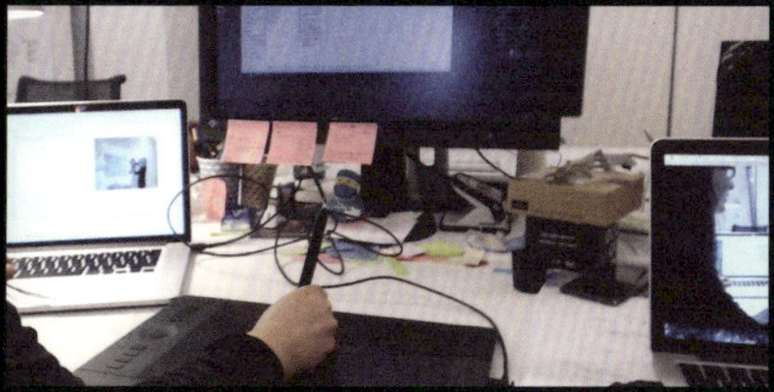

19
20

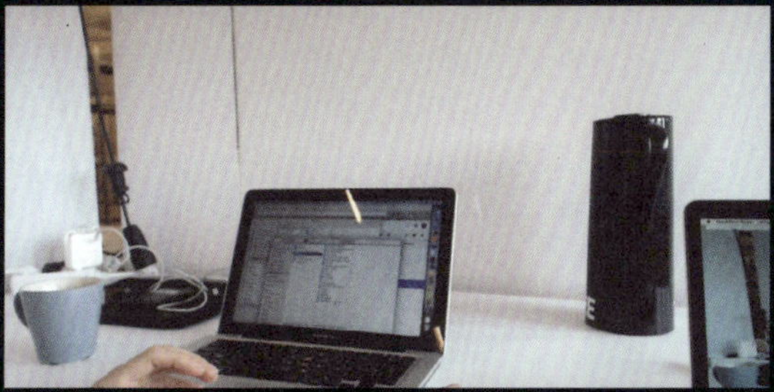

21

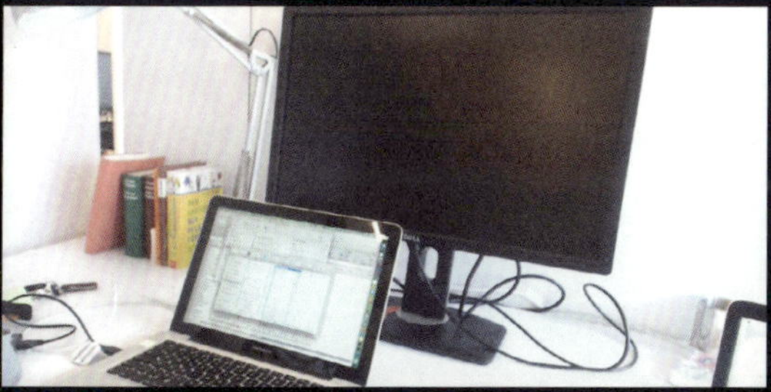

Video stills from the filmed Interviews-at-the-Computer, in which the participants gave us a tour of their computer and explained their practices. Here the different folder structures are shown (→ See Part Two, page 49).

01	Angelika, engineering sciences	11	Isabelle, design disciplines
02	Arian, natural sciences	12	Lars, Natural sciences
03	Arianna, humanities	13	Lukas, engineering sciences
04	Christine, humanities	14	Martin, design disciplines
05	Dana, humanities	15	Martina, design disciplines
06	Elani, design disciplines	16	Maximilian, humanities
07	Fabian, humanities	17	Miriam, design disciplines
08	Ferdinand, design disciplines	18	Paolo, natural sciences
09	Frieda, design disciplines	19	Robert, humanities
10	Hannah, design disciplines	20	Stefanie, humanities

Part 4

The Experimental Zone, a Shared Open Space

In this part, we address the question of how the practices described in Part Three were able to coexist in the open space of the Experimental Zone—particularly in the light of the fact that the heterogeneous properties of the individual spaces of research made such a co-presence difficult. We examine how, under these challenging circumstances, the open space of the Experimental Zone was negotiated by the participants. What did the Experimental Zone consist of beyond its four walls? Did the Experimental Zone form a space at all? Or when was it activated as a space? We investigate the ways in which the heterogenous spaces of research relate to each other when they touch, overlap, repel one another or merge with each other. Using differing levels of analyses, we identified three key dimensions of the negotiation and activation processes occurring within the shared open space:

- physically-materially, through the marking of *territories*,
- socially, through the interaction routines among the participants, and
- atmospherically, through the activation of the Experimental Zone as an assemblage of assemblages.

We used the design of eighteen different spatial settings in order to explore, on an experimental basis, whether and how specific spatial arrangements affect these three dimensions and what influence they have on the everyday knowledge production of the participants. In the process, we pinpointed certain settings which were particularly conducive to the co-presence of heterogeneous practices.

1 The Open-Plan Office: A Challenge for a Multidisciplinary Group of Researchers?

1.1 The Open-Plan Office, an Architectural Typology

As far as architectural typology is concerned, the Experimental Zone falls into the category of the *open-plan office*. However, investigating this typology was by no means our intention. When the research project commenced, we demolished all interior walls in order to create an open space that was as flexible as possible for the experiments and would permit numerous contrasting arrangements of partitions, furniture, etc. As, with one exception, we ultimately constructed all the physical experimental settings for practical reasons (costs, fire protection, sustainability) using light, temporary elements, the open-plan office became an inadvertent yet continuous feature of our research.

The open-plan office has been both omnipresent and criticized repeatedly since the 1950s. While many studies report its negative effects on work, the high proportion of seventy percent of open-plan offices in US office architecture today, as well as recent, much-publicized buildings such as Apple Campus II and the new Facebook headquarters, testify to the fact that building owners continue to expect positive effects from this typology, e.g. greater exchange and more chance encounters (Konnikova 2014). However, not all open-plan offices are alike. Considerable design differences exist with regards to parameters such as workplace density, acoustics (e.g. long vs. short reverberation time), acoustic privacy (are there acoustically screened areas?), visibility (visual connections, visual privacy, views of the outside), light (natural daylight, artificial lighting), indoor climate (temperature, ventilation etc.), materials, colors and many more. As early as the 1960s, the Quickborner Team designed the so-called "Bürolandschaft" as an alternative to the American open-plan office, intended to "strengthen informal communication channels and blur the symbolization of power and status" [1] (Kockelkorn 2008, 6). Also influential is the research by Francis C. Duffy and DEGW (Duffy and Wankum 1966; Duffy et al. 1976; Duffy et al. 1992; Duffy 1997; Laing et al. 1998; Harrison et al. 2004), who have classified office spaces according to their use (→ see page 112). Despite these attempts, the studies on open-plan offices remain contradictory. With regards to interactions and chance encounters, architectural researchers Kerstin Sailer and Alan Penn provide an overview of existing research since the 1970s (Sailer and Penn 2009). They report that studies of companies that have moved from enclosed cellular offices to an open-plan office have shown an increase in interactions (Allen and Gerstberger 1973; Brookes and Kaplan 1972; Ives and Ferdinands 1974), a decrease (Clearwater 1980; Hanson 1978; Oldham and Brass 1979; and recently Bernstein and Turban 2018) and no change (Boje 1971; Boyce 1974; Sloan n.d.; Sundstrom et al. 1982). The studies on acoustic privacy are equally contradictory: Some report negative effects of noise on office work (Banbury and Berry 1998, 2005), and others demonstrate a creativity-promoting effect (Mehta et al. 2012; Shepherd et al. 2013). While a research gap can be determined in the field of visual privacy, the existing studies agree on the necessity of natural daylight: Little daylight has been associated with health problems, poor sleep and concentration problems during the day (Boubekri et al. 2014; Elzeyadi 2011).

1 Own translation.

In the context of the Experimental Zone, the question of what effect the open space has on interdisciplinary research arose: In which spatial constellations can the participants carry out their work? And in which constellations do they interfere with each other? Especially with regards to the needs of the researchers: How much acoustic and visual privacy does scientific and design practice require? And how can one create an environment that guarantees such privacy but still promotes interaction?

1.2 Experimentalizing Space

It was clear that achieving the investigation's ultimate goal—to explore the reciprocal relationship between space and knowledge production and to elaborate the characteristics of a space promoting collaboration—would only be possible if an initial challenge were mastered, namely to enable co-presence. This is an obvious, but by no means trivial prerequisite: In order to collaborate with each other, the participants should first be able to "endure" each other and not leave the Experimental Zone due to an environment that is disturbing and prevents them from working. As demonstrated in Part Three, the scientific and creative practice is characterized by individual work and requires a favorable environment in order to permit individual impermeable spaces of research to unfold—especially for the practices of reading, writing, and drawing.

How, then, can the architectural design, particularly the functional and spatial configuration of the Experimental Zone, meet the ambivalent challenges of simultaneously promoting quiet individual work and dynamic interactions, whether formal, informal, within or between teams? By functional configuration, we mean the allocation of functions to areas in a building and thus the spatial localization of social events, while spatial configuration references the design of these areas, e.g. whether they are enclosed, open or semi-open, etc. but also how they are furnished. With this in mind, we tested different ways of designing spaces for quiet individual work such as thinking, reading or writing, and for communicative teamwork such as conceptualizing, discussing or planning, for formal or informal exchanges, etc.

01
02
03
04
05
06
07
08

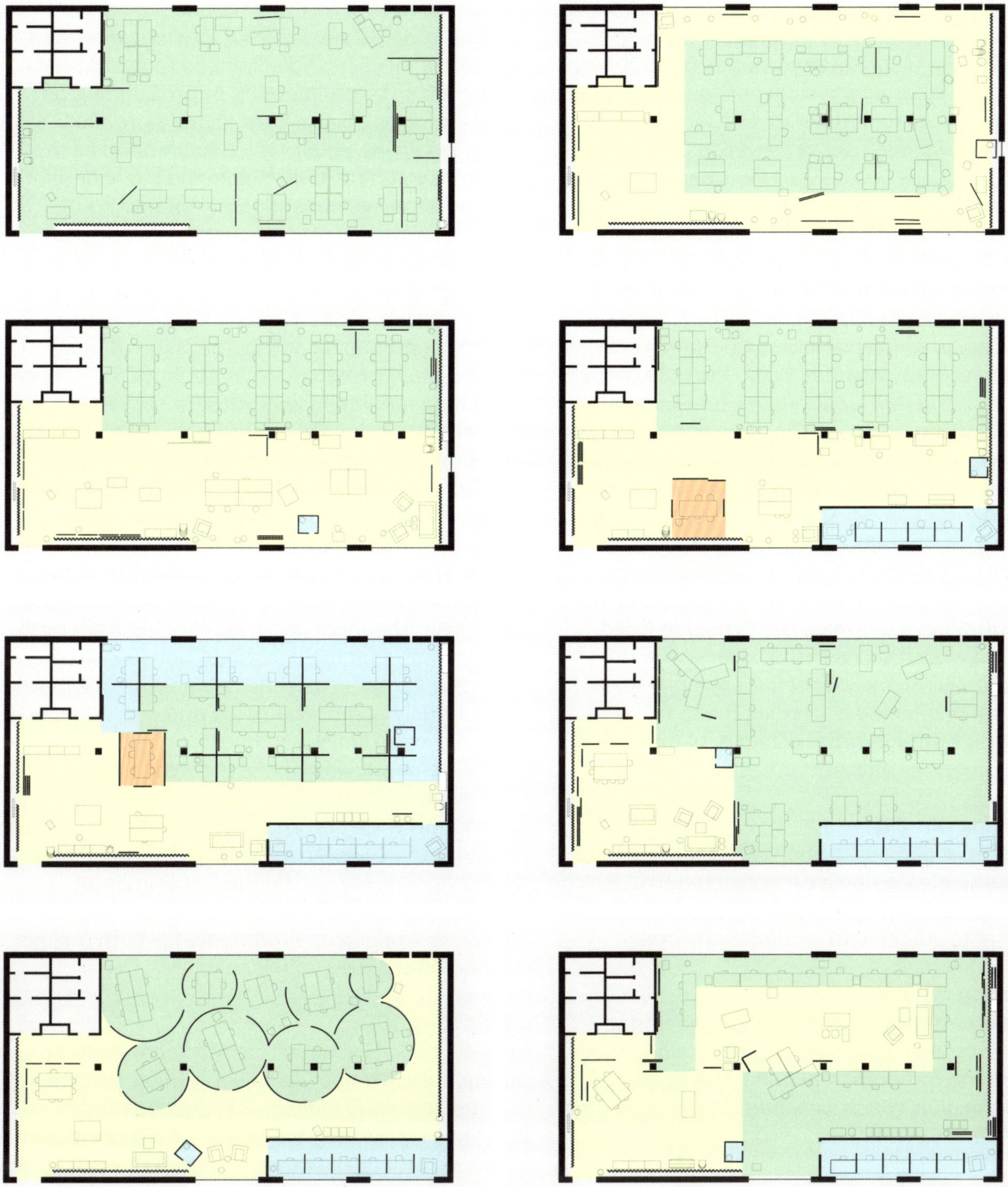

Figs. 4.1–4.8: Analysis of the configurations based on Francis Duffy (cell = blue, reef = green, club = yellow, den = orange)

Within the eighteen experimental settings (→ see Catalogue of Settings, pages 52–60), we tested eight different physical configurations. The settings were designed iteratively, setting by setting, and reflected our observations during the research process (→ see Part Two, pages 38–40).

Which spatial and functional configurations were tested? Francis Duffy identified four types of office layouts: *Hive, cell, den* and *club*[2] (Duffy 1997). In the Experimental Zone, too, four different spatial types can be found according to working style, which contrast with Duffy's categorization in one key respect: While the categories of *club, cell* and *den* are identical, the scientists' individual workstations in the open space do not fit into any category. The scientists' working style is more interactive and autonomous than *hive*, more autonomous than *den*, and far less nomadic than *club*. We therefore propose an additional category for the context of the spaces of research: The *reef*[3] describes highly autonomous and highly interactive activities performed at fixed or flexible workstations in the open space or in group rooms. An analysis of the eight physical configurations tested according to these categories (figs. 4.1–8) shows the diversity of the spatial configurations examined:

#1 (Setting 00–02)
The first spatial configuration was characterized by its complete openness: It consisted exclusively of one type of space, the *reef*, within which the participants set up their workstations freely.

#2 (Setting 03–04)
In the second spatial configuration, we added a second spatial type that we placed along the edges of the Experimental Zone: The spatial type of the *club*, which was intended to promote informal and spontaneous exchange.

#3 (Setting 05–10)
For the third spatial configuration, the Experimental Zone was divided into two parts: A *reef* with personal workplaces and a *club*, a so-called "trading zone" (Galison 1999) that was intended to promote a more multidisciplinary range of practices such as experimenting or prototyping as well as informal exchanges. In addition, a telephone booth was built, which functioned as a single workstation *(cell)*. Within the same spatial configuration, we subsequently examined the transversal theme of 'exchange' in three successive experimental settings by focusing on the relationship between formal, informal and fleeting exchange and concentrated individual work.
It quickly became clear that the issue of noise was the most problematic. In setting 08, "Temporal", a time regulation was introduced: While the morning was primarily intended for quiet individual work, the afternoon was available for noisy collaborative activities. In the subsequent setting 09, "Permeable", a spatial rather than a temporal separation was made by constructing a meeting room for formal exchange (*den*) with temporary and translucent partitions and a sound-absorbing ceiling. The most important finding from both settings was that the exchange between the participants, especially the designers, took place continuously at the workplace and could therefore neither be limited in time nor moved to another place. It was one of the main causes of conflicts with the humanities scholars who wanted more silence and concentration. The new meeting room—even if it was heavily used and encouraged teamwork in the Experimental Zone—was not sufficient as a measure to create adequate working environments for both designers and humanities scholars.

#4 (Setting 10)
In setting 10, "Hermetic", we therefore tested a strong acoustic and visual separation between collaborative and individual practices for the first time, by building the so-called Silent Space conceived for concentrated individual work (*cell*), which was constructed with permanent drywalls and contained individual work booths. The meeting area (*den*) introduced in setting 09 was preserved.

2 According to Francis Duffy, *hive* is characterized by "individual, routine, process work with low levels of interaction and low autonomy" and is situated in an open-plan setting (Duffy 1997, 62). *Cell* refers to "individual, concentrated work with little interaction" and high autonomy in enclosed individual offices (ibid., 63). *Den* accommodates group work, which is "highly interactive but not necessarily highly autonomous" and is situated in open-plan settings or group rooms (ibid., 64). And *club* is associated with highly autonomous, highly interactive, and mostly nomadic knowledge work situated in a "time-shared task-based setting" (ibid., 65).

3 We chose this term because a reef is a biotope that organisms share. Its diversity of species has reminded us of the different disciplinary backgrounds of the participants, while the organisms are both interacting and competing with each other.

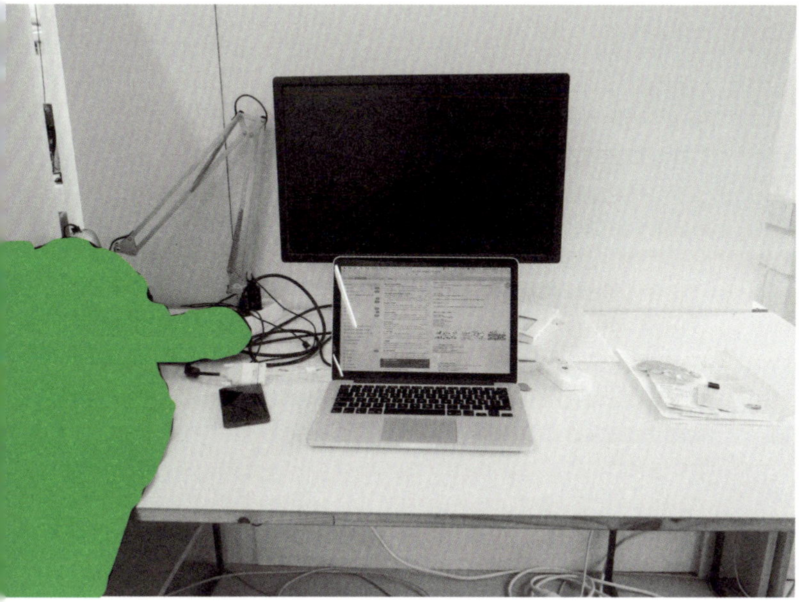

Fig. 4.9: Flexible desk use (green = clothing and bags), Paolo, Natural Sciences.
Fig. 4.10: Permanent desk use (purple = bottles and food containers), Miriam, Design disciplines.

#5 (Setting 11–13)
In the fifth spatial configuration, we examined a more subdivided configuration by building compartments for between two and four people using dividers. The predominant spatial types were spaces for individual work (*cell*) and individual and collaborative work (*reef*), in combination with areas for informal (*club*) and formal encounters (*den*).

#6 (Setting 14–15)
The sixth spatial configuration, which, like the basic setting, was arranged by the participants themselves, was again characterized by openness and consisted primarily of the spatial type for individual and collaborative work (*reef*), in combination with the spaces for informal exchange (*club*) and the quiet room (*cell*).

#7 (Setting 16)
In the seventh spatial configuration, we again examined a strongly subdivided configuration (*cell*, *reef* and *club*), but this time with lower partitions. The setting was therefore similar to the fifth spatial configuration, but created a higher visibility between the participants.

#8 (Setting 17)
The eigth spatial configuration was developed in a participatory process with the participants who were responsible for the design of the settings. The result was a combination of open workspaces (*reef*) along the edges of the room and a central trading zone (*club*) for spontaneous and informal exchanges—like an inverted variant of the second spatial configuration. The analysis of the configurations based on Duffy's categories reveals how the relationships between individual work and collaboration, or between individual and shared spaces, were experimentalized. How have these varying spatial configurations shaped social events in the Experimental Zone? And how have they been experienced and appropriated by the participants? By posing these questions, we place ourselves directly in the field of tension between space and research practices: How does the designed space influence the research practices? And, conversely, how do the research practices influence the designed space?

2 A Territorial Negotiation

As a next step, we looked at the participants' spatial practices across the different spatial configurations and see what they made of them.

In Part Three, we explored the manner in which the individual research spaces unfolded on the level of the workstation. In the following section we will place them in the context of the entire space and see how these different individual research spaces related to each other. The analysis of the spatial appropriation revealed a process of territorialization on the part of the participants that points to the anchoring of the individual research spaces in individual *territories*. It exposed a differentiated gradation between more private and more public areas.

2.1 A Fixed Territorial Marking

As an architectural endeavor, the Experimental Zone is embedded in the current discourse on the flexibilization and dynamization of the working space, "which is supposed to transform itself constantly for the flow of work without inertia, resistance and friction loss" (Schmidt 2012, 141). In this context, Robert Schmidt emphasizes a shift from a "traditional work order", in which the human body is immobilized and the office worker is constructed as a "mental" being, to a "futuristic work order", in which the human body is constantly in motion and the office is articulated as a space of flows (Schmidt 2012, 143ff). This notion of a high flexibilization of the workplace can also be found in *activity-based working* (Veldhoen and Piepers 1995), which is pursued by Microsoft, Google, etc., among others. Does the Experimental Zone form such a space of flows? Do the scientists investigated correspond to the new model of the creative, innovative employee? The answer is no.

Originally, the entire *Interdisciplinary Laboratory* with its three floors was meant to offer a flexible working environment: Each employee was given a laptop, a mobile pedestal and mobile pinboards and was supposed to be able to change their workplace depending on their current activity. The employees had strong misgivings about this concept. Despite its constant redesign process, a continuous spatial structure can be detected within the Experimental Zone whose coordinates follow a gradation between private and public. The mobile pedestals and other mobile artifacts do not strengthen the "non-territorial office" (as Schmidt claims, 2012, 142), but serve exactly the opposite purpose, providing fixed territorial markers of the individual workplace.

The Role of the Mobile Pedestals and Pinboards

The office, and therefore the Experimental Zone, is a public place. However, the workstation has a more private character, especially when it becomes stationary or part of a routine. The categories reef-cell-den-club fail to help us to understand where the boundaries between private and non-private territories lie in an open space. In other words, how do the participants create privacy/intimacy spatially? And what characteristics do these boundaries possess?

In his theory on the *territory of the self*, the American sociologist Erving Goffman defined the territory as "the claim [...· to a field of things —to a preserve [whose· boundaries are ordinarily patrolled and defended by the claimant" (Goffman 1971, 29). As a "site-bound personal space" it possesses a contour that cannot be easily crossed by others (Goffman 1971, 56ff.) and therefore forms a protected space.[4] This corresponds to what the American anthropologist Edward T. Hall described in his theory of *proxemics* (1969) as a "fixed-feature space"—where it becomes clear to everyone that an area is in the possession of someone (Hall 1969, 101ff.). In the sense of Goffman and Hall, it was clearly observable in the Experimental Zone how such territorial markings took place on a material level, as participants strategically positioned objects that function as distance pieces forming a "possessional territory" (Goffman 1971, 38). Like in a bus where one secures a second seat by placing a bag on it, the participants secured a certain area for their personal use. These individual *territories* were created by the participants by placing objects such as desks, mobile pedestals and pin boards in a certain relationship to the immobile elements such as walls, columns, windows as well as other individual *territories*. However, permanent personal workstations (→ see Part One, page 29),

4 In *Relations in Public*, Goffman posits inter alia six different territories of the self, culturally and situationally-contingent: 1) the *personal space* as the space surrounding an individual according to the definition of Hall (1969); 2) the *use space* as the territory claimed because of apparent instrumental needs; 3) *the sheath* depicting the skin and clothing; 4) the *possessional territory* as an assortment of objects that can be identified with the self and arrayed around the body; 5) the *information preserve* as a set of facts about oneself; and 6) the *conversational preserve* (Goffman 1971, 29-41).

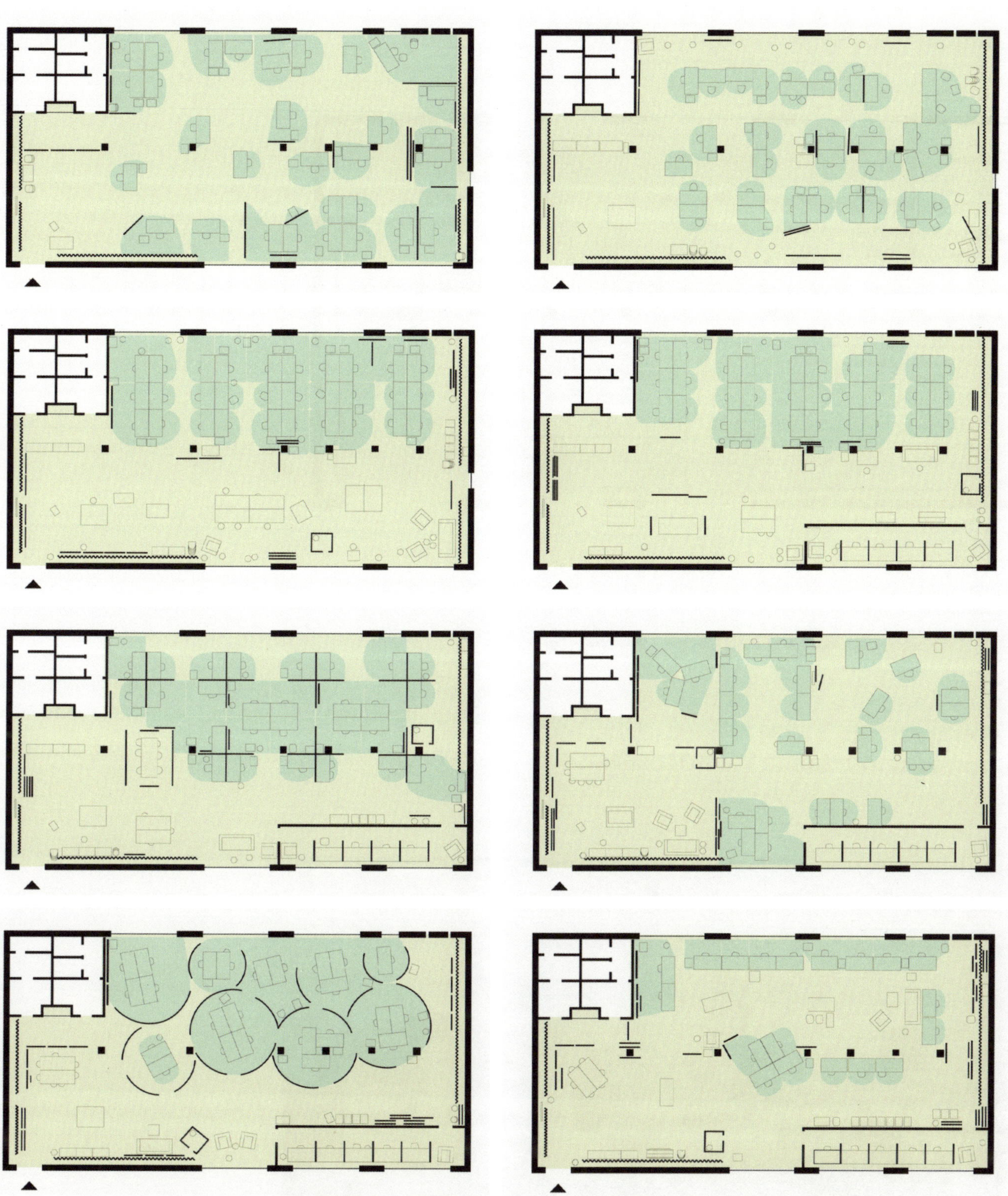

01
02
03
04
05
06
07
08

Figs. 4.11-4.18: Analysis of the individual territories according to physical configuration (individual territories = green, common area = yellow)

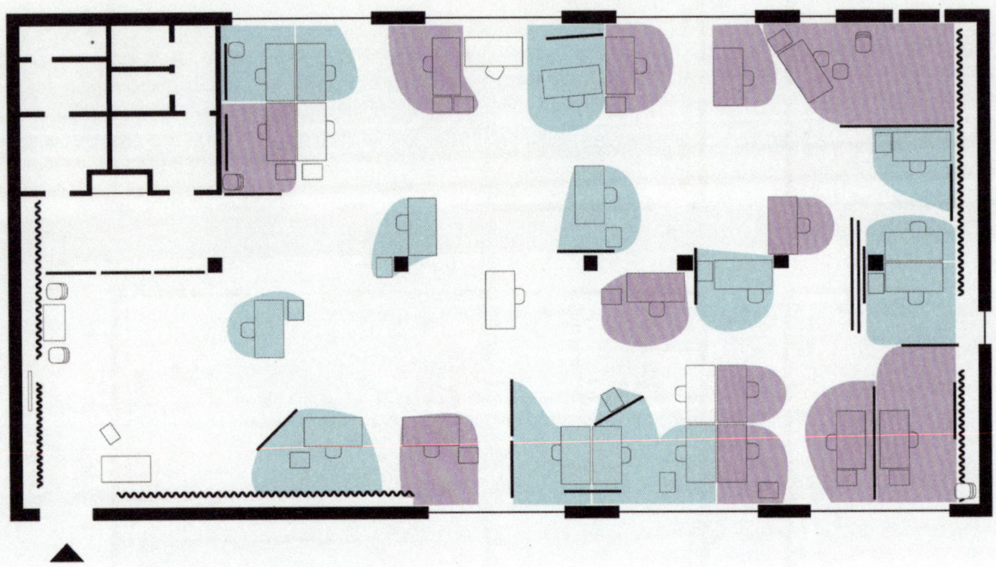

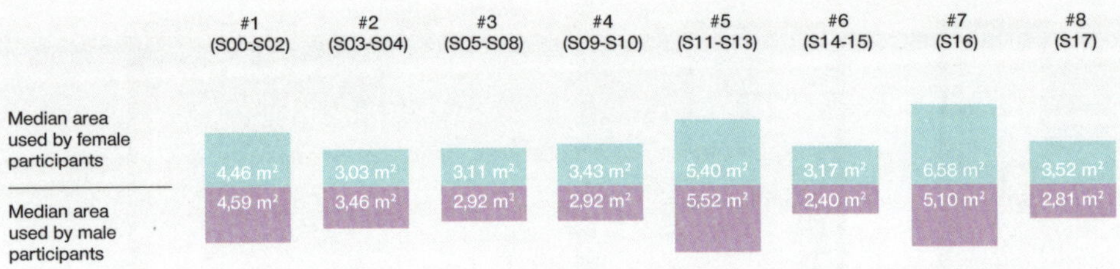

Fig. 4.19: Configuration #1, individual territories according to gender (turquoise = female, purple = male)
Fig. 4.20: Median size of the individual territories according to gender per configuration
Fig. 4.21: Pinboard placed in the open space. Photo © Fabian Scholz

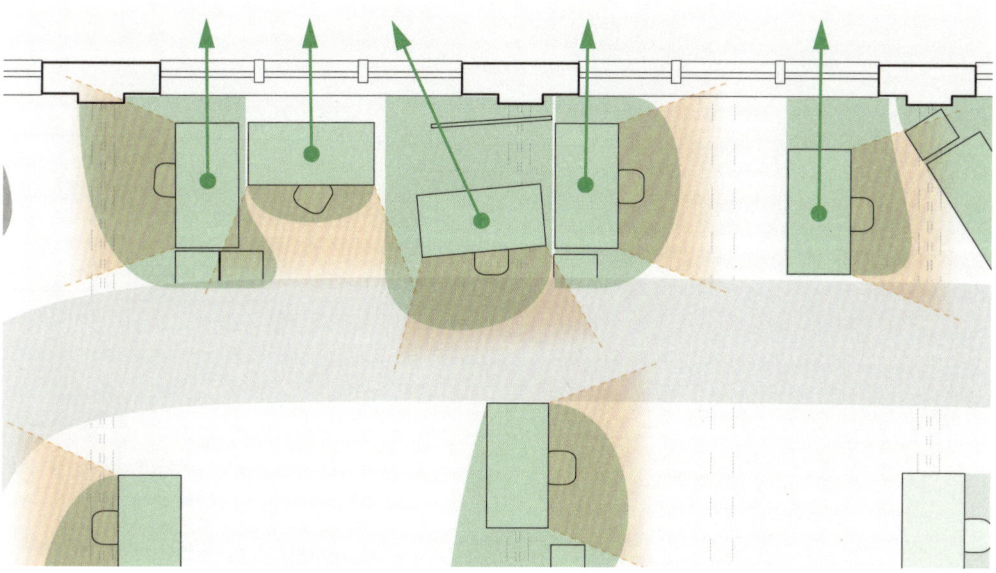

Fig. 4.22: Close-up view of exposure to the "street"

which were in addition fully equipped (→ see Part Three, page 85), had a much more expansive effect than flexible and minimalist workstations: While flexible and minimalist workstations (fig. 4.9) only contained objects necessary for the current task (e.g. a notebook), permanent personal workstations (fig. 4.10) were often equipped with materials, tools and other artifacts that cover a broad spectrum of practices. Also typical of the permanent personal workstations were the higher number of beverage bottles and food containers (violet) and the positioning of bags and clothing (green), which found a place under or next to the table. By contrast, clothes and bags were often placed on the desk at the flexible and minimalist workstations. In all types, personal belongings were used to draw the boundaries of the individual *territories*.

The Size of the Individual Territories

It is noticeable in the mapping analysis that the individual *territories* were not the same size (figs. 4.11–18). Different sizes were observed within a setting depending on the participants. What is interesting, however, is that this difference in size among the participants remained constant across the settings. Only in the compartmentalized configurations are all individual *territories* larger than in the open configurations. What was the reason for the differences in size?

The differences in size depending on status were relatively significant: The scientific staff appropriated larger individual *territories* than student assistants. According to Goffman, this demonstrates the dependent relationship between the legitimate claims to a territory and the social status of the individuals, which manifests itself in both the extent and control of the territory (Goffman 1971, 40–41). If one measures the size of the individual *territories* per participant and per setting, the following differences become apparent.

From a gender perspective, the mapping analysis shows that the men in the Experimental Zone initially made use of larger individual *territories*—especially in the first setting (fig. 4.19). Over time, however, women appropriated more space and, from configuration #6, definitively surpassed men in terms of the median size of their individual territories (fig. 4.20). Here, the actions of a research assistant who appropriated more and more space in the course of the settings until she finally occupied two or three desks are worthy of note. The extension of her individual *territory* to the surrounding workstations shows the need for a buffer zone to secure more privacy in the open space.

With regards to discipline, there is no significant difference in the size of the individual *territories*. However, what is clearly noticeable in the territorial marking is the differentiated handling

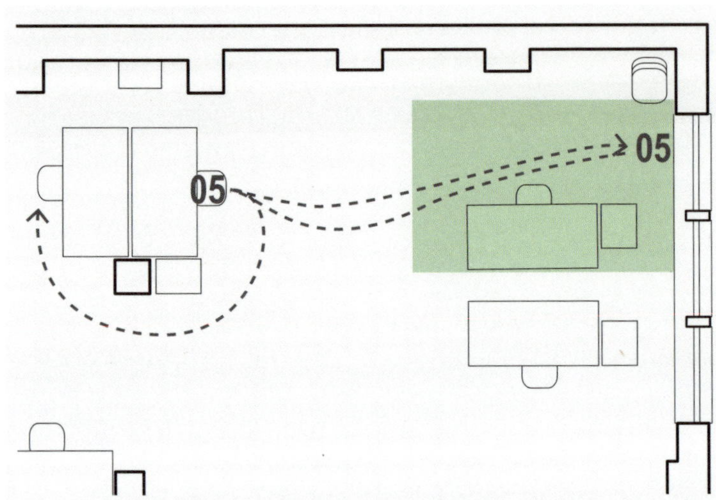

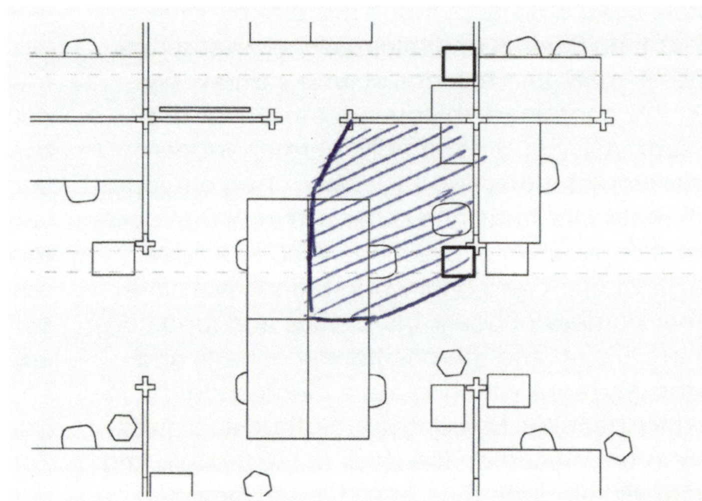

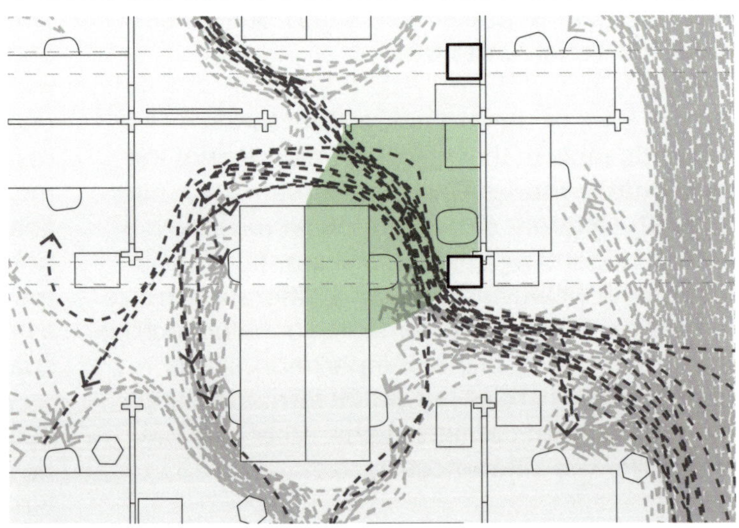

Fig. 4.23: Intrusion into an individual territory
Fig. 4.24: Perceived individual territory
Fig. 4.25: Crossing of the individual territory

of the objects, and in particular the pinboard. For the designers, the pinboard played a central role in their everyday practice, providing an overview of their work. At the same time, however, it also served as a territorial marker of their individual *territories* in so far as it limited their field of vision. The use of pinboards directly in the workplace was not envisaged in all spatial configurations, sometimes leading to unfavorable or conflict-laden situations, e.g. in the open spatial configuration of #3, when a designer sitting at the window placed her pinboard next to her desk and thus blocked both daylight and view for her neighbor (fig. 4.21). Here, it becomes obvious, that—and completely in the sense of Hall's considerations on "visual space" (Hall 1969, 65–75)—what one sees plays a major role in the formation of the individual *territories*.

View versus Exposure

The analysis of the individual *territories* reveals the participants' need to negotiate and compromise, choosing between the view from and exposure of their workstation on the one hand, and the potentially intimacy-infringing disclosure of their practices to other participants on the other. In this context, Goffman speaks of the *information preserve* as a "set of facts about himself to which an individual expects to control access while in the presence of others" (Goffman 1971, 38–39). What was meant at that time was the contents of bags, purses, containers and letters. Nowadays, the term *information preserve* applies particularly well to the computer screen of the individual participant, which has proved to be a very intimate affair. Here, Goffman refers to "penetration of the eyes" encroaching on someone else's territory (Goffman 1971, 45–46), when a participant glanced or gazed at the screen of another, for instance.

In spatial configuration #1, it is noticeable that the participants gave priority to the view, namely to an outside view. Most of the desks were oriented toward windows, as if the researchers were trying to expand their space of thinking. While some—male scientists—were able to secure places with low exposure and a good view, most had to accept a compromise of high exposure and an outside view, namely by positioning themselves with their backs to a highly frequented "street" (fig. 4.22). The workstations in the center, which had high exposure and no immediate outside view, were assigned to the student staff, further demonstrating the relationship between status and territory.

Physical configuration #2 led to a similar negotiation of view and exposure: Most participants had outside views, therefore accepting high exposure to busy streets on the inside of the table configurations. In spatial configuration #3, exposure was limited to the neighbors who had to pass by one's screen to reach their seats. Moreover, there was an impression of visibility across the rows of tables, even though the screens severely restricted the view. A view through the side windows was also available to almost everyone—except for the rearmost group of tables, which was soon abandoned. In the spatial configuration #5, the *Basic Setting II*, in which the participants arranged the configuration themselves, the outside view once again became a decisive criterion for the orientation of the desks, insofar as most desks were oriented toward the window. However, an attempt was made to limit exposure to self-formed groups—so that the screen could only be seen by a limited number of trusted colleagues. In the highly compartmentalized spatial configurations #4 and #6, both exposure and views were extremely low.

The comparison of settings illustrates that the two variables correlate in open space: Good or limited views mean a high or low exposure. The participants repeatedly emphasized that the view—whether outside or inside the room—was considered more important, even if their way of dealing with exposure became more differentiated throughout the settings and was regulated differently, i.e. within trusted groups.

Conflict-laden Situations

The fixed territorial appropriation was also observed daily in the form of crisis situations which can be described as situations of intrusion into foreign individual *territories*. Two types were observed: Firstly, the *intrusion*, understood as an invasion of a colleague's *territory*, testifies to a denial of the claim raised by the other. In the first setting, for example, the (generous) appropriation of the corner by one participant was denied by another participant by regularly entering the claimed territory and taking possession of it for a short time in order to make a phone call at the window (fig. 4.23).

Secondly, the *crossing*, understood as the brief passing through a colleague's *territory*, was relatively frequent, especially in the compartmentalized configurations, where accessibility of one's workstation was not always directly possible. In the compilation of the collected data, crisis situations become visible, as for example in configuration #5, where the individual *territory* was drawn by a participant from the desk until the partition wall (fig. 4.24), but became one of the main axes of movement in the Experimental Zone (fig. 4.25).

The claim of an individual territory was not always respected by the other participants. Are intrusions and crossings tolerated equally by all participants? Or, to put it another way: Can different ways of dealing with the individual territory be observed among the participants? And what do these depend on?

2.2 The Formation of Specific Group Territories

In the analysis of the individual *territories* and their connections, a third category has emerged. In his theory of proxemics (Hall 1969, 121ff.), Edward T. Hall carried out an analysis of "distances to man", and, based on this, distinguished between four spaces (*intimate, personal, social* and *public*) (ibid.). Following Hall's categories, the Experimental Zone only contains *personal* and *social spaces* on the basis of which the individual *territories* and the *common area* are formed (figs. 4.11–18). Although the studies by Hall and Goffman (Hall 1969; Goffman 1971) address the gradation between intimacy, privacy and sociality at the spatial level, there is a lack of differentiation here with regards to shared spaces. Our investigation shows two things: Firstly, the *common area* is characterized by different gradations and qualities; secondly, this distinction indicates a connection with disciplinary scientific cultures.

Edward T. Hall addressed the relationship between territoriality and culture, albeit with a culturalist aftertaste typical of the 1960s (1969, 121ff.). Applied to our field of research, however, the question of the connection between territory and scientific cultures arises. As already mentioned, we were unable to detect differences in the size of the individual *territories* according to discipline, only a difference in the materialization of the demarcations, i.e. with or without pinboards. Much more pronounced is the difference between the disciplines with regards to the arrangement of the individual *territories* to each other. In the early days of the Experimental Zone, the humanities scholars and natural scientists preferred an isolated place: Like in a familiar library, they integrated themselves into the anonymous collective mass, but at a distance, separately from one another. As one participant put it: "In situations in which I have to concentrate hard, I can work even more effectively in a working atmosphere [...-. But remaining on my own 'island'" (Fabian, Humanities).

By contrast, some researchers formed groups of workstations when they moved into the Experimental Zone. These groups were not based on existing social relations (some of the participants had studied together at the same college) but on project constellations and thus were team-specific group *territories* (fig. 4.26). Strikingly, each group *territory* was initiated by and mainly consisted of researchers from the design disciplines and—according to our hypothesis—emerged on the basis of a shared work culture. The first group *territories* were created by arranging two or four desks into larger tables. By sitting with their faces to each other and their backs to other colleagues, the participants physically created and emphasized a protected area. The spaces between the involved individual *territories* were characterized by a more intimate quality, distinguishing them from the *common area*. They were subject to the claim of this group of researchers and were not accessible to the other participants without a motive. From spatial configuration #3, further group *territories* were formed (figs. 4.28–33). In configurations #3 and #4, the available table groups were used by some participants as group *territories*, which were again demarcated by an inward orientation. The most overt type of demarcation was created in configuration #6, where some participants arranged eight desks in the form of a U, all facing outward. In this case, the desks formed an actual physical barrier to the others and created an interior space that could only be entered through a single entrance.

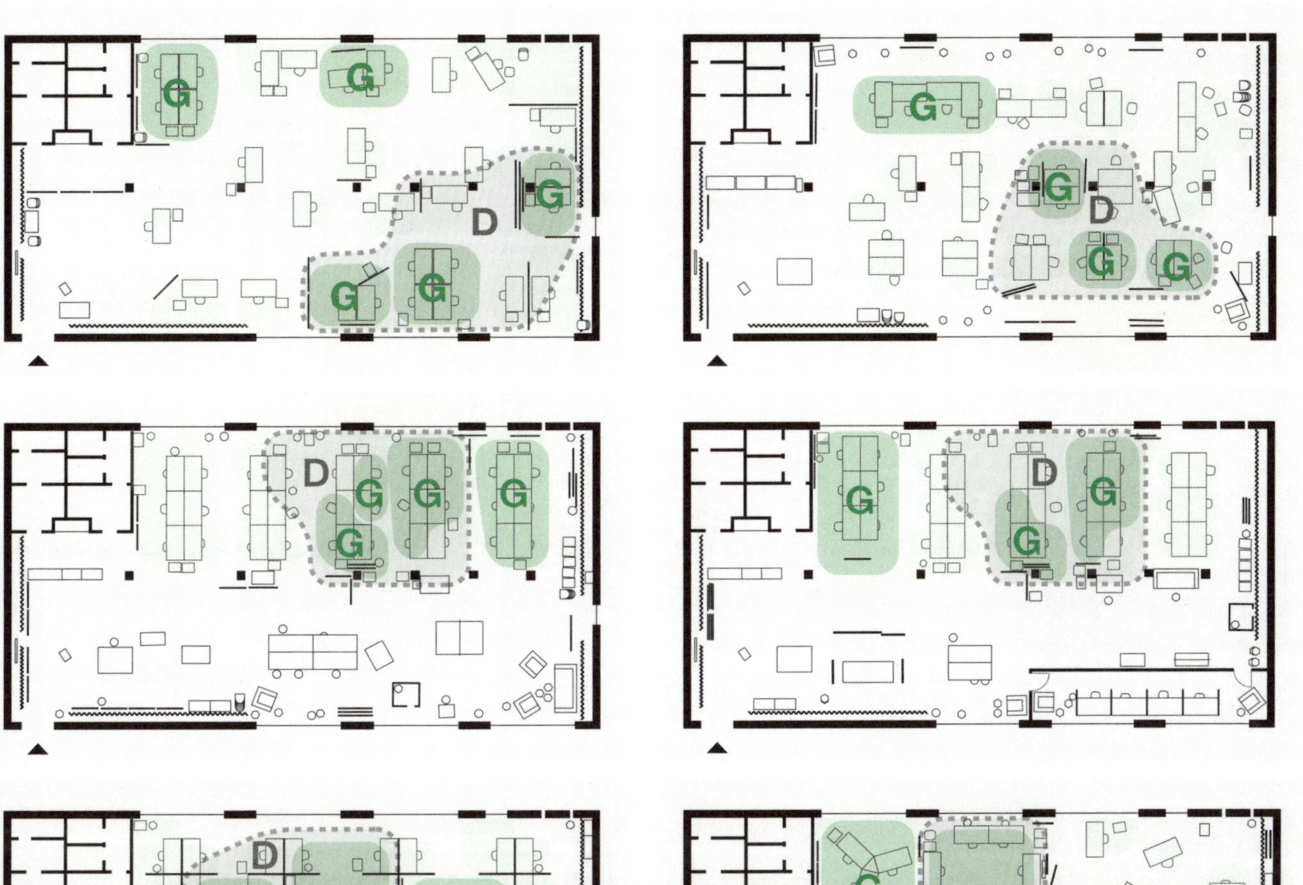

01
02
03
04
05
06
07
08

Figs. 4.26-33: Development of group territories (G) and the design cluster (D) across the eight configurations

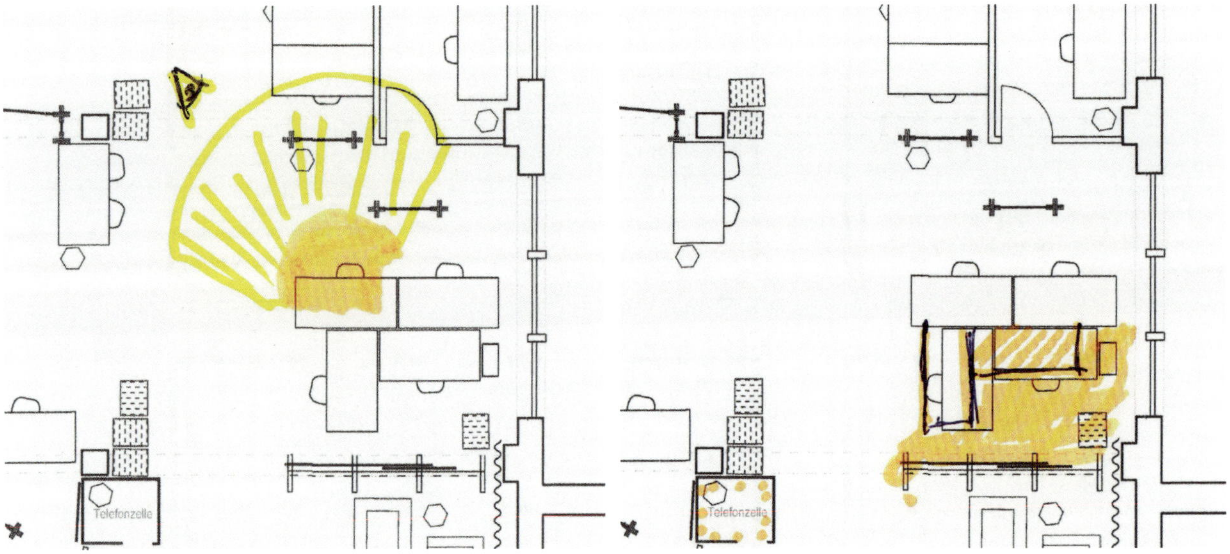

Figs. 4.34–35: Perceived individual territories of two participants (Arian, Engineering Sciences; Miriam, Design disciplines)

As the group *territories* in these later settings were not only created by scholars from the design disciplines, we draw the conclusion that they represent an acculturation process of the participants with other disciplinary backgrounds.

The acculturation process becomes visible on the one hand through the increasing emergence of new team-based table constellations, e.g. in the comparison between the open spatial configurations #1 and #6, when the participants could freely arrange their desks, and also in the comparison between the two compartmentalized spatial configurations #5 and #7. On the other hand, the acculturation process also becomes evident in an analysis of individual participants with a non-design background: A humanities scholar, who in configuration #5 always sought a place among the researchers from the design disciplines, gave up his isolation not for the purpose of taking part in a team-specific table group, but in order to open himself to other disciplines.

In addition to the phenomenon of desk groups, several groups were placed closely together forming *the design cluster* (fig. 4.26–33). This created a specific localized density in the Experimental Zone, which contrasted strongly with the isolated individual *territories* of the natural scientists and humanities scholars. While in the first two spatial configurations this cluster was still formed laterally, it gradually took over the central position within the Experimental Zone until it finally occupied the entire open space in the participatively designed configuration #08. This way, *the design cluster* shaped the entire atmosphere across most of the settings. The centrality was reinforced by the fact that the designers were those who were most frequently and continuously present.

We will develop this aspect further in Part Five, but the formation of group *territories* and of *the designer cluster* has greatly shaped the Experimental Zone as a so-called *collaborative habitat*. The consistency of the *territories* became evident in selective crisis situations. In setting 14, one participant disliked the fact that a flexible participant regularly used a flexible workstation in her group *territory*. Even if the flexible participant was within his rights to do so, it still felt like an intrusion on the space occupied by the permanent participant, as she reported in an informal conversation. In a survey of their perceived personal space, both participants addressed this conflict-laden spatial negotiation. In the drawing by the flexible participant (fig. 4.34), the incomplete coloring of his desk indicates that he was trying

	At home	Visiting	In the common area
Fleeting interaction	Fleeting, at home	Fleeting, visiting	Fleeting, common area
Informal interaction	Informal, at home	Informal, visiting	Informal, common area
Formal interaction	Formal, at home	Formal, visiting	Formal, common area

Fig. 4.36: Types of interaction

to take up little space and distance himself from his neighbors. Whereas, in the case of the permanent participant (fig. 4.35), the expansion of her individual *territory* over the surrounding desks can be understood as a claim of ownership for her team.

This analysis shows a process of territorialization by the participants that points to the anchoring of the individual spaces of research in individual *territories*: Through the placement of objects, the participants create protected territories favorable to the dynamic unfolding of their spaces of research. In the comparison of the configurations, several characteristics of these territories have become clear: Whether in terms of size, views or exposure, the design of individual territories within open space is a delicate negotiation that is, in most cases, unable to meet all the requirements of the individual practices such as visual and auditory privacy or views. The problem-solving strategy that has evolved across the settings is the formation of group *territories*—neighborly shared territories that offer protection within a group. As shown in the following section, the group *territories* also fulfil another central requirement, namely the need to interact with one another during work.

3 Social Interaction in the Experimental Zone

The interaction routines between the participants constituted a second important dimension of the negotiation and activation of the shared space. In the Experimental Zone, on the one hand, interaction took place in physical co-presence, i.e. face to face–be it verbal or non-verbal–and, on the other, through (digital) media such as telephone, e-mail, SMS, chat, etc. In the following investigation, we focused on interactions in physical co-presence, because a survey of digital interactions proved impossible for data protection and technical reasons.

With regards to the production of knowledge, the crucial role of interactions in physical co-presence, especially of informal exchange and chance encounters, has been emphasized many times (Allen and Fusfeld 1975; Allen 1977; Penn and Hillier 1992; Nardi and Whittaker 2002). In the field of laboratory architecture, the promotion of interactions has become one of the key themes, which has led both to an increase in so-called informal spaces and to their increasingly elaborate design (Rabe 2016). In our study, we would like to explore this approach in the context of interdisciplinary research: How do interdisciplinary groups interact in physical co-presence, and what influence can be exerted over these by architectural means? The interactions in the Experimental Zone were studied using participant observation and the mapping of the interactions developed by us. By experimenting with the various settings, we were able to explore whether and how specific spatial arrangements affect the interactions.

3.1 Interactions in Physical Co-presence

How did the participants of the Experimental Zone interact in physical co-presence? Firstly, it quickly became clear that different types of interactions exist. They differed not only in terms of content, but also as regards their degree of formalization and physical location. In order to investigate the influence of the spatial configurations on these dimensions, we classified the interactions based on the empirical material:

— With regards to the **degree of formalization**, three types of interaction were observed: *fleeting*, *informal* and *formal*. The *fleeting* interactions include all random and spontaneous exchanges of words, usually consisting of only a few sentences. The *informal* interactions refer to spontaneous or planned conversations. And the *formal* conversations signify planned conversations arranged by both sides in the sense of meetings. The distinction between the three degrees of formalization was made, on the one hand, on the basis of the participants' body language and comments, and, on the other, on the basis of the duration of the interaction: Fleeting interactions usually have a duration of only one or two minutes, informal conversations between five and twenty minutes, and formal interactions usually at least thirty minutes.
— Furthermore, the **physical location,** i.e. the place of interaction and the posture of the participants were considered. A distinction was drawn between three cases observed: *At home* means that all involved parties remain seated at their own workstations during the interaction. *Visiting* means that one party goes to the other party's workstation in order to interact with them. Often, the visited party sits while the visitor initially stands. However, we have often observed that, in the case of a more extended informal conversation, the visitor may, after a while, pull up a chair to sit down. And finally, *in the common area* means that during the interaction, all involved parties are located in the common area, where they either walk, stand or sit.

On this basis, nine types of interaction were identified, including *fleeting (at home)*, *informal (visiting)* or *formal (in the common area)* (fig. 4.36).

Secondly, we observed that some participants interacted significantly more than all others, both within and outside their teams. According to the research of organizational sociologist Thomas J. Allen in the field of Research & Development (R&D), interactions with people outside one's own team are essential for innovation and prove decisive for the so-called "problem-solving performance" of a team, because it is necessary to permanently import new information from outside (Allen 1977, 122ff.). Who interacted how much in the Experimental Zone, inside and outside their teams? The analysis of exemplary setting 16 reveals an interesting observation, namely that five people interact a great deal (twenty to thirty times compared to the average of 14.6 times). Four of these people have interacted with between ten and sixteen different people (here the average is eight), of which between eight and fifteen were from other projects. Since, according to the participant observation, these four people import and export information and thus promote networking between the teams, we call them *connectors*. It is not surprising, moreover, that three of these four people started new research projects in addition to their own project during the observation period (→ see Part Five, page 155). In other words, the findings indicate that connectors play a central role in the academic interdisciplinary context, not only with regards to the import and export of new information, but also to the initiation of new projects.

The interactions in physical co-presence thus exhibit very different degrees of formalization, duration and localizations and are particularly stimulated by *connectors*. What influence can be exerted on interactions by architectural means?

3.2 How does the Spatial Configuration Influence the Interactions?

Space or architecture has often been described as "active" (Niewöhner 2014, 19), a "machine" (Hillier 1996), a "medium" (Delitz 2010, 3), a "mediator" or a "connector" (Yaneva 2010, 144) with regards to interpersonal interactions. In this context, the psychiatrist Humphry Osmond distinguished two different types, *sociofugal* and *sociopetal* spaces: "Some spaces, like railway waiting rooms, tend to keep people apart. These he called sociofugal spaces. Others, such as the booths in the old-fashioned drugstore or the tables at a French sidewalk café, tend to bring people together. These he called sociopetal" (Hall 1969, 108). Which spaces are *sociopetal* in an interdisciplinary context, and which *sociofugal*?

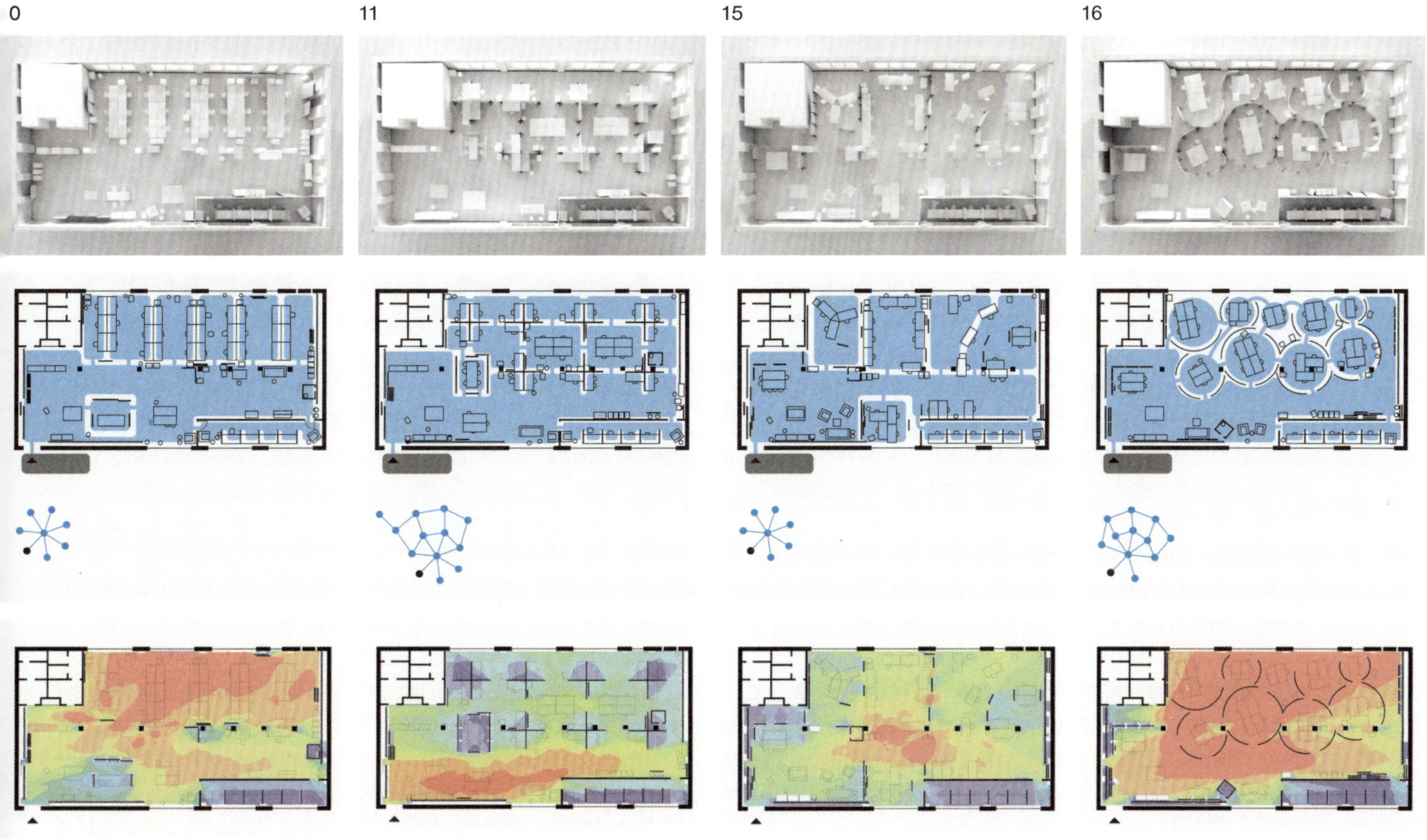

Figs. 4.37–40: Architectural models of settings 10, 11, 15 and 16
Figs. 4.41–44: Analysis of the connectivity of settings 10, 11, 15 and 16 (spatial areas and connections = blue)
Figs. 4.45–48: Visibility graph analysis for settings 10, 11, 15 und 16 (red = high visibility, blue = low visibility)

What happens if a space is completely open or divided by partitions? What happens if the connectivity of spatial areas is high or low, i.e. if the workplace of a colleague is directly accessible, or if other spatial areas have to be crossed first? What if *visibility* is high or low? How often, where and how is interaction subsequently performed?

Of course, not only the parameters *connectivity* and *visibility* had a potential influence, but also many others, such as other variables of an architectural nature (e.g. light, acoustics, room climate or colors) and of a social nature (e.g. personal relationships, status or gender). These were taken into account in our evaluation as potentially relevant influences, but were not primary objects of investigation. At this point, we would like to mention one challenge of the study: The workstations were selected by the participants themselves, so physical proximity was often related to team affiliation or personal relationships. For this reason, it was to be expected that there would be more interactions between participants sitting close together. However, since this is the case in all experimental settings, comparability was guaranteed.

With the terms *connectivity* and *visibility*, we embed ourselves in the discourse of Space Syntax:

— *Connectivity* refers to the spaces and their connections (Hillier 1996): Is a space directly accessible? Or how many spaces must be crossed in order to reach a certain space? To investigate these questions, the Space Syntax researchers have developed the justified-graph method (J-Graph method), which translates the topological relationships of spaces into graphs (Hillier and Hanson 1984). Based on floor plan drawings, spaces are translated into nodes and connections between spaces are translated into edges. In this way, the graphs show which spaces favor movement and thus chance encounters (spaces with several connections) and which spaces are more suitable for retreat (spaces with only one connection). While the J-Graph method is usually used for the analysis of buildings, we have tested its potential for the analysis of the open space. Specifically, we did not use the method to investigate the relationship between spaces, but between spatial areas in open space. Spatial areas are defined by structuring elements such as partition walls and desks, which both separate areas from each other and create connections between them.

— *Visibility* describes how visible or invisible places are in buildings. In a floor plan, first the entire interior space is rasterized and then the visibility for each raster square is analyzed with the help of a visibility graph analysis. The results are visualized in a heat map, with red representing particularly high visibility and blue particularly low visibility (Turner et al. 2001, 107).

To investigate the influence of the two parameters, we designed four spatial configurations: The settings 10, 11, 15 and 16 (figs. 4.37–40) (→ see Part Two, page 57). In these settings, the parameters *connectivity* and *visibility* were varied crosswise to permit their analysis in isolation: The *connectivity* (figs. 4.41–44) of the settings 10 and 15 follows a so-called star topology, i.e. all spatial areas are directly accessible from a central area. Settings 11 and 16, on the other hand, constitute a so-called mesh topology, i.e. many spatial areas are not directly accessible, but can only be reached by traversing other areas. The *connectivity* is higher in the first case and lower in the second. The parameter of *visibility*, on the other hand, was varied crosswise (figs. 4.45–48): It is higher in 10 and 16 and lower in 11 and 15. It follows that we created four cases in which the two parameters can be examined systematically and in isolation.

Figures 4.49–52 show the interaction mappings of the four settings.[5] A brief remark to preface what follows: The mapping could prove confusing, because it appears that interactions almost only took place between two participants sitting in the same area or who enjoyed a visual relationship. In fact, however, the floor plans show the position of the participants during the interaction and not where they came from in the Experimental Zone. This means, for example, that in setting 15 some participants were shouting their way through the room.

Firstly, a general evaluation of the interactions, depending on the degree of formalization over time, revealed the following insight. A sharp increase in the total number of interactions was observed across the four settings: While the same number of interactions was counted in the 10th and 11th settings (108 interactions each), 147 interactions and 192 interactions were counted in the 15th and 16th settings respectively. The number of interactions thus almost doubled over the entire period—despite a decrease in the number of registered participants in the 12th setting (→ see Part One, page 29). Formal interactions increased in particular, more than fivefold from the 10th to the 16th settings. In addition, an increase in informal interactions from the 15th to the 16th setting (from fifty-six to sixty-seven) was observed. However, it is impossible to relate the increase in formal and informal interactions to the *visibility* or *connectivity* in the Experimental Zone with any great certainty. Can the increase in interactions be related to the final phase of the *Interdisciplinary Laboratory*, where many worked so intensively to complete their projects and publications? Not really, because due to the staggered project periods some teams finalized their projects as early as settings 10 and 11. We therefore argue that the increasing face-to-face exchange indicates the formation of a *collaborative habitat* (more on this in Part Five). In the following, we would like to examine the role that the *visibility* and *connectivity* played in everyday interactions. An evaluation of the interactions according to the degree of formalization and physical location, taking into account the *visibility* and *connectivity* in the respective settings, resulted in the following findings.

Impaired Informality

Firstly, the ratio of informal to fleeting interactions through the settings was compared. The evaluation shows that the ratio is very similar in three of the settings (10, 15, 16): While informal interactions here account for about sixty percent in each

5 Eleven observation periods of two hours each were considered per experimental setting, i.e. a total of twenty-two hours per setting, which were spread throughout the week.

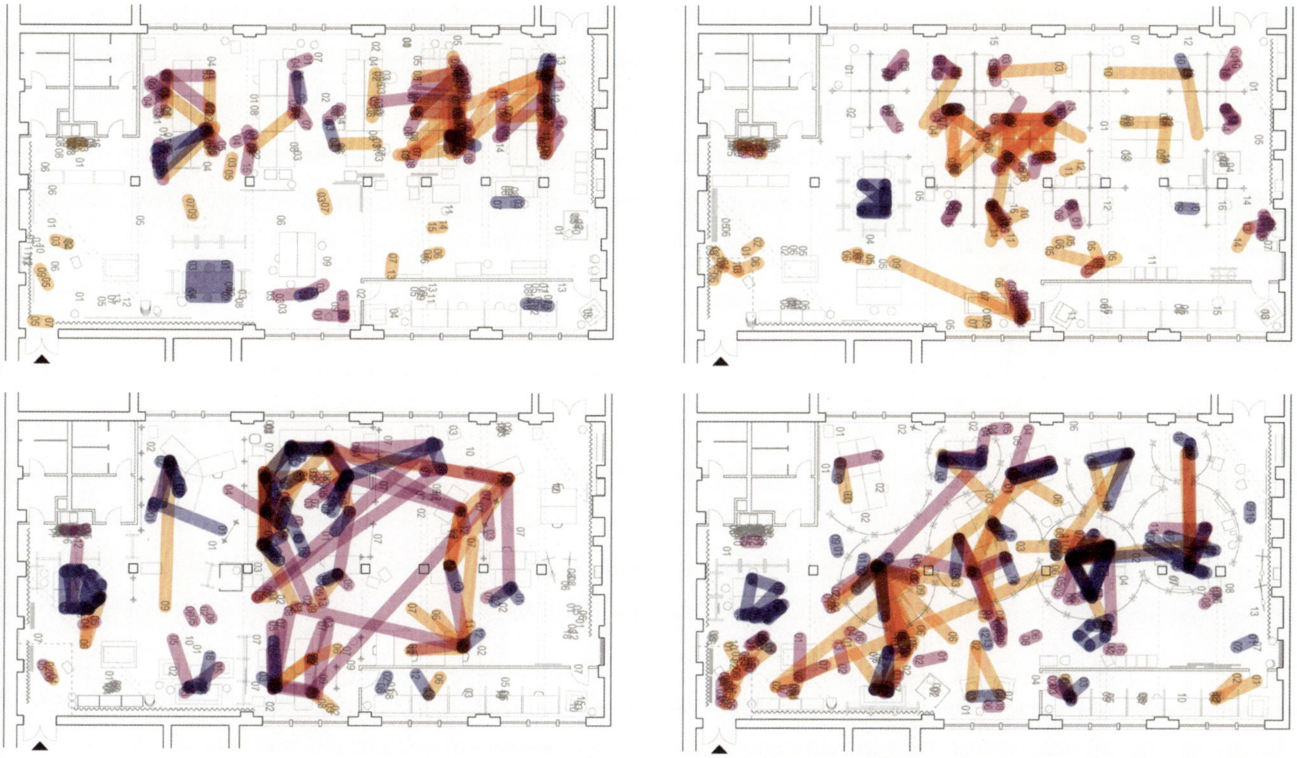

10 11 15 16

Figs. 4.49–52: Mapping of interactions for settings 10, 11, 15 and 16 (fleeting = orange, informal = pink, formal = blue)

setting, fleeting interactions account for about forty percent (fig. 4.53). However, in setting 11, the ratio is reversed: Informal interactions have shrunk to forty percent and fleeting interactions have risen to sixty percent. Precisely this setting is the only one of the four characterized by both very low *visibility* and low *connectivity*. We therefore argue that only a combination of low *visibility* and low *connectivity* can severely impair informal interactions. But why do fleeting interactions increase in such a setting?

Let us take a closer look at the two settings with a mesh topology, setting 11 and setting 16 (figs. 4.50 and 4.52). Although both are characterized by the same low *connectivity*, the height of the partitions differs: In setting 16, the partitions were lower (1.42 m), so that in a standing position it was possible to see the sitting colleagues. By contrast, the partitions in setting 11 were higher (1.94 m) and thus completely hid other people, whether sitting or standing. As described above, such a low visibility combined with a low connectivity seems to trigger a sharp decrease in informal interactions and an increase in the number of fleeting ones. Why does this have a contrasting influence on informal and fleeting interactions? In setting 16, as mentioned above, one could see the sitting scientists from a standing position, i.e. one could check who was present and who was not by standing up briefly. This was not possible in setting 11 due to the high partitions. For this reason, interactions only took place when one of the parties moved, when arriving or leaving, for example. This resulted predominantly in fleeting interactions. It can therefore be concluded that in configurations with a low connectivity the height of the partition walls has a particularly significant influence on how interaction takes place, i.e. whether fleeting or informal.

Gradation from Interaction- to Concentration-promoting Areas

Kerstin Sailer has highlighted the fact that more people tend to move through spaces that function as passageways, making interactions and chance encounters more likely (Sailer 2018). Do spatial areas that function as a passageways foster interactions, even on a small scale like in the Experimental Zone? Indeed, the analysis of the mapping of interactions confirms this hypothesis. In setting 16 (fig. 4.54), for example, which constitutes a mesh topology, it is evident that

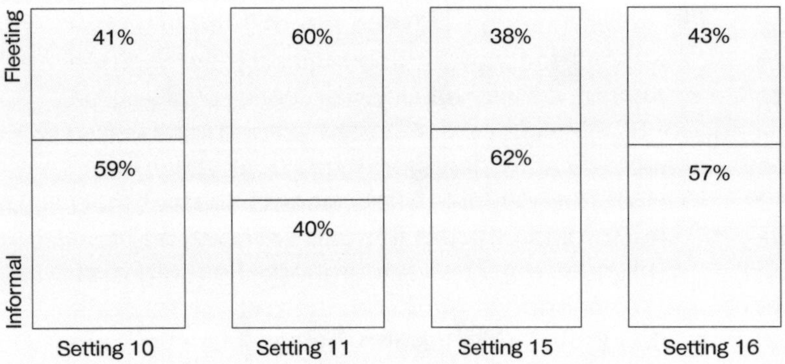

Fig. 4.53: Ratio of informal to fleeting interactions through the settings

far more fleeting and informal interactions[6] occur in those areas and compartments which have to be traversed by the users of the rear compartments, such as the common area (with thirty-five interactions) and the more central compartments (with nineteen, seven and thirteen interactions). The analysis therefore shows that configurations with a mesh topology are likely to result in a gradation from interaction-promoting or *sociopetal* to concentration-promoting or *sociofugal* areas.

The finding is further supported by another observation: The analysis of the interactions per participant shows, that in setting 16, the guest researcher Fernanda, who was not involved in any team and only worked in the Experimental Zone for a few months, interacted almost as frequently as the *connectors* mentioned above. This highlights that the spatial configuration can even place new participants with little connections at the center of attention.

On the basis of the empiric research, we were able to elaborate the characteristics of the social interactions in the Experimental Zone, i.e. categorize them and highlighted the role of so-called *connectors*. With regards to the influence of spatial configurations, the study showed that both *connectivity* and *visibility* have an influence on informal and fleeting interactions. In particular, a combination of both can severely impair informality. Relevant factors here are not only the basic spatial configuration, but also architectural details such as the height of the partitions. The study also shows how *connectivity* can be used strategically to promote interaction or retreat, or even to create *connectors*.

4 An Oscillating Atmosphere

In order to examine the participants' negotiation of the Experimental Zone as a common space, we would like to address the third and decisive dimension for its activation: The question of the atmosphere and the routines associated with it. The aim is to empirically determine which symbolic dimensions the participants assigned to the rhetorical-material configuration. In his study on programmers, Schmidt shows how "the sensual (visible, tangible and tactile) properties of artifacts and materials support and persuade this self-presentation and [possibly· motivate, stimulate, influence, challenge and impress" (Schmidt 2012, 132). To what extent does the atmosphere affect working in the Experimental Zone? As the philosopher Gernot Böhme put it, "the atmosphere is the common reality of the perceiver and the perceived" (Böhme 1995, 34). In such a dialectical relationship, the atmosphere affects the participants, but at the same time they have a strong impact on it through their practices and moods. They are connected with each other in an immediate reciprocal relationship. From this, we draw the conclusion that the atmosphere results from the assemblage of the respective individual research, i.e. from an assemblage of assemblages.

As shown previously, a cluster of designers took possession of the center of the Experimen-

6 As the analysis aimed to examine interactions occurring when crossing passageways, only interactions of the types *visiting* and *in the common area* were considered here, not of the type *at home*.

tal Zone: To what extent did this shape the entire atmosphere? The investigation shows that the atmosphere in the Experimental Zone was constantly negotiated between the opposing ambiences of a library and a design studio. Each was accompanied by certain social rules of interaction, which are made particularly manifest in the conventions of approachability, but also emerge in crisis situations.

4.1 Perception of the Atmosphere

It is relatively difficult to investigate the atmosphere empirically. In our research project, we used the methods of mental maps and participant observation. The evaluation of the mental maps shows that the atmosphere is defined according to different criteria: Visual, auditory and temporal. In fact, the first two dimensions of light and sound—in line with what Böhme defines as "non-material elements in architecture" (Böhme 2006, 34)—have proved to be central.

Visual Impression

In their mental maps depicting the atmosphere of the Experimental Zone, some participants focused on light and color. They described the Experimental Zone as rather white and grey, with cool materials. A designer, Hannah, employed the allegory of the scientific laboratory as a white and sterile space (fig. 4.55). According to her, the colorless and technical atmosphere was also enhanced by the arrangement according to a grid, as well as by the series of identical pieces of furniture (table, chair, mobile pedestral). Another participant thumbed her nose at the interview by leaving the white sheet of paper blank, arguing that "the Experimental Zone is a white sheet, undefined and pure, where everything is still to be written" (Andrea, Design disciplines). Interestingly, only designers and architects described the Experimental Zone as a typical (natural) scientific space. Here, they seem to follow Schmidt when he writes that "the color and visual homogenization [creates- an overall impression of the decidedly non-individual. Through their color and shapes, the individual furnishing elements seem like totems of rationality and functionality" (Schmidt 2012, 147). However, this effect is not emphasized by the humanities or natural scientists—certainly because it is the norm for them.

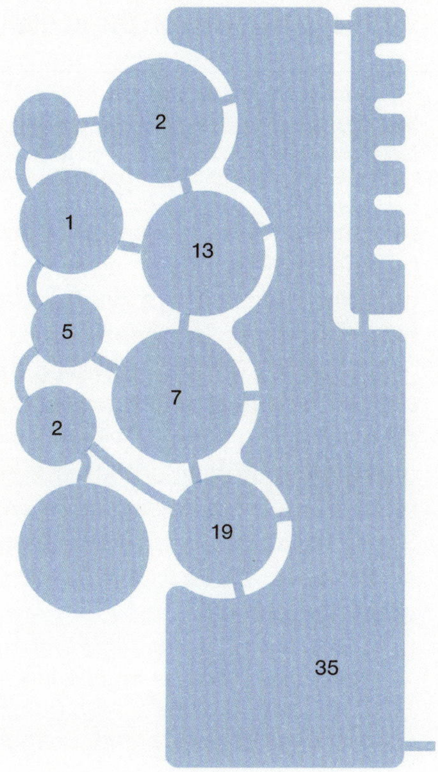

Fig. 4.54: Connectivity analysis of setting 16 showing the amount of fleeting and informal interactions per spatial area

Instead of the visual dimension of the atmosphere, they focus on the auditory dimension.

Auditory Impression

As already mentioned, noise played an important role in the negotiation of the shared space. The atmosphere of the Experimental Zone usually resembled that of a library: Little was said and people spoke softly so as not to disturb the concentrated work. The most frequent terms in the mental map interviews were "concentrated", "calm" and "curbed". However, this atmosphere was intermittent, and therefore failed to represent an overall consensus. Some humanities scholars and engineering scientists remarked that there were (disturbing) noises again and again (fig. 4.56). Some researchers from the design disciplines, on the other hand, found the atmosphere somewhat "inhibiting":

> "The atmosphere is muted, inhibited, calm. You don't want to disturb. As a result, you are not free, but rather reserved. Sounds feel more disruptive because the overall mood is so calm. There is no background noise, it is not lively."
> Mental Map, Isabelle, Design disciplines

Such contradictory perceptions became particularly noticeable when three successive experimental settings on the subject of "exchange" were carried out. The investigation has shown that the conflict-laden negotiation can be traced back to the different disciplinary cultures. In setting 08, "Temporal", the time regulation (morning for quiet individual work; afternoon for noisy collaborative activities) caused great dissatisfaction among some designers, who in turn repeatedly and actively violated the rules. However, this does not mean that the humanities scholars always prefer pure silence and the designers the babble of voices. As described in Part Three, noise tolerance depends on the activity to be performed. Nevertheless, a differentiated tolerance depending on the disciplinary background was observed in the study. Realizing that some creative activities can only be carried out by means of continuous interactions and at the computer screen, we built the silent space in setting 10 as a retreat for these concentrated practices. This spatial delimitation was far more appreciated than the temporal one. Moreover, in the participative design process for the 17th setting, some participants–especially those from the design disciplines–made further suggestions for the design of such spatial demarcation, e.g. to create a gradation of noise by zoning, i.e. from loud to quiet areas (fig. 4.57).

Oscillating Impression

Many participants also noted the oscillating nature of the atmosphere (fig. 4.58):

> "The atmosphere varies according to the days: Tuesday is rather bustling, other days rather relaxed, quiet, sometimes like in a library, sometimes like in a café or workshop, when people talk more. It is due to the number of people present, which is relevant to the general mood: The more people, the more stressful the atmosphere."
> Mental Map, Lukas, Engineering Sciences

This is where the rhythm of the entire *Interdisciplinary Laboratory* becomes noticeable, because the fixed compulsory events on Tuesdays attracted many more researchers to the house and, accordingly, to the Experimental Zone than on the other days. Despite this difference depending on the day of the week, a certain consolidation of the atmosphere can be observed, which can be analyzed on the basis of the conventions of approachability.

4.2 Conventions of Approachability

In Part Three, we established that, with different practices such as *conceptualizing, writing* or *drawing,* differing individual research spaces unfold: Sometimes the spaces are highly permeable with porous boundaries and sometimes fairly impermeable with nonporous boundaries. In an open space, how do the participants convey these dynamic characteristics of their spaces to the others? Or, more specifically: How do the participants signal to each other whether they are currently approachable or do not want to be interrupted? According to Goffman, the "conversational preserve grants an individual the right to exercise some degree of control over when he can be invited to a conversation" (Goffman 1971, 69).

The available literature suggests that the conventions of approachability may differ depending

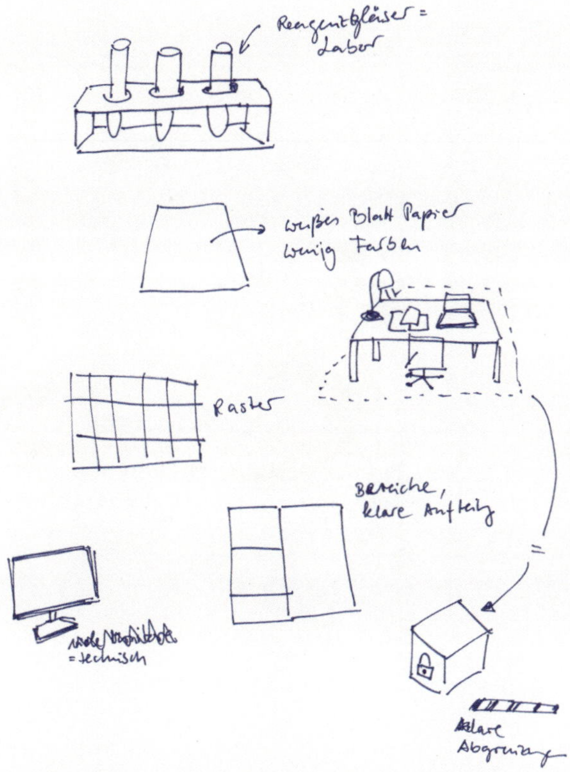

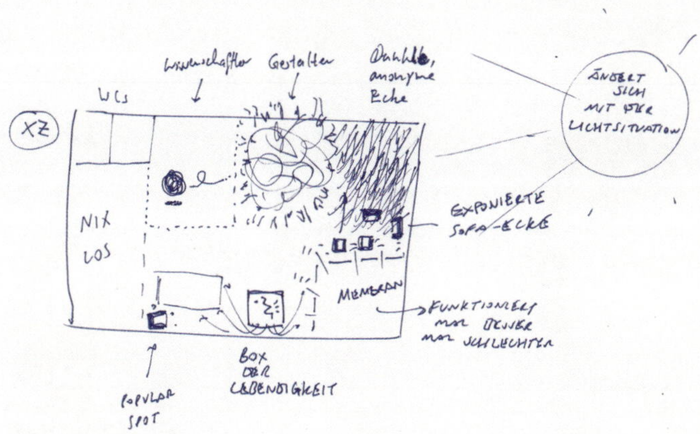

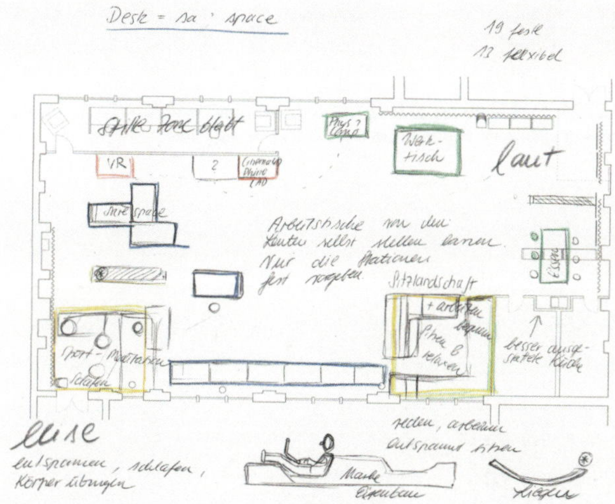

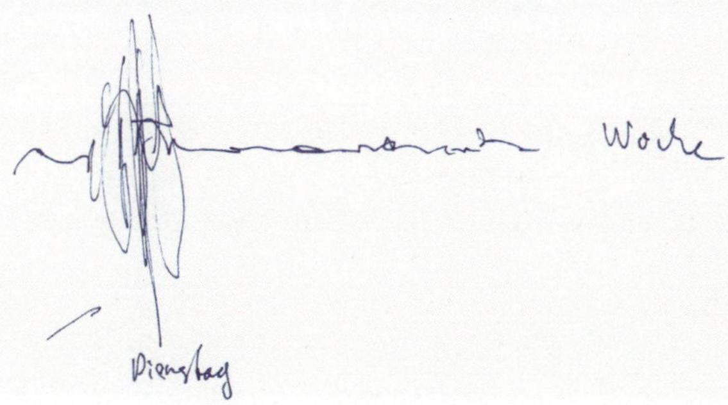

Fig. 4.55: The Experimental Zone as a natural sciences laboratory (Mental Map, Hannah, Design disciplines)
Fig. 4.56: The Experimental Zone as a sound landscape (Mental Map, Alexander, Design disciplines)
Fig. 4.57: Potential noise handling (proposal by the participant Isabelle, Design disciplines)
Fig. 4.58: Oscillating atmosphere of the Experimental Zone (Mental Map, Lukas, Engineering Sciences)

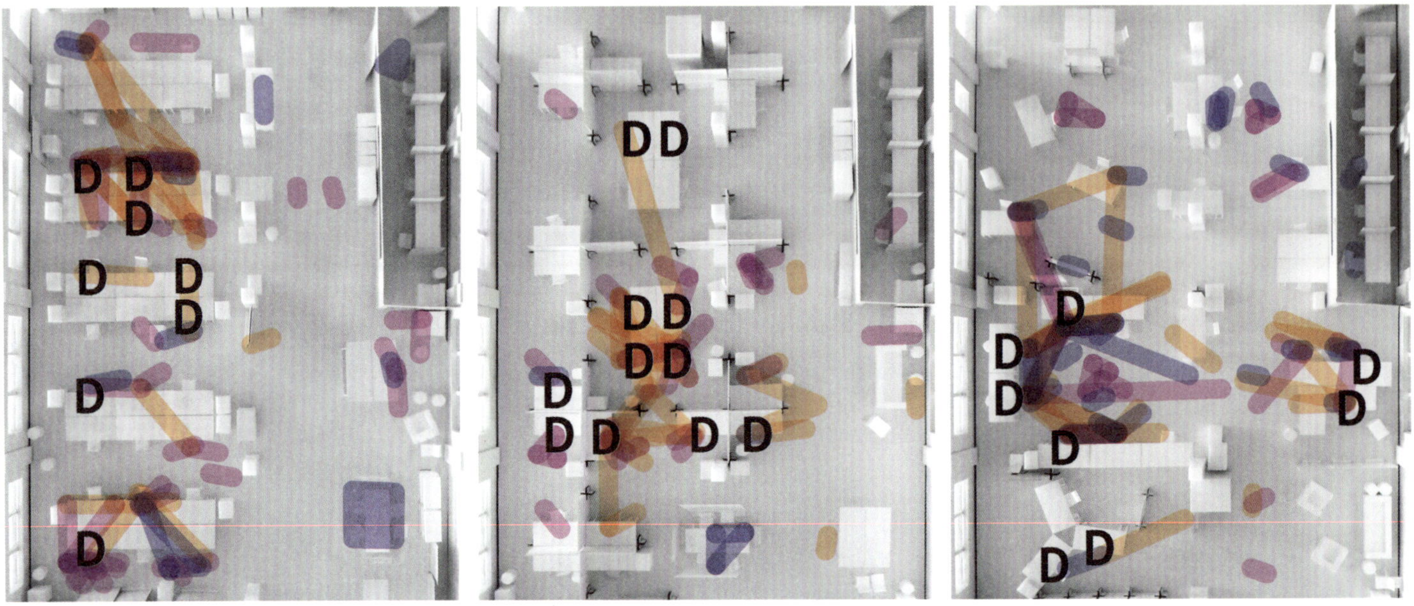

Figs. 4.59–4.61: Mapping of interactions, spatial configurations #4, #5 and #6
(D = workstations of researchers from the design disciplines)

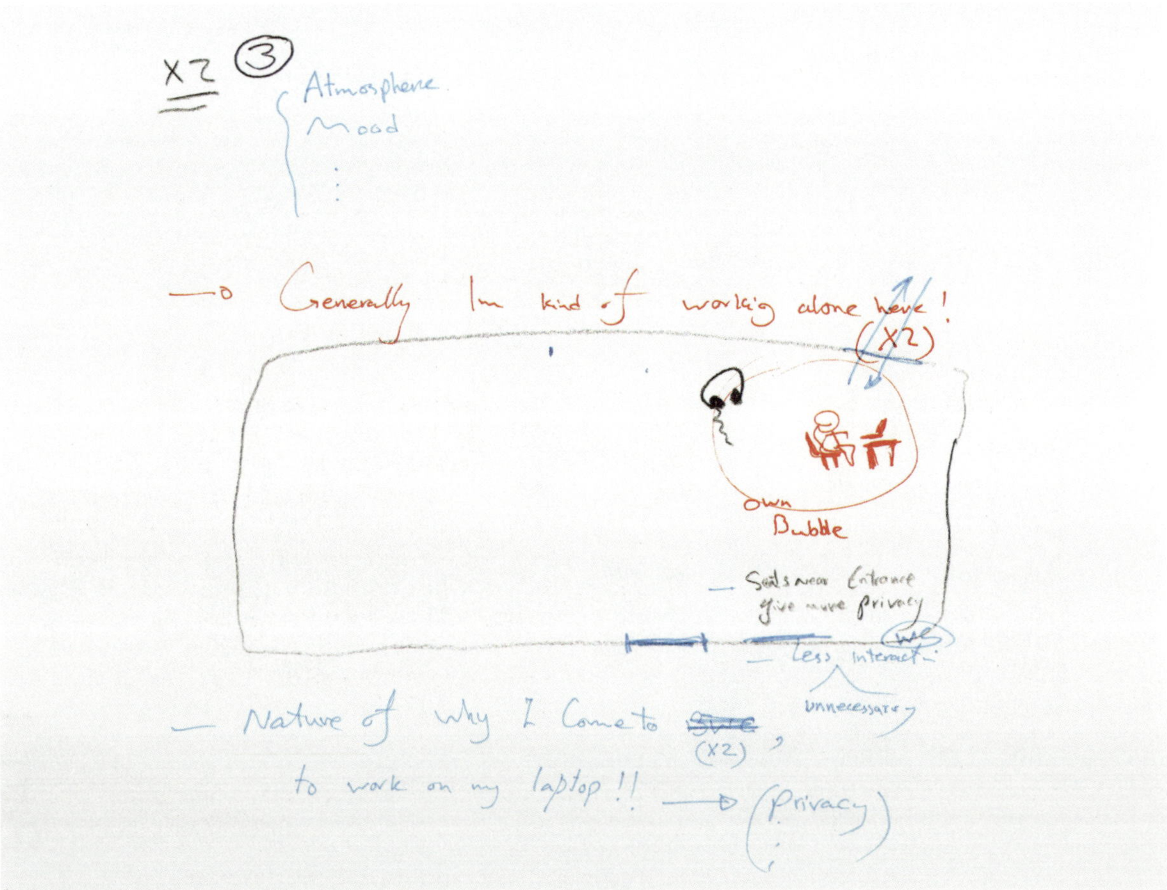

Fig. 4.62: Signaling unapproachability through the use of headphones
(Mental Map, Arian, Engineering Sciences)

on location and context. For example, in their study of an architecture firm, sociologists Alan Backhouse and Paul Drew observed that employees were primarily regarded as "available" for so-called "tasks of recruitment" when they interrupted their "task of immediate occupation", got up from their workplace and moved into the common space (Backhouse and Drew 1992, 579). In the Experimental Zone, on the other hand, the participant observation revealed the establishment of a different set of rules. In addition to verbal signals of approachability such as a greeting or an expression of unapproachability ("I'm busy right now"), participants indicated their approachability primarily using their *bodies* and certain *artifacts*.

With regards to *body posture*, the participants were considered to be approachable when they got up from the workplace and moved into the common area—just like in the study by Backhouse and Drew. However, and in contrast to the aforementioned study, they were also considered approachable when they were sitting at their workstations. In this case, the participants communicated their approachability by means of subtler body language and facial expressions: Here, we observed that a reclined, relaxed body posture and a relaxed facial expression were considered approachable, while leaning forward and a tense facial expression demonstrated immersion and thus non-approachability. In addition, the participants also signaled approachability directly by eye contact or smiling, or, conversely, avoided eye contact in order to signal unapproachability. The evaluation of the mapping of interactions reveals who was contacted frequently at the workstation and who approached others with frequency: As mentioned above, the five *connectors* were highly approachable, often, in fact, when at their workstations. Furthermore, it is evident that the designers were approached more frequently at the workplace—as if their individual *territories* were more permeable for guests than those of the researchers from the humanities and the natural and engineering sciences (figs. 4.59–61).

In addition, participants used artifacts to signal approachability: It quickly became the case that participants started wearing headphones, not only to listen to music or for noise canceling, but also as a gesture to their colleagues that they did not wish to be disturbed. The mental map of an engineering scientist is particularly exemplary in that it shows how he creates his "own bubble" through the use of headphones and makes himself unapproachable to his peers (fig. 4.62). Finally, the computer screen was also used to signalize nonresponsiveness, for example by participants staring intensely at the screen or by hiding behind it.

The conventions described collectively regulate the atmosphere of the Experimental Zone, creating a rather calm environment. The participants speak to each other either directly at their workstation or while walking, in both cases rather softly.

> "The bells chime at noon. Alexander gets up and addresses Fabian. They talk about a potential cooperation. At first Alexander speaks rather loudly, and Fabian answers loudly, at the same volume. But it feels too loud. Alexander is uncomfortable, he turns around, then sits down, opposite Fabian. They lower their voices significantly for a while."
>
> Field notes, participant observation

The Experimental Zone was thus characterized by a generally calm atmosphere similar to that of a library. This basic atmosphere developed in the initial settings as a result of the routines for dealing with noise. However, repeated instances in which these patterns were broken existed, such as periods of exuberance, which swiftly overturned the quiet atmosphere:

> "A new colleague arrived today. She is sitting next to her new team. She and Alexander speak very loudly. She has a very powerful voice. Her voice fills the whole room. In English. A humanities scholar is troubled by this. He searches for headphones, finds none and walks out. The designers are particularly loud today. Miriam has also just arrived with two guests and they talk relatively loudly, too. A third group, infected by the designers, also begins to talk. Everyone is now talking very loudly. This is a kind of take-over by the designers!"
>
> Field notes, participant observation

Crisis situations like these provide an indication of the relatively low threshold of atmospheric change in the Experimental Zone, depending on who was present: When many designers were present, the atmosphere tended to be louder than when researchers from the humanities, natural sciences or engineering were present exclusively. It validates our hypothesis of the atmosphere as an assemblage of assemblages. This constant delicate negotiation was observed in the oscillation between a quiet atmosphere, in the sense of a library, and a livelier atmosphere, similar to that of a design studio.

Conclusion

The challenges of the spatial design of interdisciplinarity become particularly clear in the open space of the Experimental Zone: How can interdisciplinary collaboration be promoted and heterogeneous practices be fostered at the same time? Encounters between different practices initially revealed a certain incompatibility of the different spaces of research—whether individual or collaborative, permeable or impermeable etc. The participants negotiated the open space on three levels, namely by establishing *territories*, engaging in interactions and creating atmospheres. With regards to the territories, the study has shown that the participants created individual *territories* and increasingly also group *territories* that offer more protection in the open space. Both types enabled the fixed anchoring of the participants as described in Part Three, allowing a rapid retrieval of their assemblages, which contradicts the image of the nomadic and highly flexible knowledge worker or the trend of activity-based working (→ see Part Three, page 96). As far as the interactions are concerned, the study provided indications for the formation of a *collaborative habitat* and for the central role of so-called *connectors* in the exchange between teams. On the basis of a fine-grained categorization of the interactions, it was demonstrated that, firstly, a combination of low visibility and low connectivity strongly inhibits informality, and, secondly, that a more complex connectivity such as a mesh topology causes a gradation from interaction-promoting to interaction-inhibiting areas. And with regards to the atmosphere, it has been highlighted that routines have evolved through the settings that permit an oscillation between the mood of a library and that of a design studio.

The differentiated cultures of spatial appropriation between scholars from the design disciplines and the sciences became evident at all three levels of negotiation. In addition, we were able to identify settings which proved particularly suitable for the co-presence of the heterogeneous research spaces. These are, in particular, the spatial configurations that show a high diversity of areas with different characteristics, insofar as they specifically promote the emergence of heterogeneous research spaces—the 16th setting, for instance, combines areas with varying degrees of connectivity and visibility, as well as acoustically open and isolated areas (fig. 4.54). However, the investigation was not so much aimed at enabling the co-presence of heterogeneous practices, but above all at the question of how co-presence becomes collaboration: What are the characteristics of a space that promotes interdisciplinarity? Part Four has already afforded us some insights, including the identification of spatial configurations that promote or inhibit informality or of acculturation processes between the disciplines, such as the emergence of *group territories* or an "interdisciplinary" atmosphere. In Part Five, we will complete the investigation by examining the collaborative research spaces as well as by reviewing the Experimental Zone as a collective experience in order to explore and further develop the characteristics of the *collaborative habitat*.

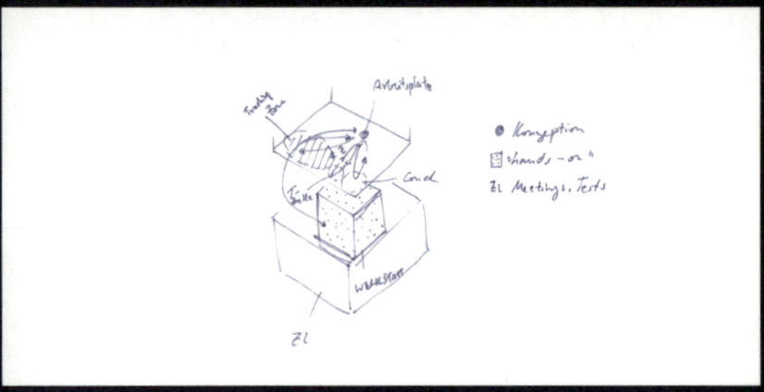

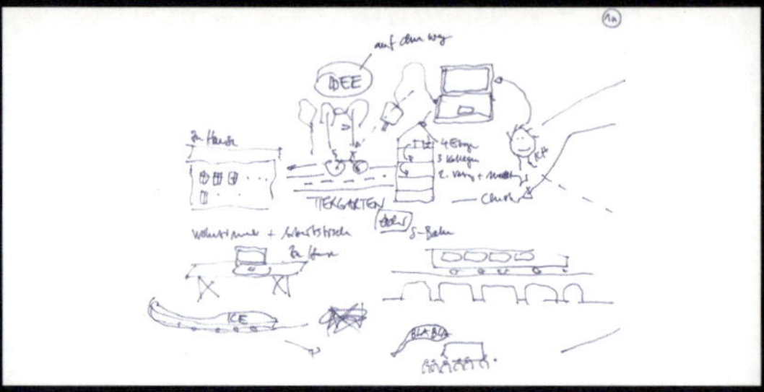

01
02

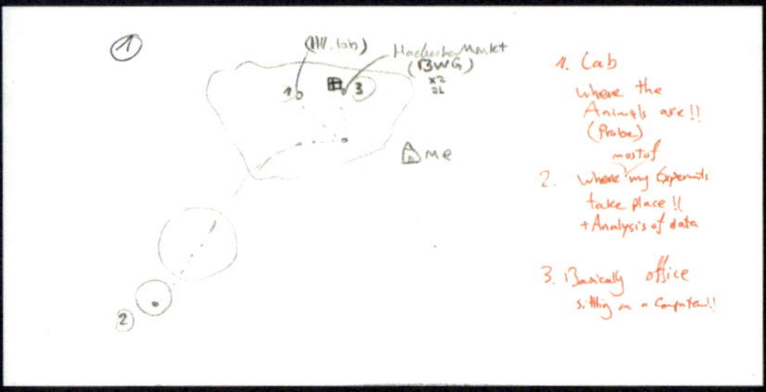

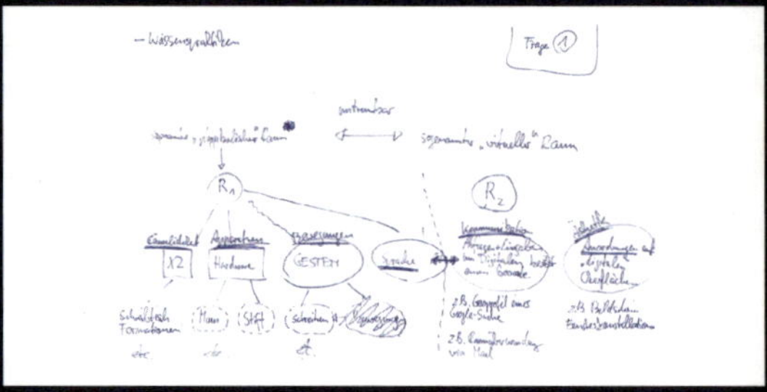

03
04

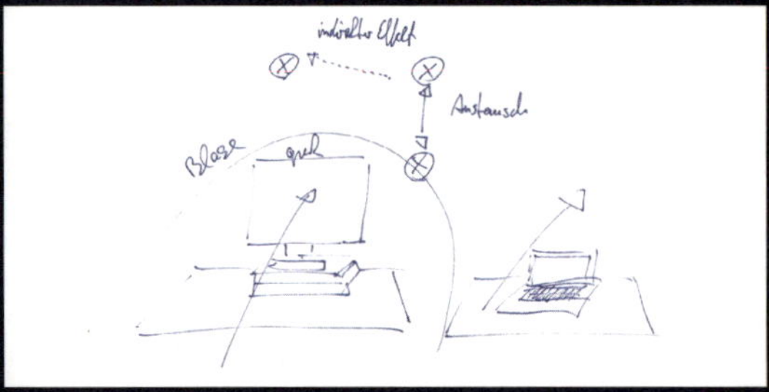

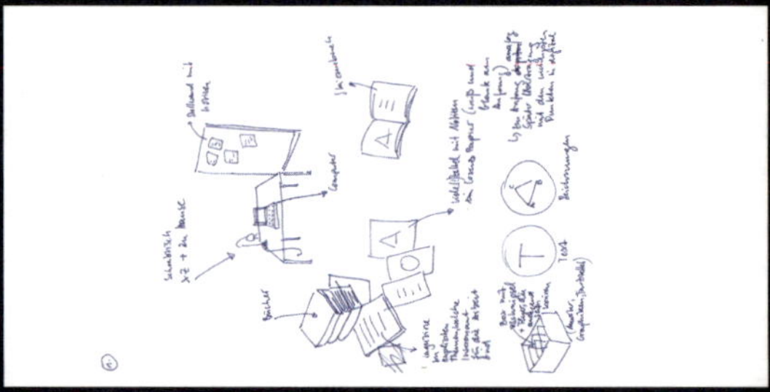

05
06

07
08

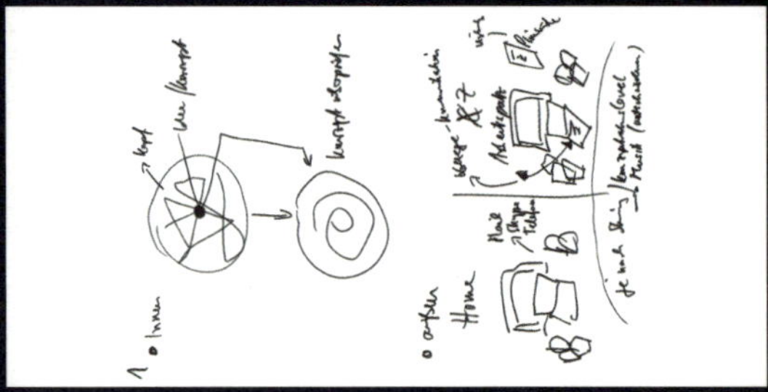

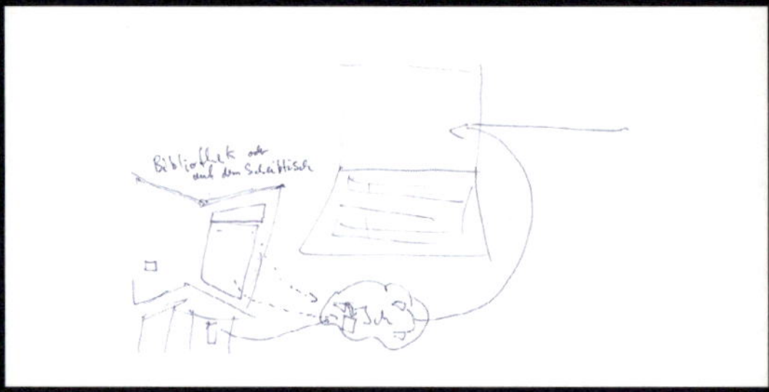

09
10

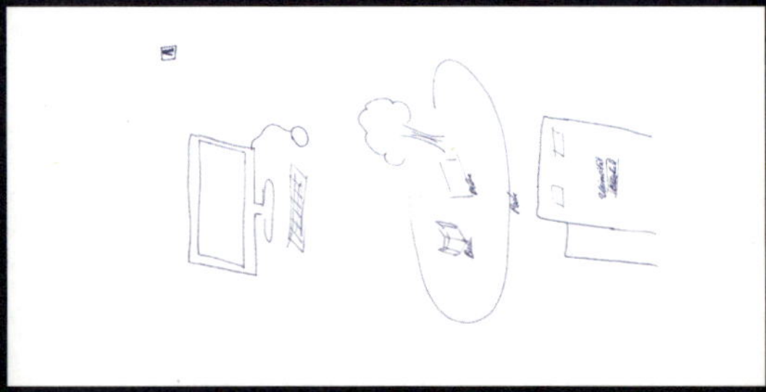

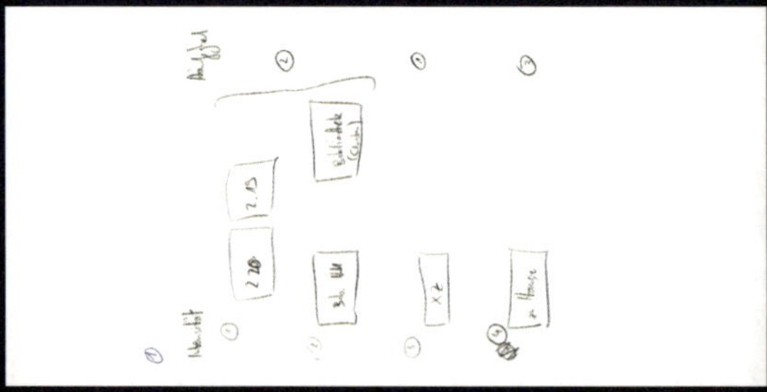

11
12

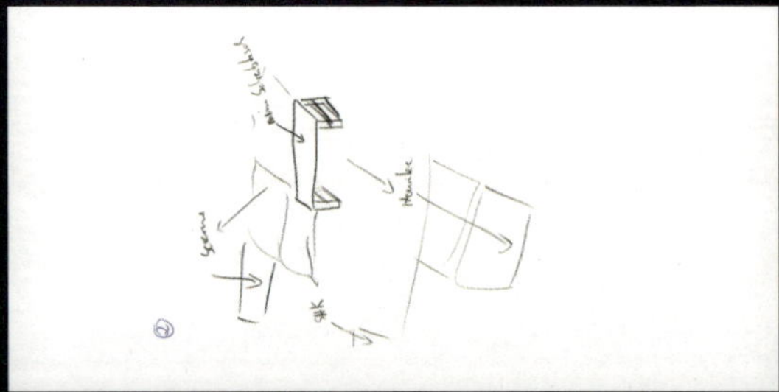

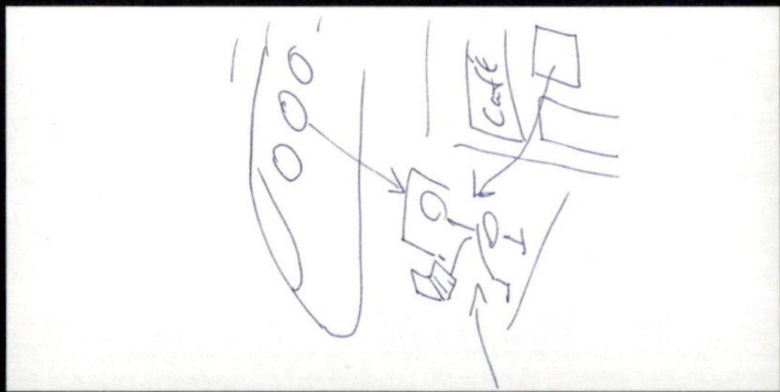

13
14

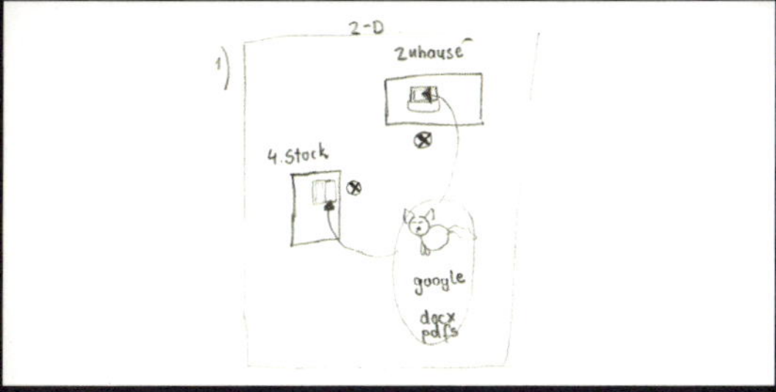

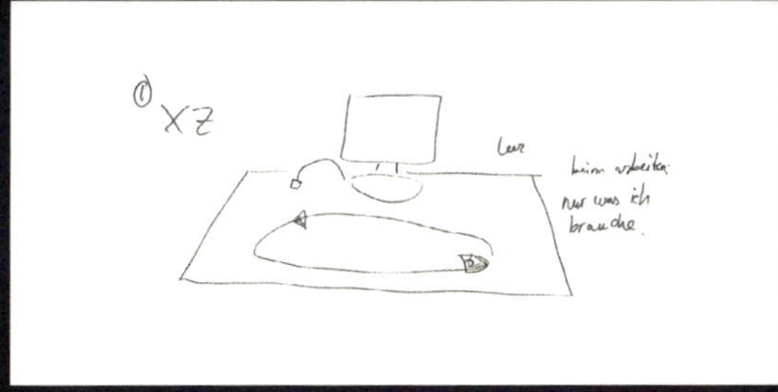

15
16

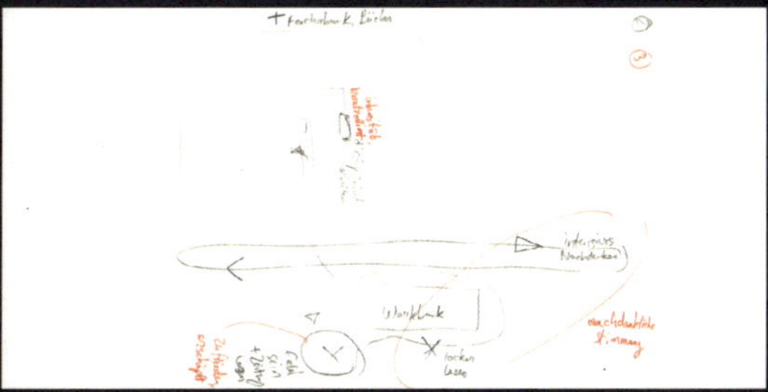

17
18

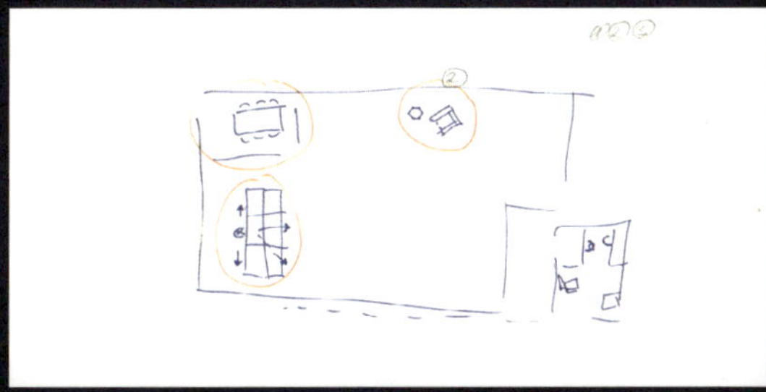

19
20

Mental maps of the physical workplace. The method of mental map is used in order to collect spatial perceptions of the subjects on the basis of drawings. The participants were asked to draw the spatialization of their research practices (→ see Part Two, page 48).

01	Alexander, design disciplines	11	Mara, humanities
02	Andrea, design disciplines	12	Mark, humanities, page 1
03	Arian, natural sciences	13	Mark, humanities, page 2
04	Fabian, humanities, page 1	14	Oliver, humanities
05	Fabian, humanities, page 2	15	Petra, humanities
06	Hannah, design discipline	16	Ralf, humanities, page 1
07	Isabelle, design disciplines	17	Ralf, humanities, page 2
08	Julian, humanities	18	Stefanie, humanities
09	Laura, design disciplines	19	Steffan, engineering sciences
10	Lukas, engineering sciences	20	Veronika, natural sciences

Simulation of Movement

00

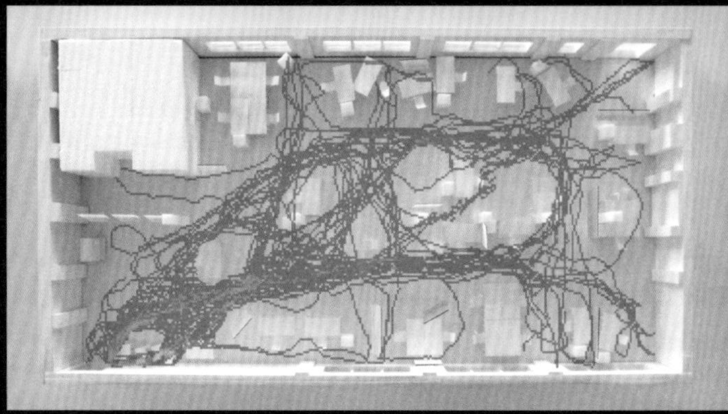
01

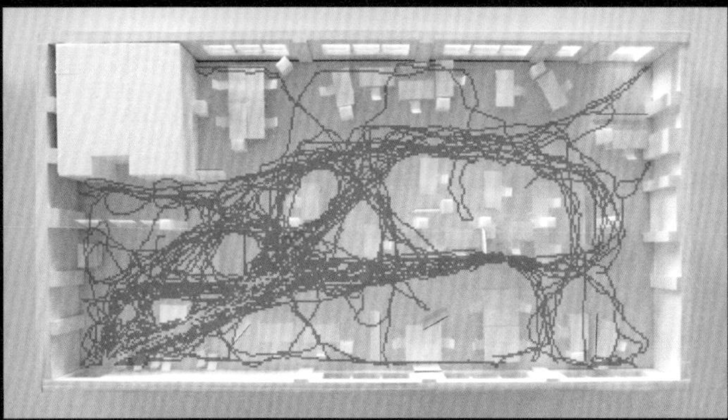
02

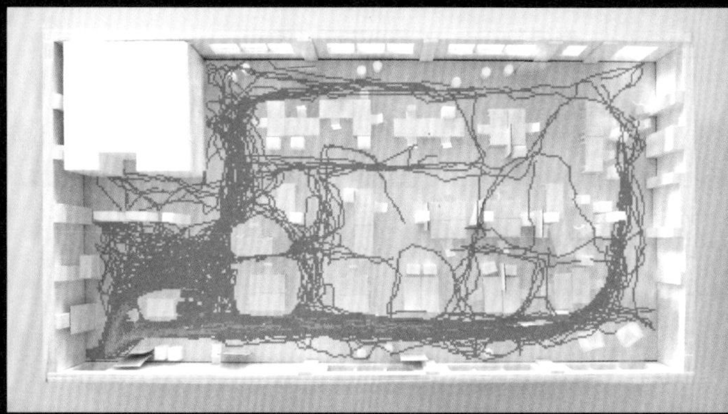
03

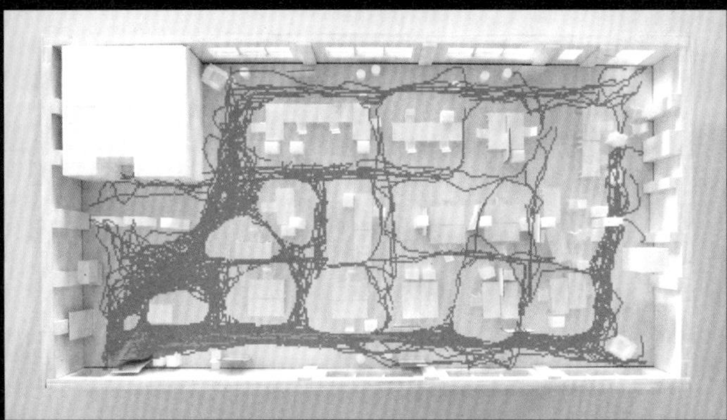
04

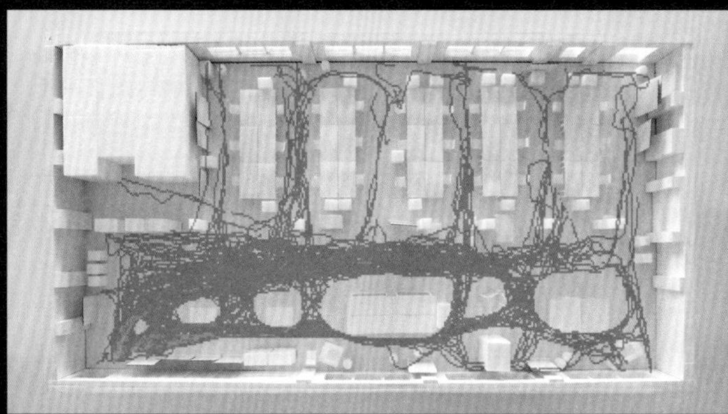
05

06

07

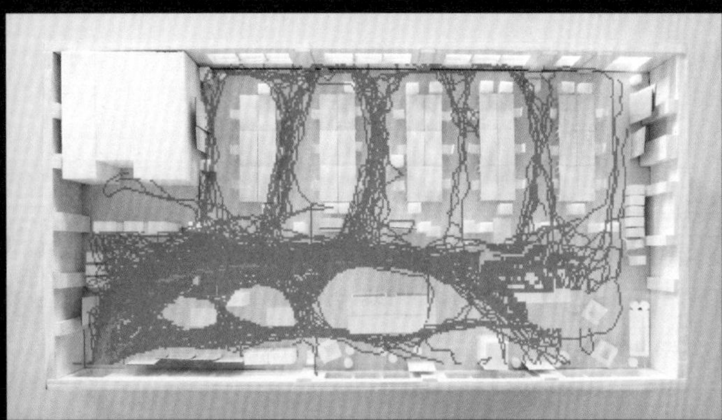
08

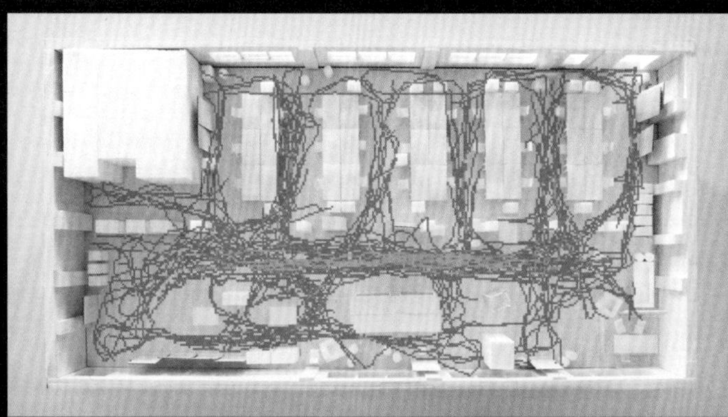
09

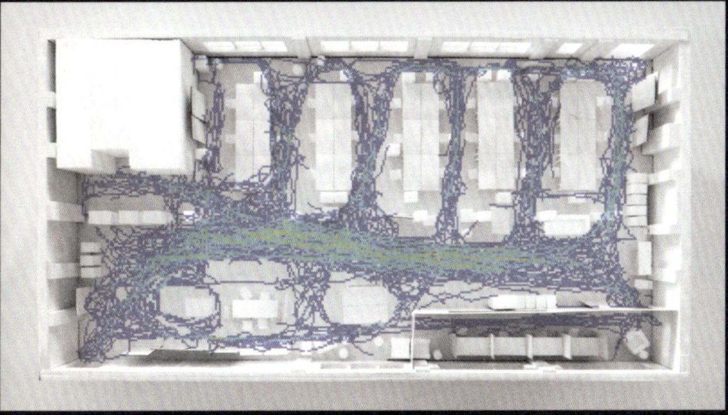
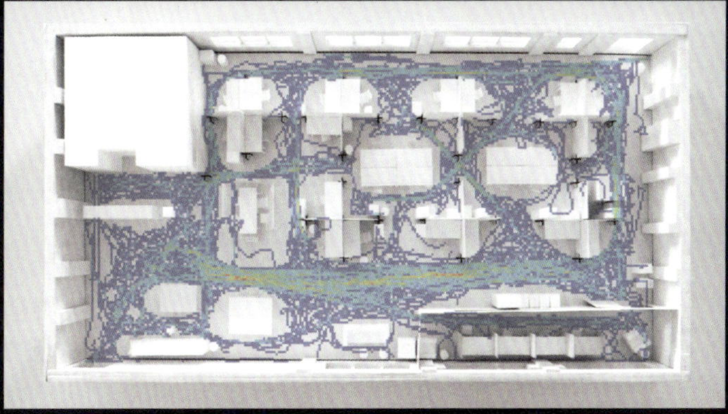

10
11

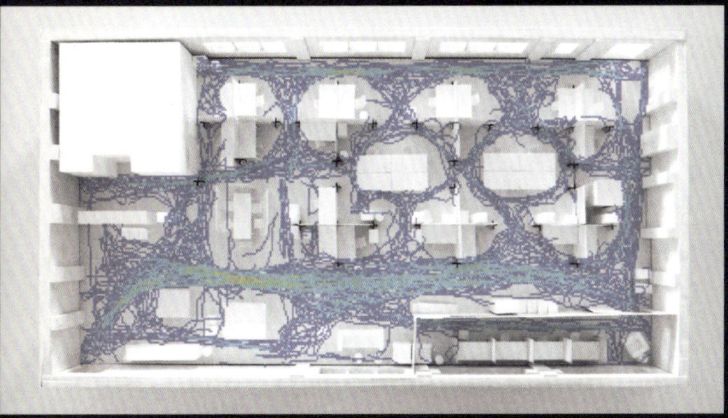
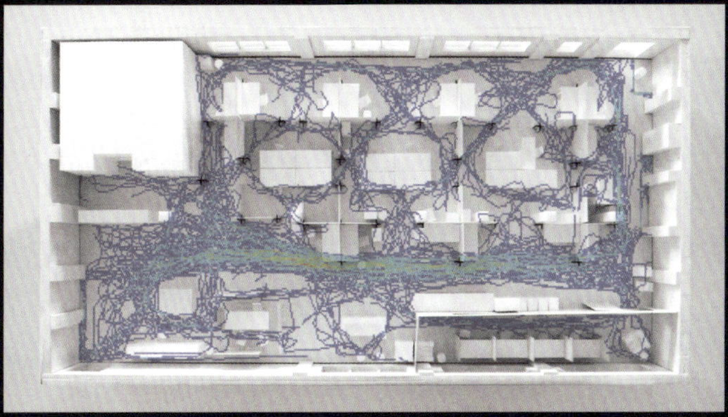

12
13

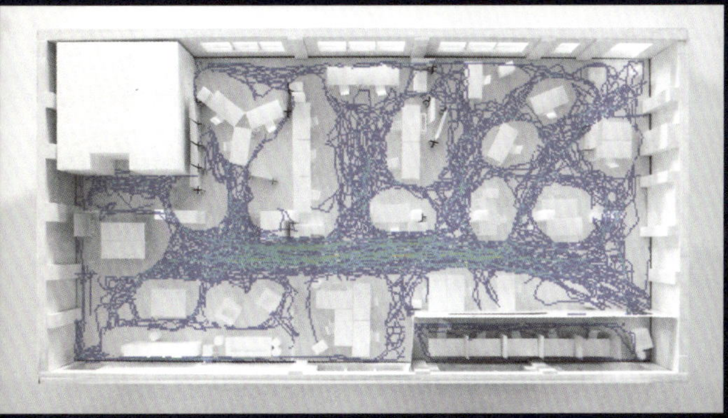
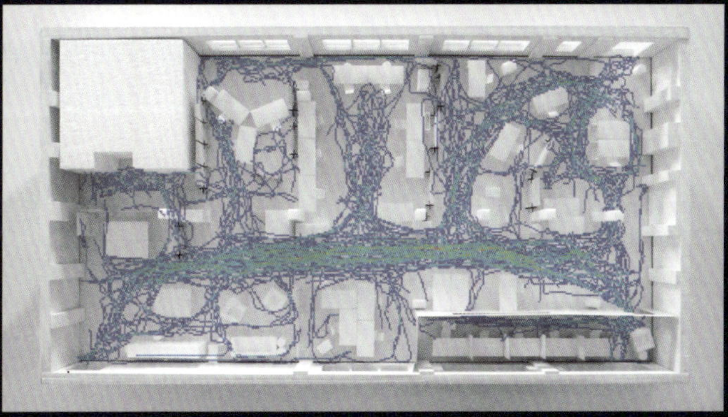

14
15

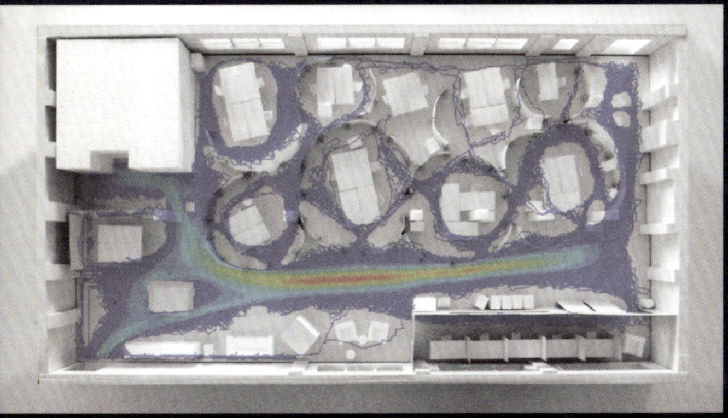
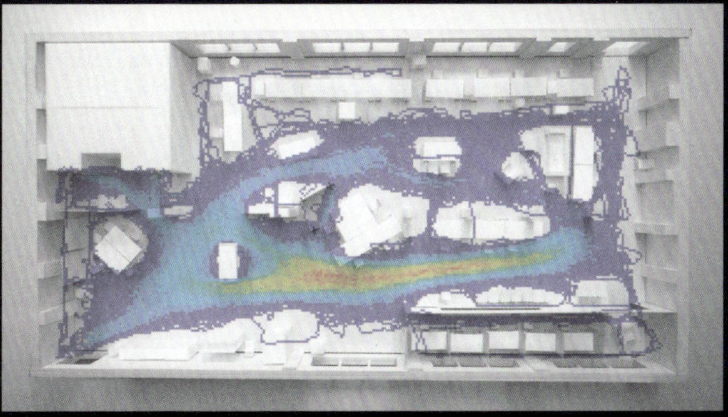

16
17

Agent-based simulation of human movement, created with the Space Syntax software depthmapX (→ see Part Two, page 48), overlaid on model photos of the settings. Graphic © Patryk Kujawa, Dimitra Megas, Benjamin Meurer, Fabian Scholz, Catherine Slusher

Experimental setting 00 “Basic Setting”
Experimental setting 01 “Activity Wall”
Experimental setting 02 “Working Topics – Working Methods”
Experimental setting 03 “Newspaper, Sun & View”
Experimental setting 04 “Navi”
Experimental setting 05 “Practices”
Experimental setting 06 “Diary”
Experimental setting 07 “Work & Play”
Experimental setting 08 “Exchange: Temporal”
Experimental setting 09 “Exchange: Permeable”
Experimental setting 10 “Exchange: Hermetic”
Experimental setting 11 “Compartments”
Experimental setting 12 “Strange Objects”
Experimental setting 13 “Tools”
Experimental setting 14 “Basic Setting II”
Experimental setting 15 “@experimental zone”
Experimental setting 16 “Clockwork”
Experimental setting 17 “Participatory Setting”

Mapping of Movement

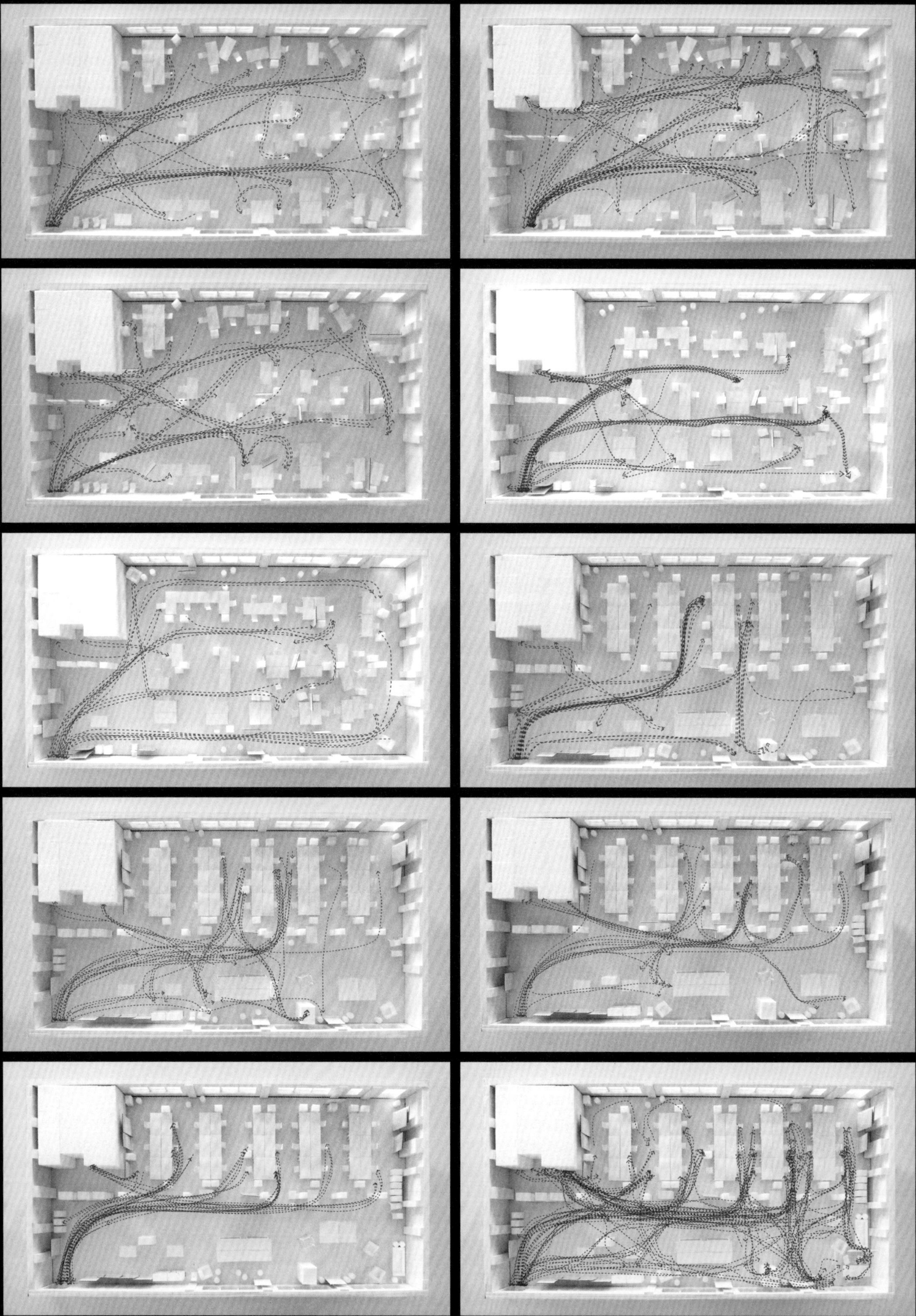

00
01
02
03
04
05
06
07
08
09

10

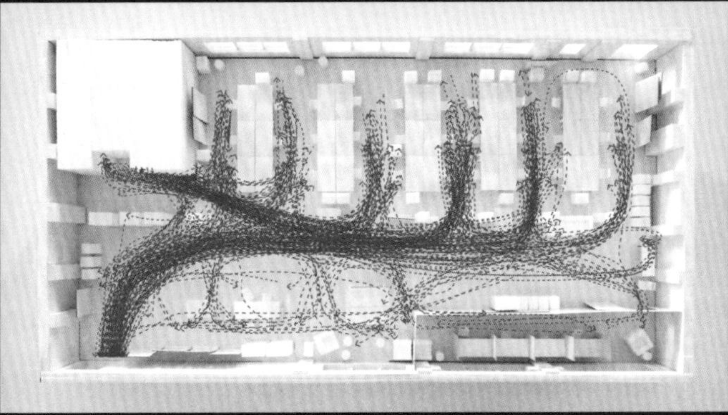

11

12

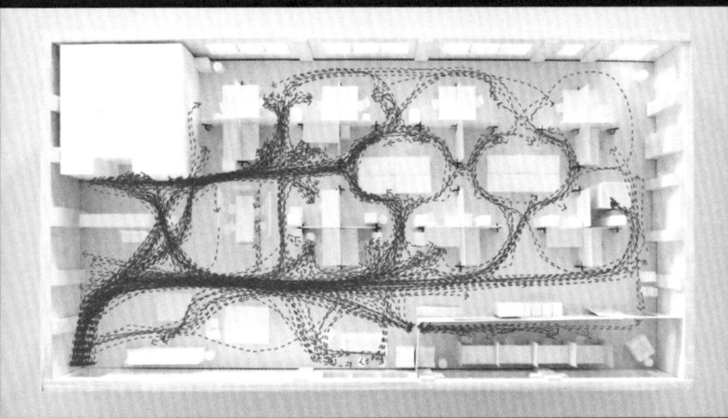

13

14

15

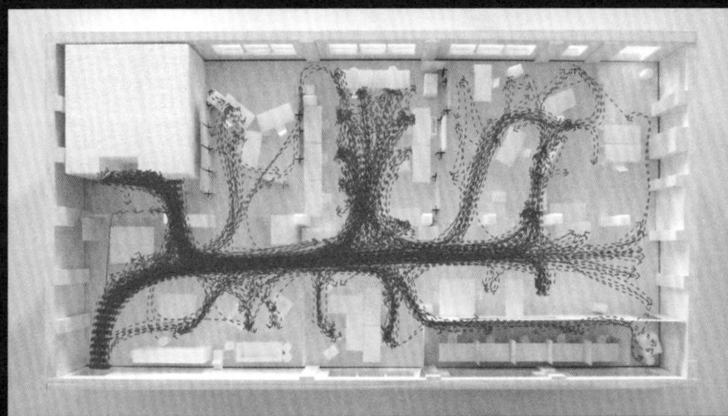

16

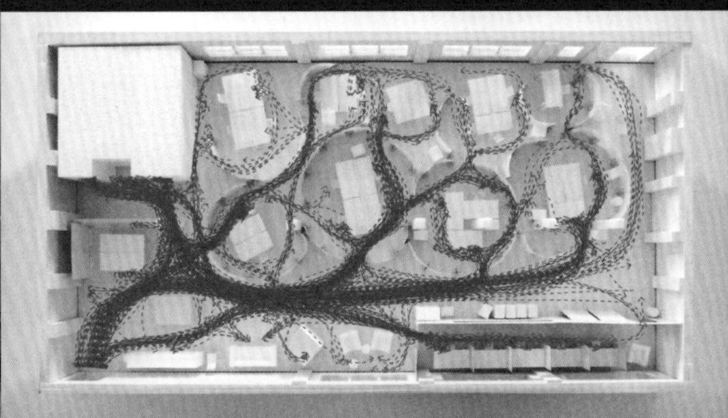

Manual mapping of the participants' movements (→ see Part Two, page 48), overlaid on model photos of the settings. While the two-hour mapping was initially carried out 1–2 times per setting, from setting 10 it was carried out 8–11 times per setting due to a change in the observation protocol (for the exact number of observation periods see the captions). Graphic © Patryk Kujawa, Dimitra Megas, Benjamin Meurer, Fabian Scholz, Catherine Slusher

Experimental setting 00 "Basic Setting" (2x2h)
Experimental setting 01 "Activity Wall" (1x2h)
Experimental setting 02 "Working Topics – Working Methods" (1x2h)
Experimental setting 03 "Newspaper, Sun & View" (1x2h)
Experimental setting 04 "Navi" (1x2h)
Experimental setting 05 "Practices" (1x2h)
Experimental setting 06 "Diary" (1x2h)
Experimental setting 07 "Work & Play" (1x2h)
Experimental setting 08 "Exchange: Temporal" (1x2h)
Experimental setting 09 "Exchange: Permeable" (3x2h),
Experimental setting 10 "Exchange: Hermetic" (8x2h)
Experimental setting 11 "Compartments" (7x2h)
Experimental setting 12 "Strange Objects" (8x2h)
Experimental setting 13 "Tools" (9x2h)
Experimental setting 14 "Basic Setting II" (8x2h)
Experimental setting 15 "@experimental zone" (11x2h)
Experimental setting 16 "Clockwork" (11x2h)

Mapping of Interactions

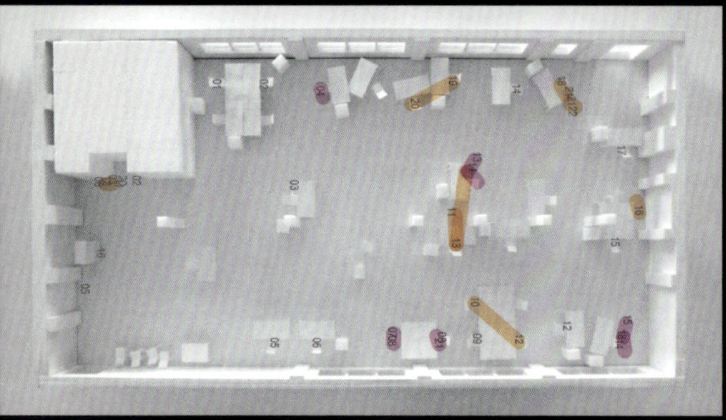
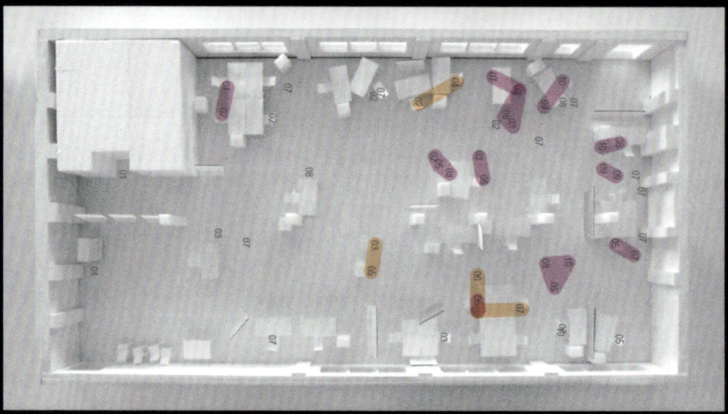

00
01

02
03

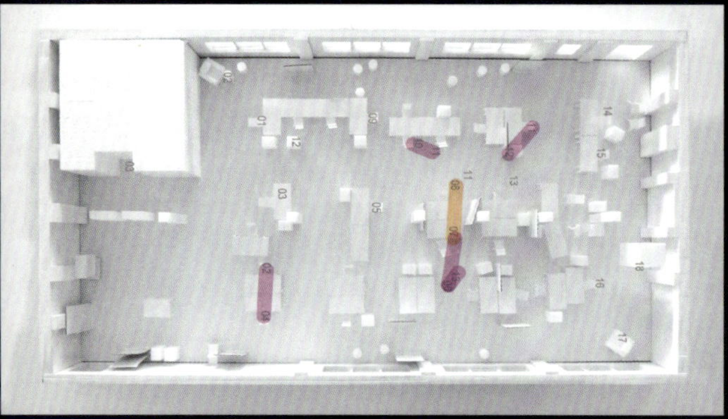
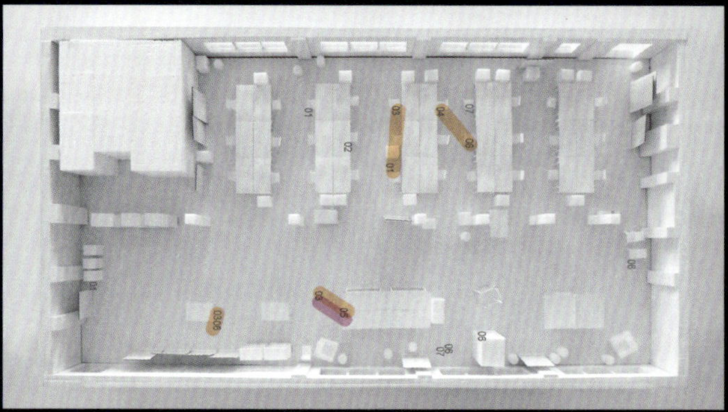

04
05

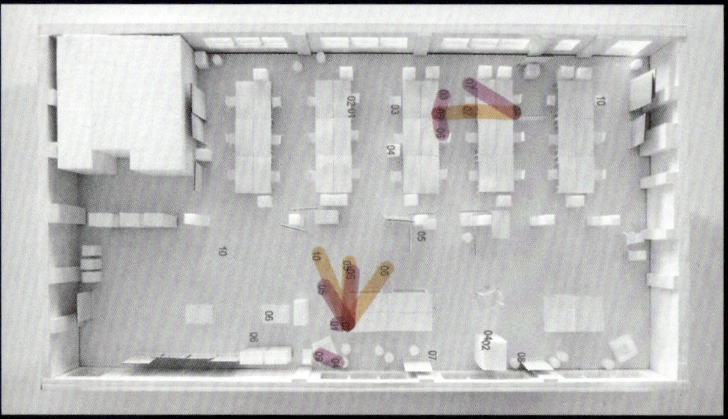
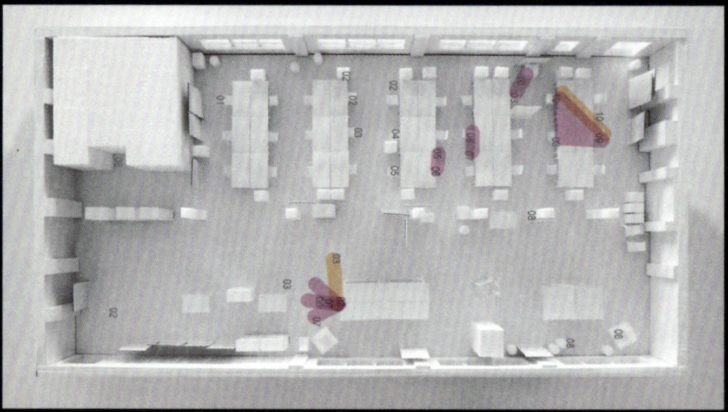

06
07

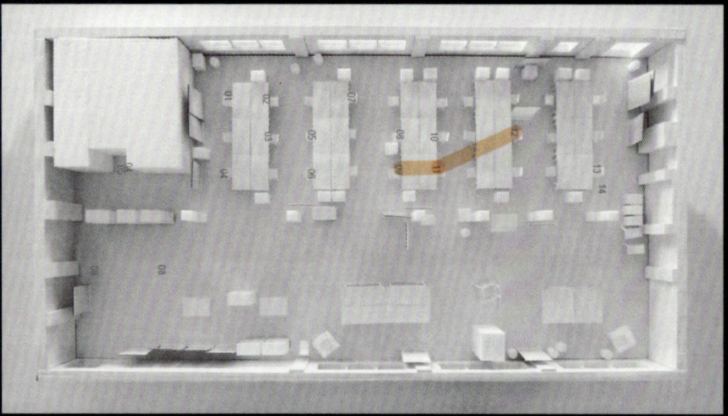
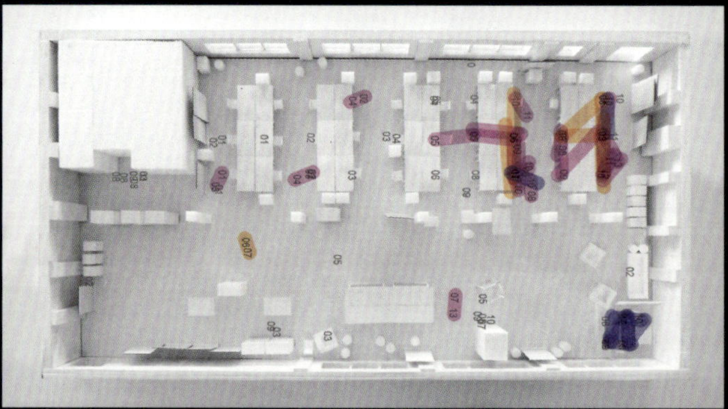

08
09

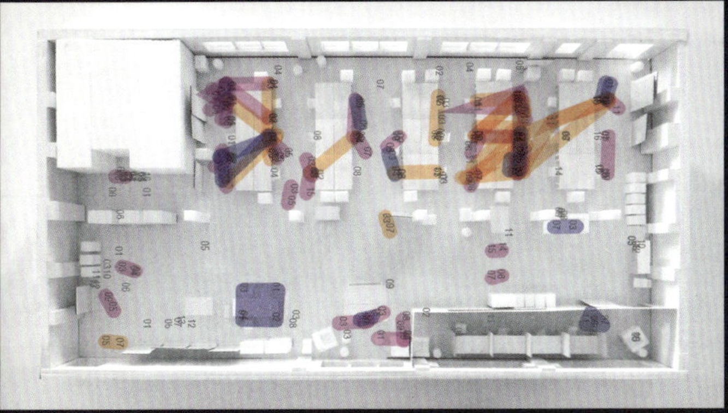

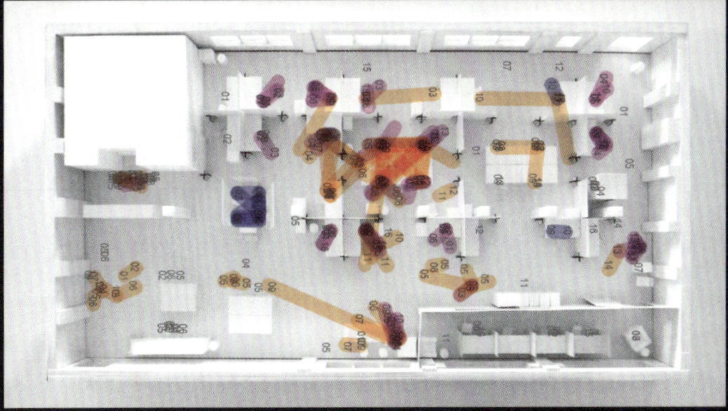

10
11

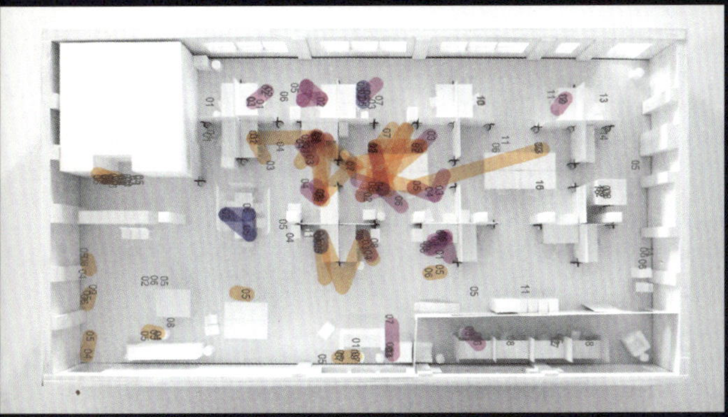

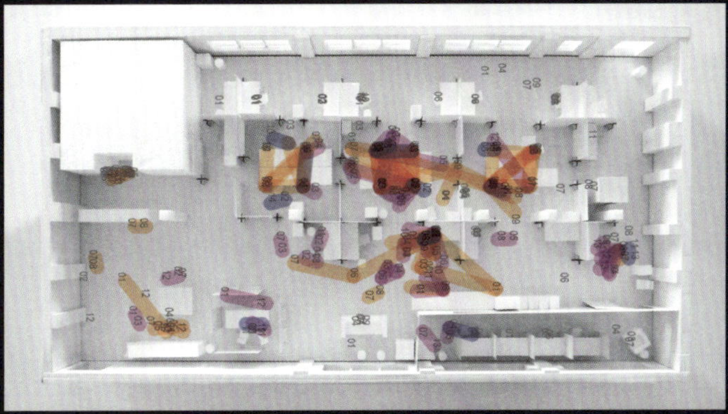

12
13

14
15

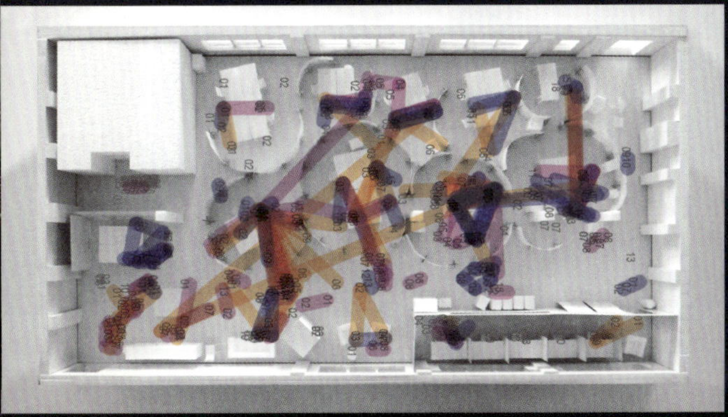

16

Manual mapping of the participants' interactions per experimental setting (→ see Part Two, page 48), overlaid on model photos of the settings (orange = brief interactions, pink = informal interactions, blue = formal interactions). While the two-hour mapping was initially carried out 1–2 times per setting, from setting 10 it was carried out 8–11 times per setting due to a change in the observation protocol (for the exact number of observation periods see the captions). Graphic © Patryk Kujawa, Dimitra Megas, Benjamin Meurer, Fabian Scholz, Catherine Slusher

Experimental setting 00 "Basic Setting" (2x2h)
Experimental setting 01 "Activity Wall" (1x2h)
Experimental setting 02 "Working Topics – Working Methods" (1x2h)
Experimental setting 03 "Newspaper, Sun & View" (1x2h)
Experimental setting 04 "Navi" (1x2h)
Experimental setting 05 "Practices" (1x2h)
Experimental setting 06 "Diary" (1x2h)
Experimental setting 07 "Work & Play" (1x2h)
Experimental setting 08 "Exchange: Temporal" (1x2h)
Experimental setting 09 "Exchange: Permeable" (3x2h),
Experimental setting 10 "Exchange: Hermetic" (8x2h)
Experimental setting 11 "Compartments" (7x2h)
Experimental setting 12 "Strange Objects" (8x2h)
Experimental setting 13 "Tools" (9x2h)
Experimental setting 14 "Basic Setting II" (8x2h)
Experimental setting 15 "@experimental zone" (11x2h)
Experimental setting 16 "Clockwork" (11x2h)

Visibility Analysis

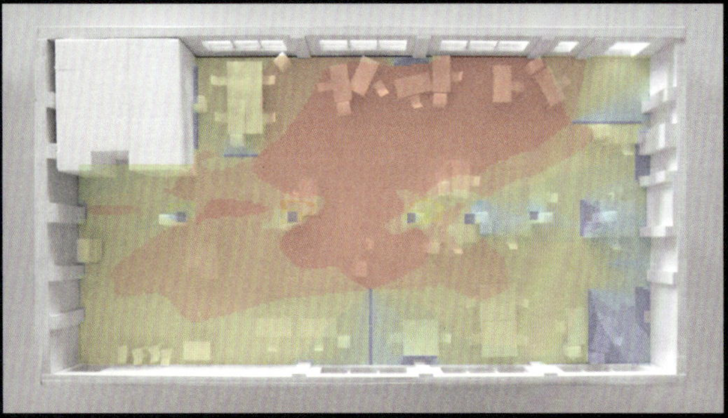
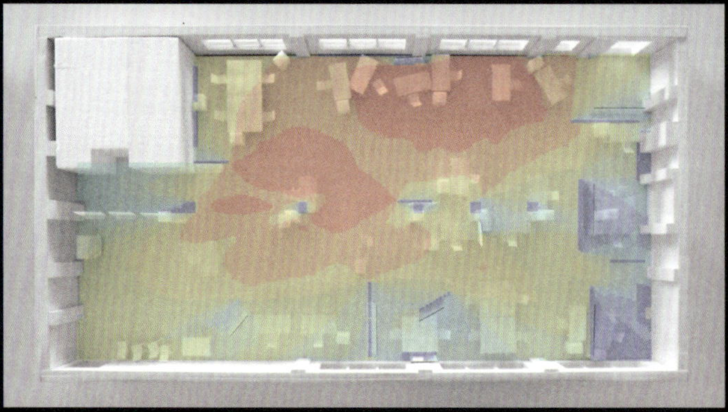

00
01

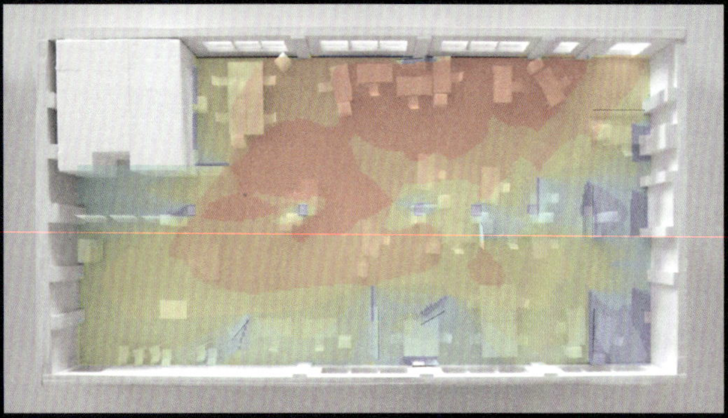
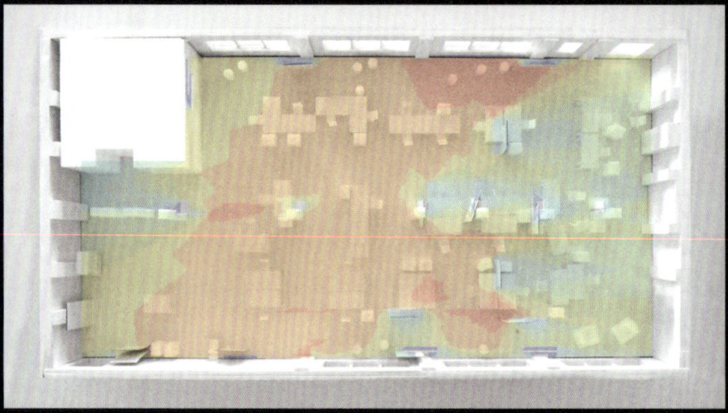

02
03

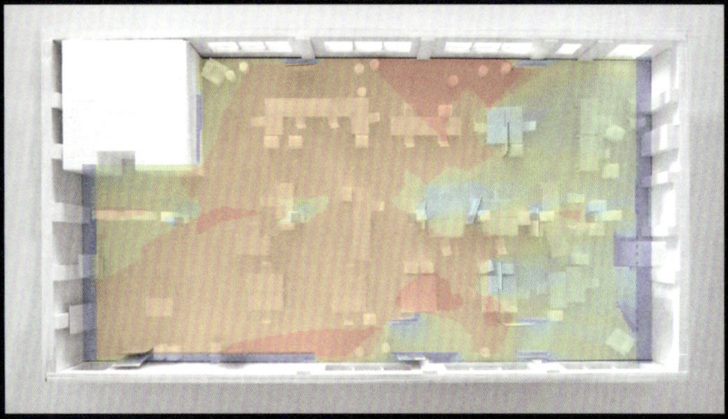

04
05

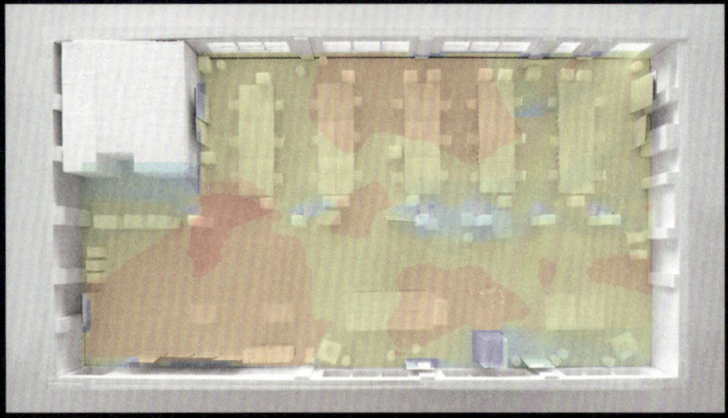

06
07

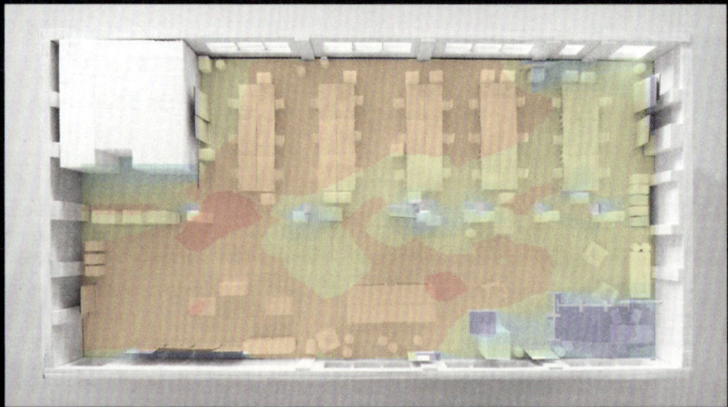

08
09

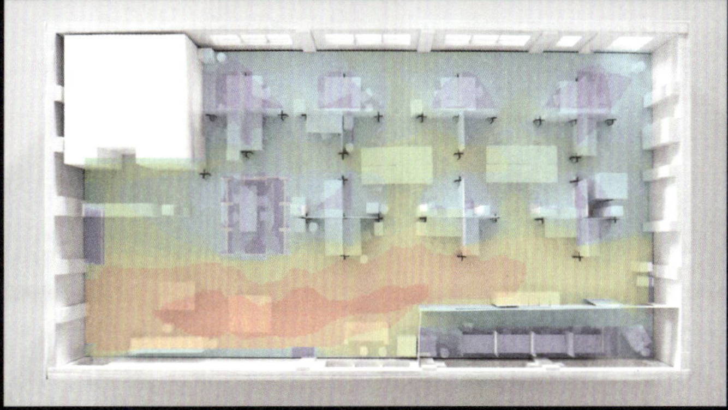

10
11

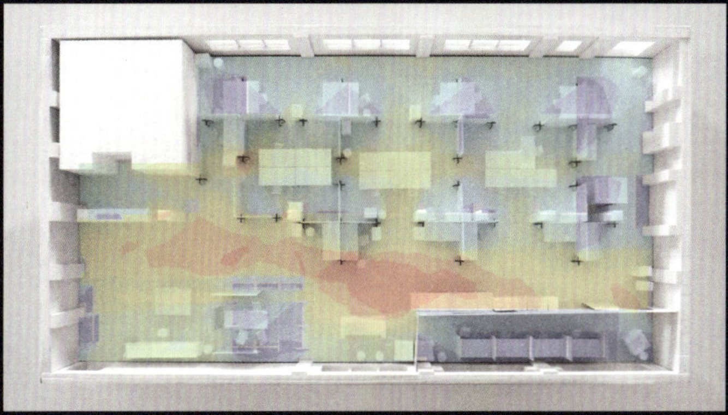

12
13

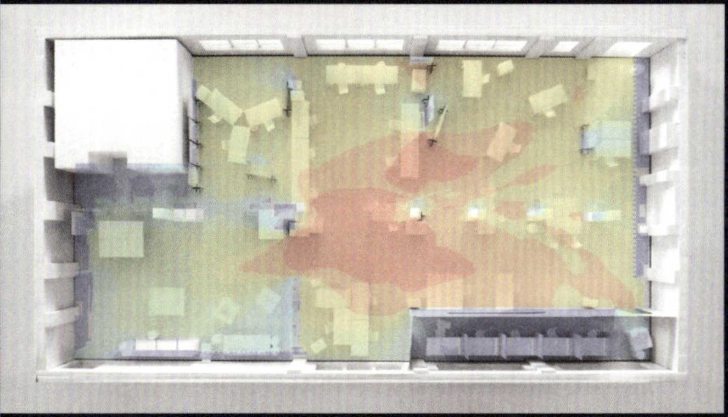

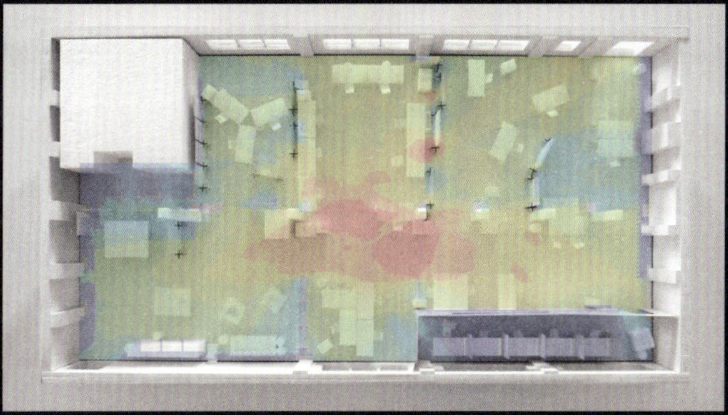

14
15

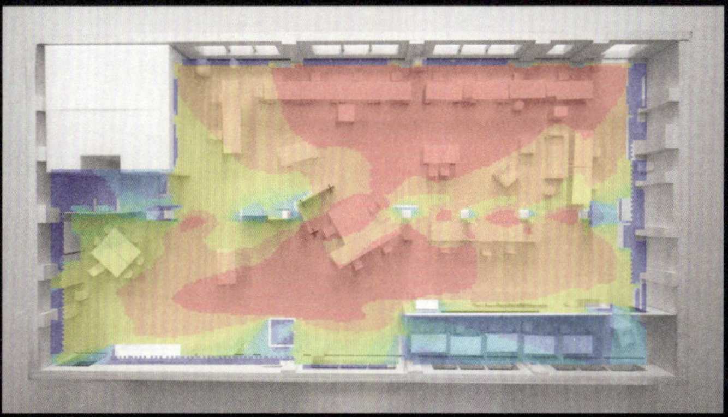

16
17

Visibility graph simulation created with the Space Syntax software depthmapX (→ see Part Two, page 48), overlaid on model photos of the settings. Graphic © Patryk Kujawa, Dimitra Megas, Benjamin Meurer, Fabian Scholz, Catherine Slusher

Experimental setting 00 "Basic Setting"
Experimental setting 01 "Activity Wall"
Experimental setting 02 "Working Topics – Working Methods"
Experimental setting 03 "Newspaper, Sun & View"
Experimental setting 04 "Navi"
Experimental setting 05 "Practices"
Experimental setting 06 "Diary"
Experimental setting 07 "Work & Play"
Experimental setting 08 "Exchange: Temporal"
Experimental setting 09 "Exchange: Permeable"
Experimental setting 10 "Exchange: Hermetic"
Experimental setting 11 "Compartments"
Experimental setting 12 "Strange Objects"
Experimental setting 13 "Tools"
Experimental setting 14 "Basic Setting II"
Experimental setting 15 "@experimental zone"
Experimental setting 16 "Clockwork"
Experimental setting 17 "Participatory Setting"

Connectivity Analysis

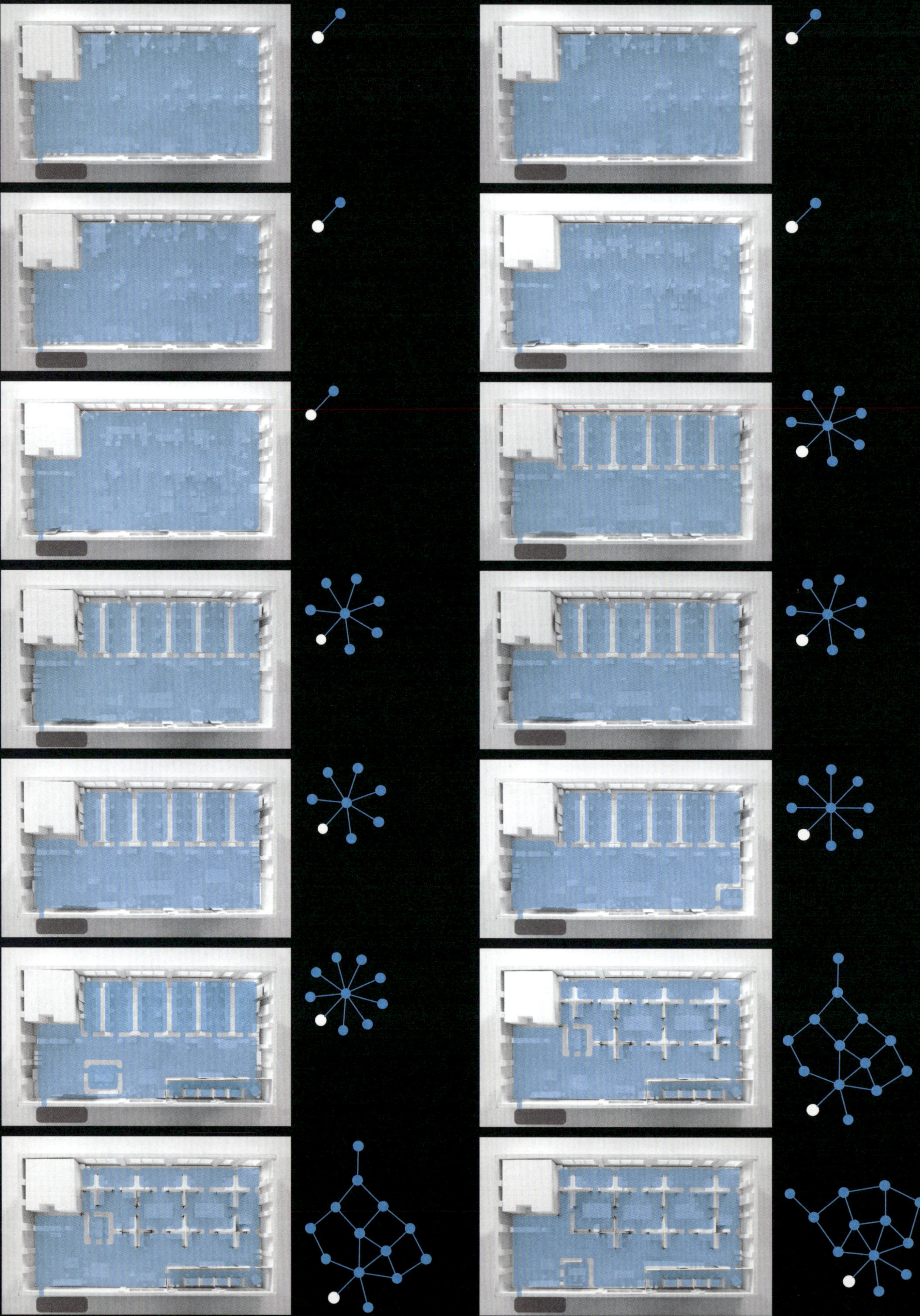

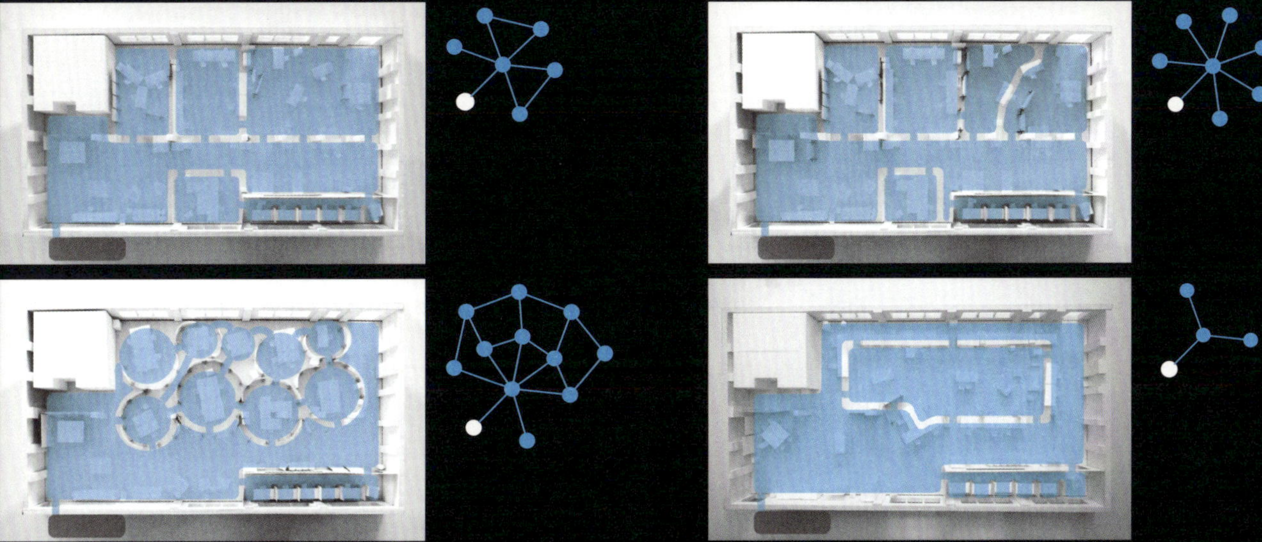

Analysis of the connectivity of the spaces within the Experimental Zone using the justified graph method by Space Syntax (Hillier and Hanson 1984) (→ see Part Four, page 126), overlaid on model photos of the settings. Graphic © Theodora Georgopoulou, Dimitra Megas, Fabian Scholz

Experimental setting 00 “Basic Setting”
Experimental setting 01 “Activity Wall”
Experimental setting 02 “Working Topics – Working Methods”
Experimental setting 03 “Newspaper, Sun & View”
Experimental setting 04 “Navi”
Experimental setting 05 “Practices”
Experimental setting 06 “Diary”
Experimental setting 07 “Work & Play”
Experimental setting 08 “Exchange: Temporal”
Experimental setting 09 “Exchange: Permeable”
Experimental setting 10 “Exchange: Hermetic”
Experimental setting 11 “Compartments”
Experimental setting 12 “Strange Objects”
Experimental setting 13 “Tools”
Experimental setting 14 “Basic Setting II”
Experimental setting 15 “@experimental zone”
Experimental setting 16 “Clockwork”
Experimental setting 17 “Participatory Setting”

Part 5

From Co-presence to Collaboration or the Design of a Collaborative Habitat

This concluding chapter summarizes our findings on the interrelationship between space and knowledge practices as we address our core questions: What is the influence of space on interdisciplinary knowledge production? Which spaces and spatial qualities are required in order to develop new knowledge at the interface between the disciplines? The investigation has shown that interdisciplinarity in the sense of a co-production of knowledge between different disciplines can only emerge when—as a first step—co-presence is achieved. But how can the second step be taken; i.e. how can a mere co-presence be transformed into a collaboration? The aim of this chapter is to develop the characteristics of a *collaborative habitat*, in the sense of a space that promotes collaboration but nevertheless allows withdrawal. Firstly, the study shows that a *collaborative habitat* is, in large part, predicated on the participants' appropriation of space and their attribution of a collective identity—or how the Experimental Zone became "their" habitat through sociality and discursive negotiation. Secondly, the spaces of collaboration are synthesized according to type and analyzed spatially in order to elaborate the characteristics of collaborative research spaces.

1 Appropriation of the Experimental Zone as a Familiar Habitat

Over the course of time, the investigation revealed that the Experimental Zone had acquired a collective identity, specifically by promoting sociality among participants and by encouraging mutual knowledge of the participants' research materials. What is remarkable is that two of these dimensions have emerged as effects from experimental settings. The decisive role played by our research project in the appropriation process of the Experimental Zone is also worthy of note. This appropriation as a familiar habitat was strongly influenced and promoted by the participants' reflections on the spatial conditions of research and their own workspaces, which were stimulated by our study.

1.1 The Emergence of a Collective Identity

On the one hand, the collective identity was promoted through eventization. Joint activities and events were the subject of experimental setting 07, which took place from December 2015 to January 2016. During this period, many opportunities for informal exchange were offered, thus imitating and caricaturing the start-up culture: Firstly, a loud gong was sounded daily to signal

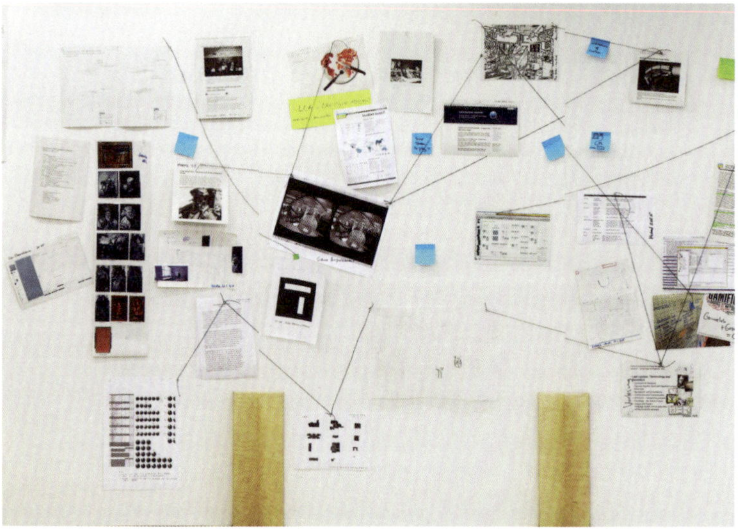

Fig. 5.1: Galette des Rois event. Photo © Henrike Rabe
Fig. 5.2: Table tennis tournament. Photo © Henrike Rabe
Fig. 5.3: Setting 01, “Activity wall”. Photo © Friedrich Schmidgall
Fig. 5.4: Setting 04, “Navi”. Photo © Fabian Scholz

Figs. 5.5–6: Pinboards used by researchers from the design disciplines. Photos © anonymous participant (5.5), Dimitra Megas (5.6)

the start of a joint lunch break, inviting the participants to eat together or play table tennis. Secondly, regular social events were organized, including a Christmas party, a Galette des Rois party, a Russian breakfast and a table tennis tournament (figs. 5.1 and 5.2). In the setting-specific questionnaire, many participants indicated that they had met new people. Most of them highlighted the improved atmosphere and social inclusion, while only a few deemed the meetings during working hours onerous. Some of the questionnaire respondents stated that they would continue to get together after the setting's conclusion in order to eat, drink or play table tennis—which they actually did. Setting 07 thus proved a turning point as far as the familiarity between the participants was concerned. This familiarity among the participants of the Experimental Zone became particularly evident at the *Interdisciplinary Laboratory's* subsequent annual retreat: The participants sat together during meals, talked intensively during coffee breaks and played table tennis in the evening. In this sense, they formed a new group within the *Interdisciplinary Laboratory* that could also be observed outside its walls. They had something in common that the other scientists did not: They shared a certain way of working, which had both developed and materialized in the flexible open space of the Experimental Zone (→ see Parts Three and Four).

On the other hand, the collective identity benefited from a high content-related visibility. In addition to event-based experiments, we conducted content-based experimental settings in which a high visibility of content was tested. In experimental setting 01, the visualization and entanglement of work topics was investigated. Once a week, the participants were asked to pin an object representing their current work topic on a so-called activity wall in the entrance area (fig. 5.3). In experimental setting 04, the physical space was equipped with a "commenting navigation system". By means of suspended signs, the participants were able to pinpoint what was happening at this position, also with regards to content (fig. 5.4). In both settings, an attempt was made to encourage the participants to explore those topics worked on by the others and discover potential intersections. Even if the participants demonstrated a basic interest in these methods, it was difficult to implement them in everyday life and to keep the visualization of the research material up to date. A certain

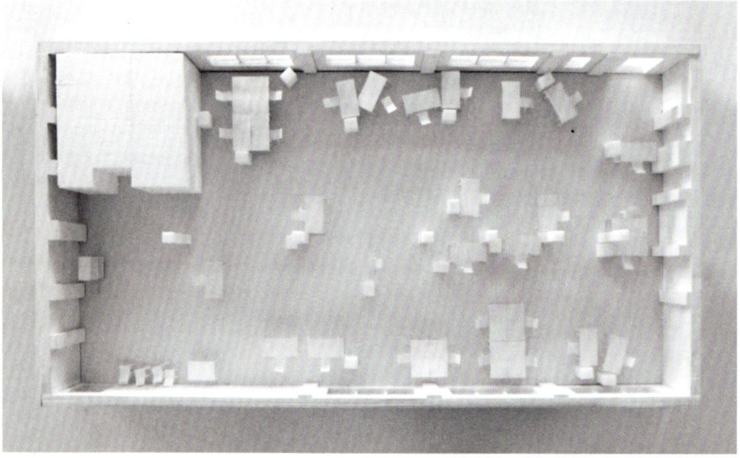

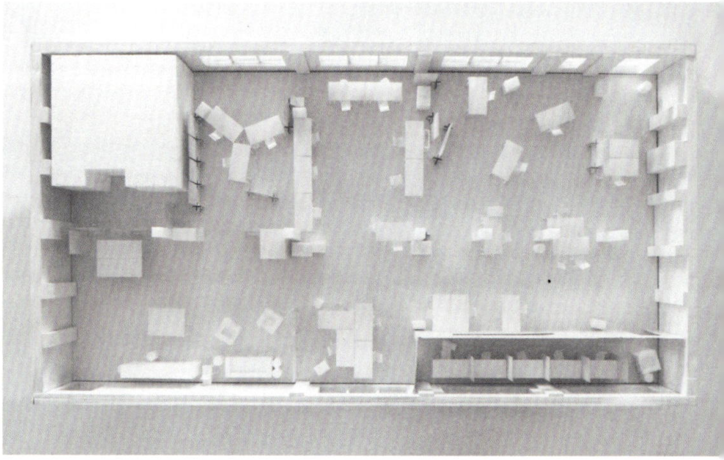

Figs. 5.7–8: Comparison of Basic Settings I and II.
Photo © Dimitra Megas, Fabian Scholz
Fig. 5.9: Participative workshop for the design of the 17th setting.
Photo © Friedrich Schmidgall

reluctance to reveal their research material was observed among scholars from the humanities and natural sciences.

Indeed, the study demonstrated a discipline-specific approach to the disclosure of ongoing work. Researchers from the design disciplines frequently used pinboards to visualize their work in progress, such as sketches, text passages or materials, arguing that pinboards provide an overview and function as "joint displays" of data, thoughts and materials (figs. 5.5 and 5.6). Researchers from the fields of humanities and natural sciences did not engage in such a practice, justifying this on the grounds that it was too intimate. We hypothesize that this is related both to a certain notion of an anticipated sophistication as regards their work, and to the protection of their individual authorship. Researchers from the design disciplines perceived the need for intimacy as a considerable obstacle to collaboration, inasmuch as it ensured that the working themes of the scientists remained opaque as opposed to transparent. Interestingly, a process of acculturation became apparent on the part of the scholars from the humanities and natural sciences, who used more pinboards as time passed.

The visualization and mutual awareness of the contents resulted in a shared sense of togetherness. Thematic, but also theoretical, technical, and methodological overlaps between the participants became visible: Some of them, for instance, investigated new technologies from perspectives including media science, computer science and design. Others worked on the topic "space", investigating contexts such as museums,

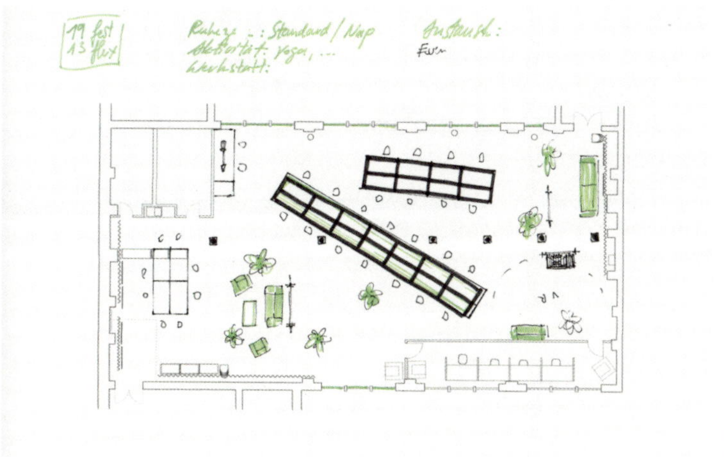

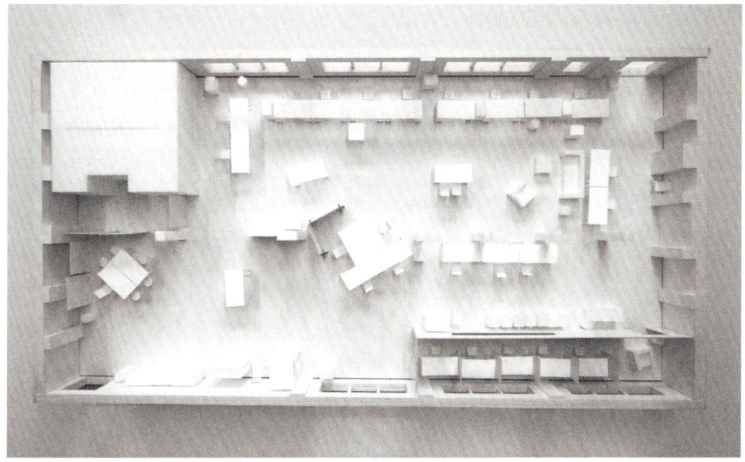

Fig. 5.10: Initial design sketch by the participants
Fig. 5.11: Architectural model of setting 17. Photo © Theodora Georgopoulou, Fabian Scholz

science and food practices. On the one hand, familiarity with the research of the others and possible overlaps contributed strongly to the appropriation of the Experimental Zone while constituting an important factor in the emergence of new collaborations on the other (→ see page 155).

Finally, the collective identity was further strengthened by public exposure. In the Experimental Zone, external visitors were extremely frequent because of the showcase character of the research project for the *Interdisciplinary Laboratory*. These guided tours were perceived by the participants as intrusive because they made them feel "as if they were in a zoo". They therefore responded by secretly exchanging amused glances, which in turn created a new confidentiality and contributed to the collective identity.

1.2 Spatial Appropriation and Reflexivity

The emergence of a collective identity was accompanied by an increasing appropriation of the Experimental Zone: The more the sense of social belonging increased, the more the participants took spatial possession of the Experimental Zone. This act of increasing appropriation was reinforced by our investigation, e.g. through the regular collective set up or dismantlement of settings or when negotiating the distribution of workstations for subsequent settings. Besides this collective spatial appropriation, the investigation itself—in particular the discussions of new settings, methodological approaches or interim results with the participants, but also the different interview formats (discursive interviews, mental map interviews, interviews-at-the-computer)—inspired the participants to reflect continually on the spatial conditions of research. They became more aware of their working context, began to think along with us and to reflect on the effect of space—exactly in the sense of *co-laborative* research, where the researchers become co-producers of knowledge (Niewöhner 2015). Two particularly exemplary moments are described below.

First of all, when the so-called "Basic Setting II" was carried out two years after the first "Basic Setting" (→ see Part Two, pages 52 and 59), the participants approached the task in a completely different manner. Once again, they had the entire open space at their disposal and were able to appropriate this as they wished. While the construction of the first "Basic Setting" was accompanied by very little exchange, as everyone hurriedly and eagerly chose his or her own place, everything was decided collectively from the outset in "Basic Setting II". This time, the tables were not placed individually and isolated (fig. 5.7), but table groups were formed (fig. 5.8) (→ see page 120). Over time, it was fascinating to observe that the participants' reflexivity on space had increased immensely, allowing them not only to think about their own workstation, but to place it in relation to the *territories* of the others. They immediately realized that, as a social group, they would benefit from forming a group *territory*, which should display certain characteristics, regarding e.g. boundaries, orientation and visibility.

Secondly, experimental setting 17, "Participative Setting" stimulated an intensive reflection on the spatial conditions of knowledge production, as the participants were asked to transpose their experiences of interdisciplinary workspaces into the design of a setting (fig. 5.9). In the design discussions, the participants collectively negotiated the ideal image of the Experimental Zone, highlighting three themes in the first round: The activation of the body, the division into functional zones and the implementation of social rules for the purpose of exchange. In the second round, further recurring topics (noise, color/nature, practices) were addressed. Eventually, "informal exchange" was decided on as the central theme, without us as investigators having guided the participants to this outcome. They developed the hypothesis that making practices visible is a fundamental prerequisite of interdisciplinary research. The concept therefore envisaged a *trading zone* (Galison 1999) as a shared area in the center, surrounded by individual workstations (figs. 5.10 and 5.11).

During the course of the investigation, the participants developed a collective identity and a sense of belonging, reinforced by eventization, making content visible and public exposure. At the same time, the *co-laborative* investigation strengthened the participants' reflexivity with regards to the spatial conditions of research and their own workspaces. As a result of both, they increasingly appropriated the space and began to feel familiar with it, inspired by it and secure in it. We hold that this is the prerequisite for further interdisciplinary connections.

2 Collaborations in the Experimental Zone

In Part Four, we examined how the participants interacted with each other. However, interacting does not necessarily mean collaborating. What do we mean by collaborating? As the sociologist Jessica Pflüger highlights, "very different terms and conceptions are used: […] 'co-operation' (e.g. Furney 1950), 'collaboration' (e.g. Gottlieb 1995; Shrum et al. 2007), as well as 'scientific teamwork' (e.g. Hagstrom 1964) or 'team research' (e.g. Luszki 1958; Bradley 1982). These terms are usually not precise […]. It can be determined, however, that 'cooperation' and 'collaboration' often refer to network-like structures, especially interdisciplinary cooperation in large-scale projects or with industrial partners" [1] (Pflüger 2013, 18). In the following, we define collaboration as a collective co-production of knowledge.

Despite the persistent myth of the lone scientific genius, collaboration and teamwork are the rule these days, or rather, as referenced by the sociologists of sciences Natasha Mauthner and Andrea Doucet, "the academic mode of production" (Stanley 1990, 4; cited in Mauthner and Doucet 2008, 972): The reasons for this, which have been well known for some decades, are the complexity of the problems to be treated (Eaton 1951), the need for a differentiation of researcher knowledge and skills (Bahrdt 1971) and a change in the economic and technical framework (Hagstrom 1964). This corresponds precisely to the reasons attributed to interdisciplinary working constellations (Bredekamp and Schäffner 2017).

Despite its increasing relevance, the phenomenon of collaboration has not been extensively studied, this almost certainly because "scientific teamwork appears to be one of the taken-for-granted aspects of research" (Barry et al. 1999, 27). Most research focuses on the field of natural sciences and, in particular, on interdisciplinary constellations (Blackwell 1955; Luszki 1958; Parthey and Schreiber 1983; Crow et al. 1992). The latter are placed in the spotlight because they "present a special challenge" (Pflüger 2013, 17). Even though all these studies have provided analyses of the "selection of a suitable interdisciplinary research topic, differences in content and methodology, as well as characteristic status differences and competitive mechanisms between the disciplines, up to communication difficulties of multidisciplinary teamwork" (Pflüger 2013, 18), the influence of space on interdisciplinarity remains very sparsely illuminated.

The aim of this final chapter is to trace the spatial conditions required by an interdisciplinary collaboration. Worthy of note is the fact that four new research projects were "born" in the Experimental Zone over the course of time in addition to the original research proposal, pointing to its strong potential for innovation. The coexistence of different types of collaborations allows us to present a differentiated and complex picture of the *collaborative habitat*.

2.1 Differing Types of Collaboration

In the Experimental Zone, three types of collaboration could be distinguished, depending on whether they occurred inside or outside existing or new teams: The first type refers to *collaborations within research teams*, understood "as integrated, clearly delimitable groups with at least two members who for a limited period of time attempt to achieve a common research goal and also interact with each other" (Pflüger 2013, 24). It thus refers to the project work announced in the research proposal, which is to be carried out through routine everyday content interactions. The Experimental Zone housed several research teams, two of them complete with all their team members, a few more with only part of the team present. As described in Part Four, most of them formed spatial clusters over time to be able to interact face to face. One of the research teams, for instance, which formed a table group, exhibited a well-coordinated workflow characterized by a certain hierarchy with a vertical division of labor between the members and a relative stability over time (Platt 1976, 69): The student assistants completed interchangeable tasks, while the postdoctoral researchers were responsible for the content-related guidance of the project and for compiling the results. This "authoritarian" ethos (Platt 1976, 78) was relatively typical of all projects in the Experimental Zone.

The second type concerned *collaborations between participants with the same disciplinary background* who were not in a team. It consisted of specialist exchanges on problems encountered by the participants. Interestingly, this was observed particularly among scholars from the design disciplines, computer science and natural science. As shown in Part Four (page 133), the work of researchers from the design disciplines was characterized by frequent short interactions necessary to the completion of their tasks. In this sense, the communicative nature of the creative production of knowledge was observed—in contrast to scholars from the humanities, who were left more to their own devices.

The third type involved *emerging collaborations* that were initiated within the Experimental Zone. Four new research projects which started with a brief exchange of words were officially established, and for which new research applications were subsequently submitted during the course of the *Interdisciplinary Laboratory*, demonstrating their momentum. It is noteworthy that all these projects enfolded at the interface between the humanities and design disciplines and were initiated by at least one *connector*. How did these new collaborations evolve? We would like to outline the background to one of these research projects by way of example, which was described vividly by a participant:

> "'*Playing with Virtual Realities*' [...- was born by chance inside the Experimental Zone [...-. One day in [...- 2016, I was writing at my table and observed Christian Stein, a computer scientist [and- linguist playing an arcade game [...-, while using the VR technology HTC VIVE in the other corner of the room. At the time I saw him, I was working on a lecture presentation which dealt with my research on dance and embodied

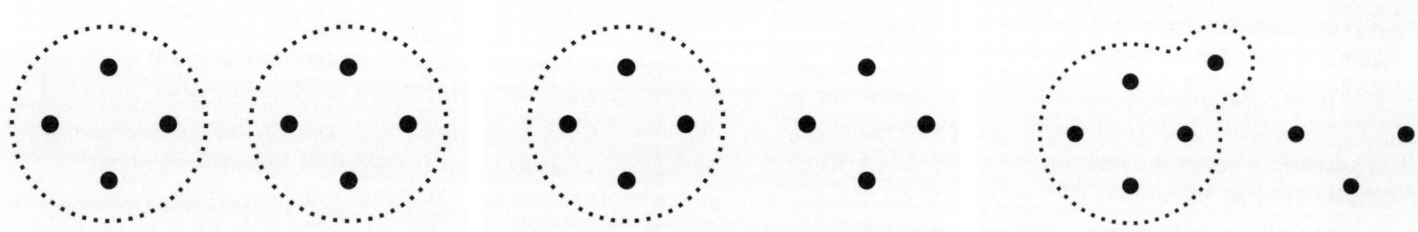

Fig. 5.12: Coexisting of two research spaces (dots = human and non-human elements, dotted lines = boundaries of research spaces)
Fig. 5.13: Interrupting of a research space by another
Fig. 5.14: Docking to another research space
Fig. 5.15: Merging of two research spaces

> cognition. […] [Stein's] vision [was] so absorbed by the game that he was oblivious to the physical surroundings in the studio space. He wore goggles and used controllers in order to shoot and to protect himself from drones that huntedhim in a virtual universe. […] Yet, to my eyes, Stein looked as if he were dancing. I felt joy at seeing a fellow researcher move in this scientific environment. Without […] thinking of the potential for a mutual research project, I left my working table and started to improvise dancing movements with him. When he left the virtual setting, I told him about my playful experience, in which he participated without knowing. […] By following my influential first encounter with a new engaging interaction, [our] intermedial and interdisciplinary research collaboration […] was born."
> Katan-Schmid 2019, 95–96

This report highlights how the initiation of encounters and collaborations was facilitated and accelerated by the experimental environment of the Experimental Zone. It highlights how the *collaborative habitat* has permitted specific communicative practices, in the form of verbal or non-verbal exchanges, which facilitate the empowerment of new endeavors. Moreover, the analysis of the three types of collaboration raises another point: The leading group of participants in charge was characterized by a strong status homogeneity consisting exclusively of doctoral and postdoctoral researchers. This allowed a coexistence characterized by horizontality. Here, we suggest that this has stimulated collaborations. How can such collaborations, whether inside or outside existing teams, be spatially analyzed? In other words: How does a collaborative space of research unfold?

2.2 Coexisting, Disrupting, Docking and Merging of Research Spaces

We would now like to examine the moment when two research spaces meet, as in the case of Einav and Christian, but from a spatial point of view: How do the spaces react to each other? How do collaborative spaces evolve? And what effect does the physical configuration have on these? Before proceeding to the actual analysis, we would like to introduce four types of encounters between research spaces that we have identified based on the data collected: *Coexisting, interrupting, docking* and *merging*.

The first two types—*coexisting* and *interrupting*—are based on the analyses in Part Three: The *coexisting* of two research spaces refers to the simultaneous execution of two practices in proximity to one another (fig. 5.12). By contrast, *interrupting* signifies the deactivation of one research space by another (fig. 5.13). This occurs when the characteristics of two research spaces are incompatible. Above all, spaces that require impermeable boundaries, such as spaces of reading, writing or drawing, tend to be interrupted by spaces of collaboration.

The analysis of interactions revealed two further types: The third type, *docking,* means to join another individual's space of research (fig. 5.14). We frequently observed how participants temporarily deactivated and left their own research

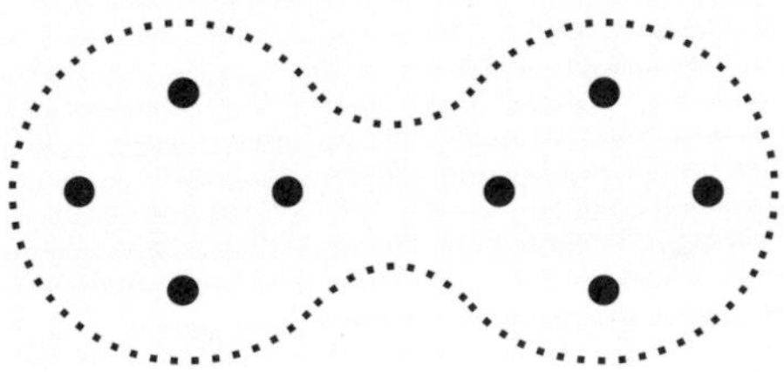

spaces in order to join those of others. The aim of docking can be an informal meeting, to ask or answer questions, to help the other person, etc. The fourth type, *merging*, references the union of two individual spaces of research into a collaborative space of research (fig. 5.15). In contrast to docking, the researcher does not leave and deactivate his own research space, but, instead, the new space comprises the assemblages of both participants. The two types clearly illustrate the difference between interaction and collaboration, which leads us back to the question of the spatial conditions under which an interaction becomes a collaboration.

2.3 What Does the Space do with the Collaborations?

In the following, we will explore the impact of the physical configuration on the interactions: In which configurations do collaborative research spaces unfold? And in which is this not the case? In order to explore these questions, we looked at various interactions and analyzed the configurations in which collaborative research spaces unfold and those in which they do not. The digital interactions, i.e. the synchronous editing of a collective text, e.g. in Google Docs, while carrying on an exchange simultaneously via chat (Slack, Skype, etc.), constituted something of a blind spot in our observation. It unfortunately proved impossible to capture this empirically. As a result, the investigation is limited to interactions which could be observed within the framework of the participant observation and mapping of interactions.

The first case study constitutes a comparison of interactions between Alexander (design disciplines) and Isabelle (design disciplines) across two settings: In physical configuration #5, which was characterized by a marked compartmentalization, Alexander and Isabelle had moved into a four-person compartment together with two further colleagues. They set up four tables as a table island and selected the workstations diagonally opposite each other (fig. 5.16). In physical configuration #6, on the other hand, Isabelle and Alexander built a "table-U" together with six further colleagues. They chose two workplaces opposite one another, with the result that they sat with their backs to each other (fig. 5.17).

In an exemplary situation in configuration #5 (fig. 5.16), both initially worked silently at their workstations in the four-person compartment until Isabelle addressed Alexander:

> "Then Isabelle asks something and looks at Alexander. He reacts immediately, says, 'go to perspective...' while still sitting in his seat, from where he has no view of her screen. When Isabelle continues to ask, he gets up and goes to Isabelle's workstation. He stands next to her and guides her through the menu until she can find her way around. After about two minutes both say ok, Alexander goes back to his place and sits down."
>
> Field notes, participant observation

In this example, Alexander left his workstation in order to help Isabelle at hers (fig. 5.18), thus deactivating his individual research space and

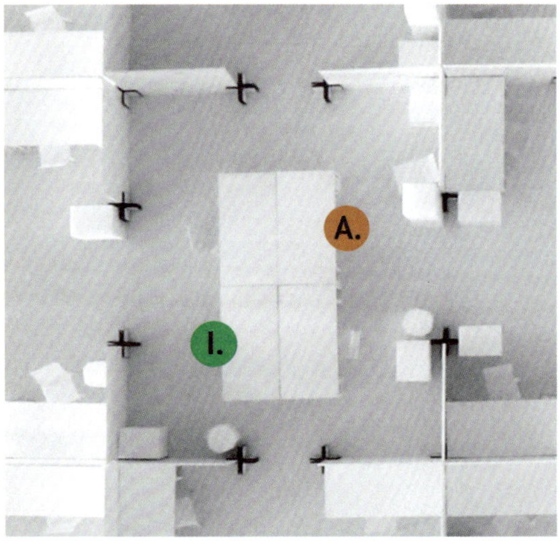

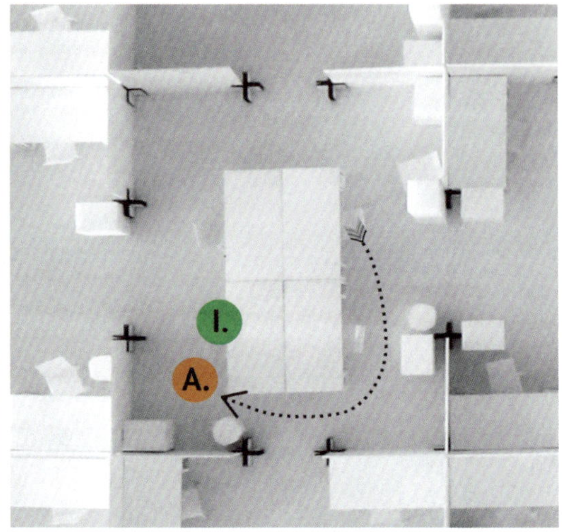

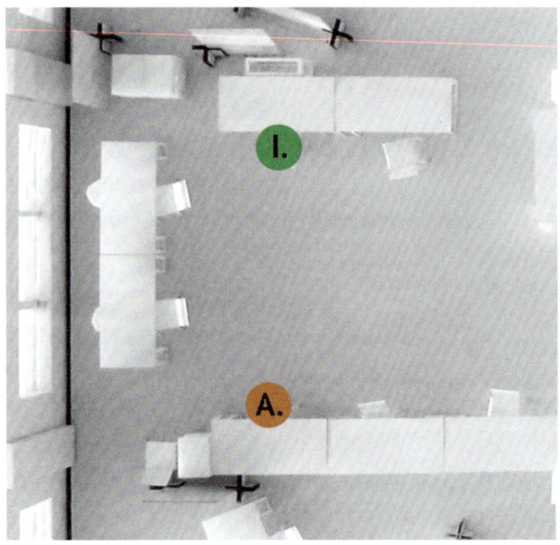

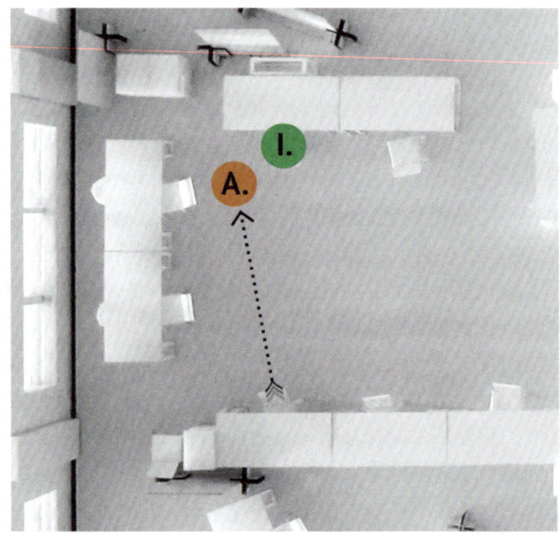

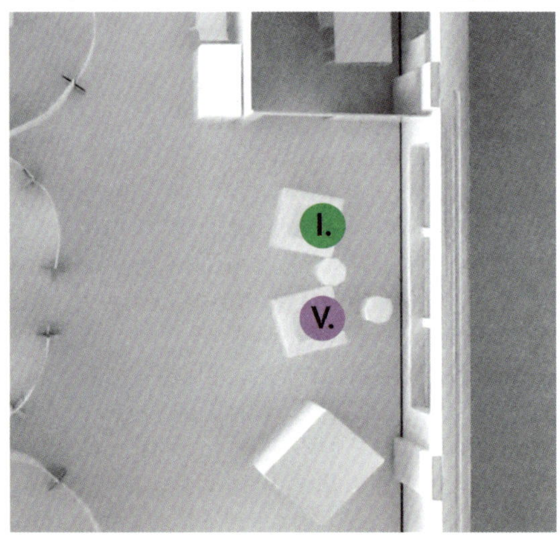

Fig. 5.16 (top left): Alexander (orange) and Isabelle (green) at their workstations in configuration #5
Fig. 5.17 (bottom left): Alexander (orange) and Isabelle (green) at their workstations in configuration #6
Fig. 5.18 (top right): Alexander (orange) goes over to Isabelle (green)
Fig. 5.19 (top middle right): Alexander rolls up to Isabelle
Fig. 5.20 (bottom right): Collaborative space of Isabelle (green) and Vid (purple)

joining Isabelle's individual research space in an example of *docking* (fig. 5.14). Another interaction, in physical configuration #6 (fig. 5.17), proceeded completely differently. As in the previous case, each of them worked quietly alone at their places in the "table-U" until one spoke to the other:

> "Alexander just rolled up to Isabelle with the chair, crossing the space between them. He found it quite loud, the rolling, he made a funny facial expression and tried to do it more quietly. He slowly arrived at Isabelle's side and waited until she turned to him. He wanted to show her something, a device or tool he bought the other day. 'Good tip' says Isabelle and thanks him. They discuss together at the screen. Alexander says goodbye and rolls back."
> Field notes, participant observation

As in the previous example, both scientists were immersed in their individual research spaces until one of them addressed the other. In this case, however, Alexander did not leave his own assemblage: By remaining seated and bridging the distance only by rolling over, he maintained the connection to his workplace (fig. 5.19). In this way, their spaces of research merged into a collaborative research space (fig. 5.15).

The comparison of the two workstation constellations provides indications of the physical configurations in which individual research spaces can merge and form a collaborative space: In both configurations, the distance between the two scientists was similar, about 2.6 meters in configuration #5 and 3.6 meters in configuration #6. The connectivity between the two workstations was also similar: In both constellations, the scientists were within the same space. Differences could be found above all in the orientation of the workstations: The orientation of the workplaces and bodies was different, diagonally opposite in configuration #5 and with their backs to each other in configuration #6. Accordingly, the visual relationship between the scientists differed: They could see each other in configuration #5, while they had to turn around to do so in configuration #6. However, this act of turning not only permitted a view of the colleague, but also shared view of his screen, drawing etc. In addition, Alexander's workplace was equipped with a rolling office chair that allowed him to shorten the distance to Isabelle for a brief period without completely leaving his own assemblage. Here, the office chair functions entirely in the spirit of Robert Schmidt, who deemed it an invention for the adaptation of bodies at work (Schmidt 2012, 138).

A second case study underlines the fact that the shared view of media is not only favored in the "table-U" configuration, but also by sitting side by side, as the following example, a collaborative space of Isabelle and Vid, demonstrates (fig. 5.20):

> "Isabelle and Vid are working together on an article, contents-wise, in the armchairs by the window. They both have a laptop on their laps and switch back and forth between talking and quiet work in Google Docs. Sometimes one looks up and faces the other to ask something. It's a collaborative physical-virtual space."
> Field notes, participant observation

In this case study, Isabelle and Vid have created a collaborative space through merging in which they can seamlessly switch back and forth between individual and collaborative work. The example also illustrates how coherently digital media are integrated into knowledge production and that research spaces are indeed highly *physical-virtual* spaces.

Both examples are characterized by a seamless alternation between individual and collaborative practices. The aforementioned physical-spatial characteristics—proximity, a high connectivity, a certain orientation and rollable office chairs—allow a seamless transition between individual and collaborative spaces and thus an embedding of the collaboration within the workflow.

Moreover, in both case studies, the shared view of media is crucial for the formation of the collaborative space. We have frequently observed the use of various digital and analog media in conversations, e.g. displays, books, printouts, sketches, models and prototypes. However, the act of revealing content on one's own screen or notebook is not at all trivial in a scientific context: Individuals must let the others into their individual *territories* and allow them a view of their own *information preserve* (Goffman 1971, → see page 119). In this sense, this act constitutes a powerful gesture that creates familiarity between two researchers. In addition, as language-based communication is often difficult in interdisciplinary collaborations due to different specialist languages, "items like a local oscillator can function as a binding element between subcultures when stripped from its original context and coordinated with a new one" (Galison 1999, 156). Based on the empirical material, we thus consider the facilitation of a shared view of media one of the main characteristics of the collaboration-promoting space.

3 Characteristics of a Collaborative Habitat

The aim of our research project was to experimentalize the effects of space on interdisciplinary knowledge practices and to develop the characteristics of a *collaborative habitat*. We introduce the notion of the *collaborative habitat* to describe a synecological system for interdisciplinary knowledge production, which encourages interdisciplinary collaborations and synergies between individualized researchers, both in the context of existing teams as well as regarding the creation of new projects. The *collaborative habitat* is fundamentally based on the cultivation of a *collective identity* manifested in a sense of belonging and mutual trust among the researchers. This is an expected result. What our study has revealed, however, are the spatial implications and consequences associated with this. To summarize the characteristics of the *collaborative habitat*, we have developed five statements that include recommendations for the design of interdisciplinary research spaces.

STATEMENT 1:
Interdisciplinary collaboration is facilitated by physical co-presence, which, particularly in the context of a high visibility, promotes a gradual rapprochement with others and an acquaintance with their practices as well as informality and chance encounters. Physical co-presence is the prerequisite for existing and new collaborations: On the one hand, it makes it possible for scientists to gradually get to know the others and their working methods. We postulate that a gradual progression of encounter and rapprochement with this otherness facilitates acculturation processes as well as the emergence of new collaborations. On the other hand, our study concurs with the literature in confirming the fundamental role of interactions in physical co-presence, especially as far as informal exchange and chance encounters are concerned. The role of so-called connectors is crucial here, insofar as they ensure the exchange between existing teams and accelerate a dense interlinking of the researchers—whether thematic, epistemological or methodological. With regards to the influence of spatial configurations on the interactions, the study showed that a combination of a low connectivity and a low visibility severely inhibits informality.

As a design consequence, the results suggest that the open space is essentially an interdisciplinarity-promoting typology, as its high visibility stimulates both a gradual rapprochement with the others and informal exchange. However, it is essential to achieve an appropriate balance between this high visibility and the scientists' need for visual privacy.

STATEMENT 2:
The co-presence of heterogeneous practices requires a pluri-functional space that offers areas of retreat and is regulated by routines of approachability. A multidisciplinary group of researchers from the humanities, design disciplines, engineering and natural sciences performs a wide variety of practices, such as reading, writing, designing, thinking, conceiving, researching, drawing, sketching, collecting, analyzing, building models, mapping, programming, and computing. Depending on the practice, the individual research spaces show varying degrees of (im)permeability leading to problems of compatibility. However, the co-existence of such heterogeneous practices is the prerequisite for collaboration. In the literature, a high flexibilization of workstations, known as activity-based working (Veldhoen and Piepers 1995), is praised as the solution to the compatibility problem of the heterogeneous practices in the open space. However, our research has clearly shown that, in contrast to this new model of the flexible and innovative employee, the majority of the scientists investigated needs a fixed individual territory that allows them a quick retrieval of their assemblages and is thus favorable for the dynamic unfolding of their spaces of research. Through the placement of objects, the scientists create protected individual

but also group *territories* that offer protection in the open space and the view outside this space, as well as a certain visual and auditory privacy.

As a design consequence, the experimentalization process has shown that, in particular, two measures allow highly incompatible practices to be performed in an open space: Firstly, silent areas such as the room constructed in setting 10 allow scientists to withdraw temporarily in order to carry out concentrated practices. This stands in striking contrast to the traditional architecture of science, in which group practices (e.g. meetings, etc.) are usually spatially isolated. Secondly, an open space characterized by a high diversity of areas with different characteristics promotes the emergence of heterogeneous research spaces. The investigation has shown, for example, that instead of creating an open space with a homogeneously high connectivity, a so-called mesh topology can create both interaction-promoting and concentration-promoting areas. For example, the interconnected compartments of the 16th setting resulted in a gradation of this nature, from livelier and more communicative to quieter, more concentrated areas.

In addition, the co-existence of heterogeneous practices creates heterogeneous atmospheres. For their regulation and negotiation, the emergence of specific conventions of approachability has proven to be highly relevant: As a result, the atmosphere in the Experimental Zone oscillated dynamically between that of a library and that of a design studio. For the pluri-functional space it is therefore essential to allow diverse atmospheres and the emergence of specific conventions of approachability.

STATEMENT 3:

A research environment with a high visibility of work-in-progress content can stimulate the rapprochement between the disciplines and the emergence of new collaborations. Beyond the high visibility of the scientists and their practices described in statement 1, we were able to observe the effects of a further step, namely the visualization of the contents themselves: If the content currently developed is visualized outside the computer—e.g. through the use of highly visible analog and digital media such as pinboards or collective displays—and thus visually shapes the research environment, the researchers are passively and gradually confronted with foreign working themes and methods. The passive confrontation leads to an unconscious adoption, which can then be followed by an active appropriation. As described in statement 1, the gradual confrontation facilitates both acculturation processes and the emergence of new collaborations. Driven by the designers, such a visualization was first encountered with reluctance on the part of the scholars of the humanities and natural sciences, since their knowledge culture is characterized by a different way of dealing with the protection of their own work against third parties and the view into the unfinished is therefore perceived as intrusive. Over time, we were able to observe a process of acculturation, i.e. an opening of the humanities and natural scientists in this respect. Here, we put forward the hypothesis that the homogeneity of the participants' status was an important factor in the establishment of a culture of allowing others into one's own *information preserve* (Goffman 1971).

STATEMENT 4:

Seamless transitions between individual and collaborative spaces help co-presence to evolve into collaboration. The investigation has shown how collaborative spaces unfold as individual research spaces *merge*. The collaborative space benefits in particular if none of the researchers has to leave their individual research space in order to interact. What can be done to prevent the individual assemblages from breaking? The analysis revealed that the fundamental prerequisites for the emergence of collaborative spaces are the seamless transition between individual and collaborative practices, as well as the possibility to look at media together. In terms of spatial design, this means that physical proximity is crucial. What is remarkable here is that the group *territories* and the so-called *design cluster* initiated by the participants themselves offered exactly that: They created a high proximity between the workstations. Furthermore, the analysis has shown that constellations in which scientists sit next to each other or—contrary to expectations—with their backs to each other, are particularly beneficial, since they facilitate a shared view of media such as screens or notebooks.

STATEMENT 5:
A participative design approach contributes both to the collective identity and spatial reflexivity of the researchers and thus to the appropriation and formation of a collaborative habitat. In the course of the investigation, the participants developed a collective identity and a sense of belonging, which were particularly stimulated by eventization, a high visibility of the contents and public exposure. At the same time, the *co-laborative* investigation strengthened the participants' reflexivity with regards to the spatial conditions of research and their own workspace. As a result of both, they increasingly appropriated the space and began to feel familiar, inspired and secure. As this is the prerequisite for further interdisciplinary connections, we put forward the hypothesis that a participative design approach contributes to the appropriation and formation of a *collaborative habitat.* Moreover, the fact that we conducted an experiment and named the building wing "Experimental Zone" accordingly resulted in a certain experimental culture among the researchers, who were then more inclined to embark on apparently "audacious" collaborations. In this respect, the project created a research environment that encouraged risk-taking.

Concluding Remarks

In addition to the exploration of the characteristics of the collaborative habitat, the investigation provides two further contributions, firstly, in the context of spatial research and secondly, in the context of science studies.

From the perspective of spatial research, we have developed a theoretical position on the concept of space as well as a new interdisciplinary method: Based on empiricism, we question the dichotomy between the physical and the virtual, and propose the concept of the *physical-virtual* space in the sense of an integrative continuum (→ see Part One). We have thus transferred Stefan Beck's reflections on the entanglement of analog and digital media (Beck 2015) into a spatial perspective and analyzed what this means for the enactment of research practices. A central contribution of our study is the development of a new interdisciplinary method for spatial research: *Experimental design-based field research* has allowed us to conduct research at the interface between design and observation, as well as between hypothesis-driven and explorative procedures (→ see Part Two). The interdisciplinary and visual survey methods developed, such as the color coding of auto-photography and the mapping of movements and interactions, make it possible to reveal previously hidden spatial and visual characteristics and interrelationships.

From the perspective of science studies, the study offers a contribution to the analysis of collaboration and interdisciplinarity—especially in the context of the *Design Turn* (Schäffner 2010) and its implications for knowledge production in the humanities and natural sciences. In the investigation and evaluation of results, it has repeatedly become evident that scholars in the fields of the humanities and natural sciences can learn a great deal from their peers in the design disciplines. Various acculturation processes were observed, e.g. how scholars from the humanities and natural sciences began to work with pinboards; how they arranged themselves in table groups and also, more fundamentally, how they appropriated new topics and tools and thus gained "new" insights. The designers naturally also benefited considerably from the encounter with their colleagues from the humanities and natural sciences, be it in dealing with discourses, texts or methodology. Our research project *ArchitecturesExperiments* has shed a practice-theoretical light on the *Interdisciplinary Laboratory's* mission to investigate the encounter between science and design, revealing the extent to which a visual and communicative working method can contribute to the classical production of scientific knowledge. This should not be misunderstood as a plea for scientific knowledge production to follow the cult of innovation or to submit to market logic. Rather, the investigations reveal—as this book hopefully illustrates—the benefits of interdisciplinary work.

01
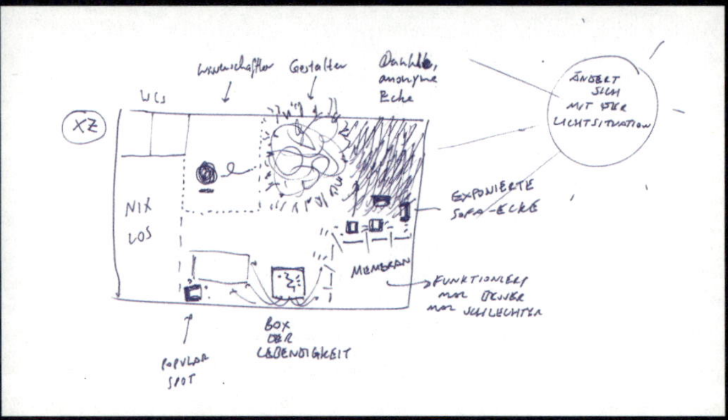

02

03
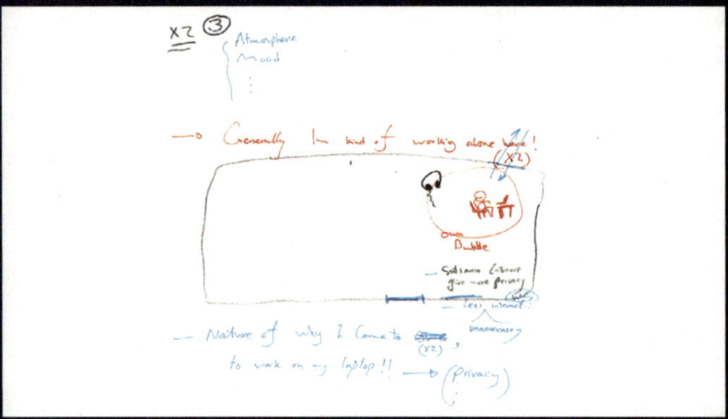

04
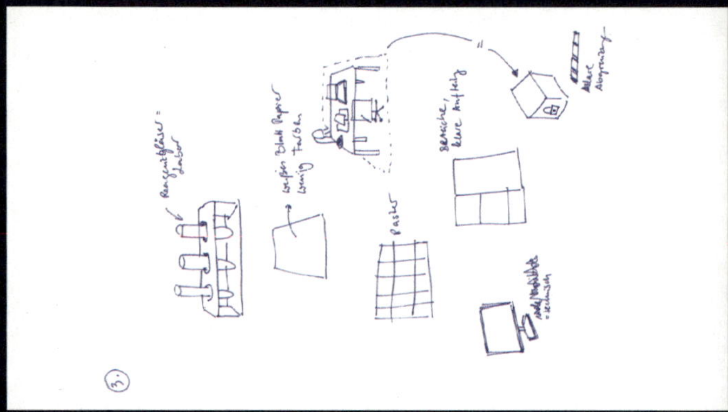

05

06

07
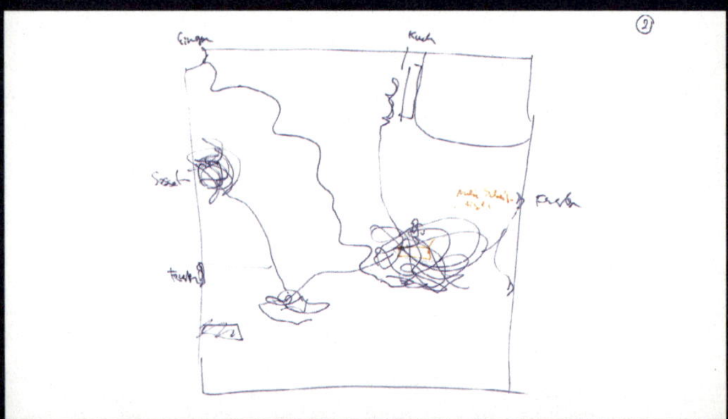

08

09
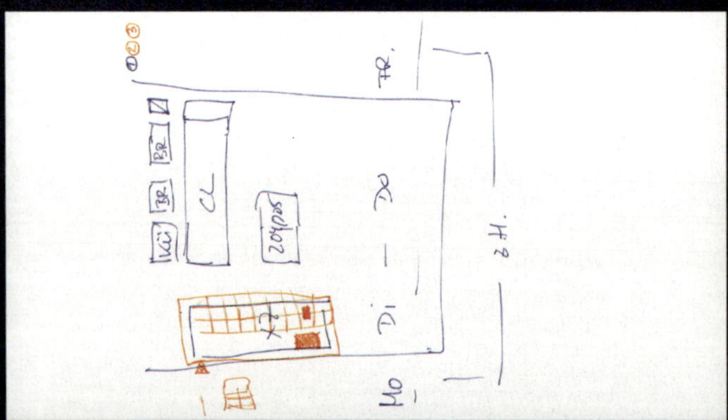

10
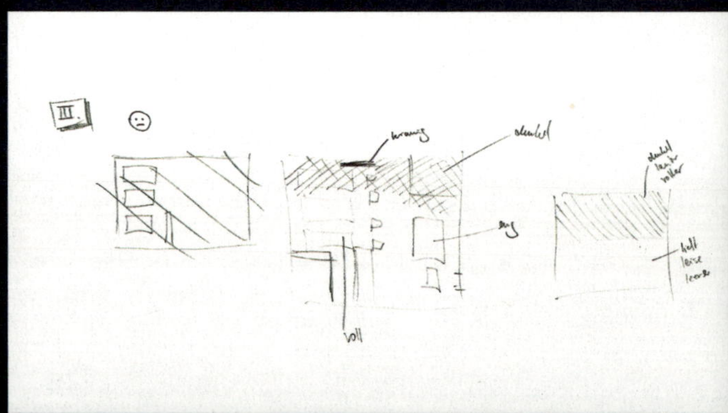

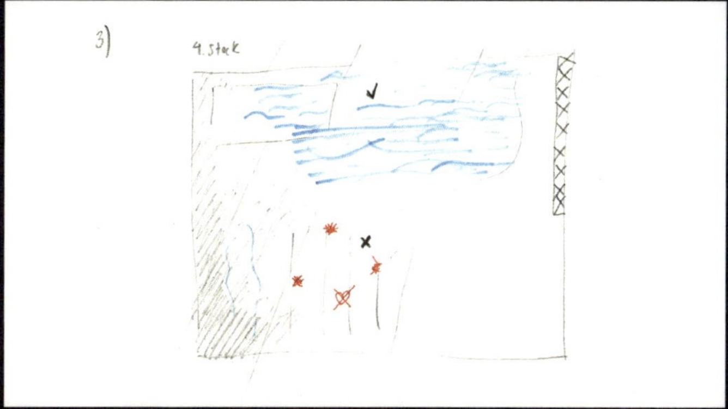

11
12

13

View into the Experimental Zone

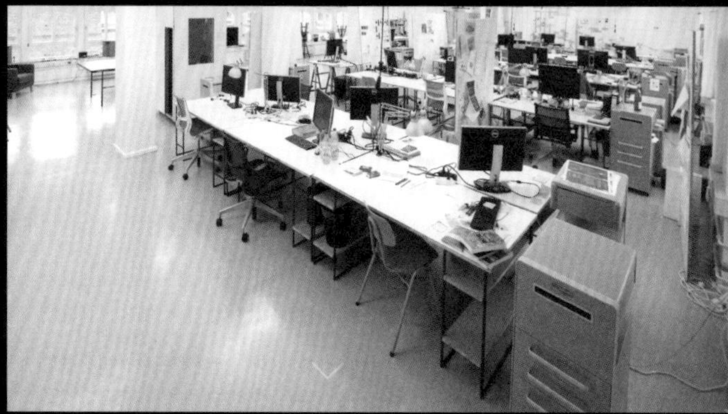

06
07

08
09

10
11

12
13

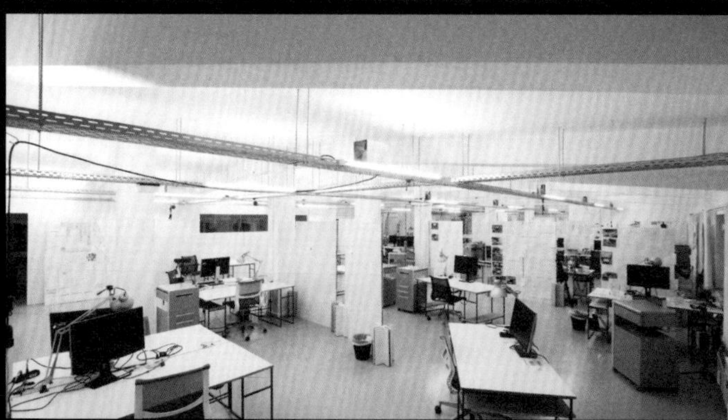

14
15

View from the south-west corner of the Experimental Zone per setting. Photographic documentation from 38 fixed angles (→ see Part Two, page 46) was introduced in October 2015, therefore only the settings 06 to 17 are documented. Photos © Susanne Friedl, Patryk Kujawa, Benjamin Meurer, Dimitra Megas, Fabian Scholz

Experimental setting 06 “Diary”
Experimental setting 07 “Work & Play”
Experimental setting 08 “Exchange: Temporal”
Experimental setting 09 “Exchange: Permeable”
Experimental setting 10 “Exchange: Hermetic”
Experimental setting 11 “Compartments”
Experimental setting 12 “Strange Objects”
Experimental setting 13 “Tools”
Experimental setting 14 “Basic Setting II”
Experimental setting 15 “@experimental zone”
Experimental setting 16 “Clockwork”
Experimental setting 17 “Participatory Setting”

View into the Experimental Zone

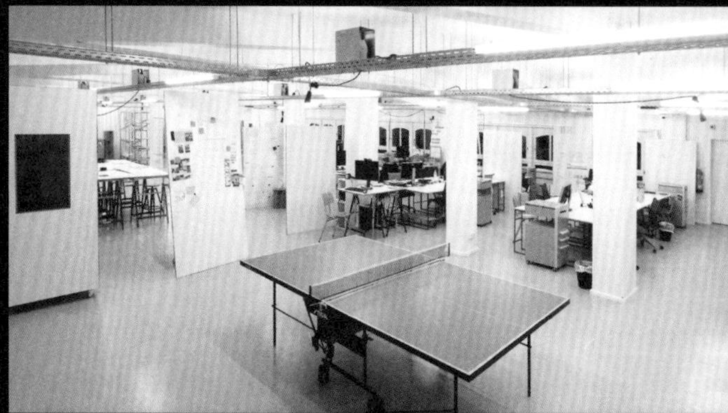

05
06

07
08

09
10

11
12

13
14

15
16

17

Allen, Thomas J. 1977. *Managing the Flow of Technology: Technology Transfer and the Dissemination of Technological Information within the R&D Organization*. Cambridge, Mass.: MIT Press.

Allen, Thomas J., and Alan R. Fusfeld. 1975. "Research Laboratory Architecture and the Structuring of Communications." *R&D Management* 5 (2): pp. 153–64.

Allen, Thomas J., and Peter G. Gerstberger. 1973. "A Field Experiment to Improve Communications in a Product Engineering Department: The Nonterritorial Office." *Human Factors: The Journal of the Human Factors and Ergonomics Society*, no. 5: pp. 487–98.

Alvesson, Mats, and Kai Sköldberg. 2016. *Reflexive Methodology. New Vistas for Qualitative Research*. 2nd edition. London: SAGE Publications.

ARCH+. 1992. "Vilém Flusser. Virtuelle Räume - Simultane Welten." *ARCH+* 111.

Ash, James. 2016. "Theorizing Studio Space: Spheres and Atmospheres in a Video Game Design Studio." In *Studio Studies. Operations, Topologies and Displacements*, edited by Ignacio Farias and Alex Wilkie, pp. 91–104. New York: Routledge.

Backhouse, Alan and Paul Drew. 1992. "The Design Implications of Social Interaction in a Workplace Setting." *Environment and Planning B: Planning and Design* 19: pp. 573–84.

Bahrdt, Hans Paul. 1971. *Wissenschaftssoziologie - Ad Hoc*. Düsseldorf: Bertelsmann.

Banbury, Simon, and Dianne C. Berry. 1998. "Disruption of Office-Related Tasks by Speech and Office Noise." *British Journal of Psychology* 89 (3): pp. 499–517.

——. 2005. "Office Noise and Employee Concentration: Identifying Causes of Disruption and Potential Improvements." *Ergonomics* 48 (1): pp. 25–37.

Barry, Christine, Nicky Britten, Nick Barber, Collin Bradley, and Fiona Stevenson. 1999. "Using Reflexivity to Optimize Teamwork in Qualitative Research." *Qualitative Health Research* 9 (1): pp. 26–44.

Baur, Nina, Linda Herring, Anna Laura Raschke, and Cornelia Thierbach. 2014. "Theory and Methods in Spatial Analysis: Towards Integrating Qualitative, Quantitative and Cartographic Approaches in the Social Sciences and Humanities." *Historical Social Research* 39 (2): pp. 7–50.

Beck, Stefan. 2015. "Von Praxistheorie 1.0 zu 3.0 – oder: wie analoge und digitale Praxen relationiert werden sollten." presented at the Conference "Digitale Praxen", Goethe Universität, Frankfurt am Main. Accessed May 15, 2019: https://hu-berlin.academia.edu/StefanBeck/Talks.

Berg, Gunhild. 2013. "Experimentieren." In *Über die Praxis des kulturwissenschaftlichen Arbeitens: Ein Handwörterbuch*, edited by Uta Frietsch and Jörg Rogge, pp. 140–44. Bielefeld: transcript.

Berger, Peter L., and Thomas Luckmann. 1969. *Die gesellschaftliche Konstruktion der Wirklichkeit: Eine Theorie der Wissenssoziologie*. Frankfurt am Main: Fischer.

Bernstein, Ethan S., and Stephen Turban. 2018. "The Impact of the 'Open' Workspace on Human Collaboration." *Philosophical Transactions of the Royal Society* B 373 (20170239): n.p.

Blackwell, Gordon W. 1955. "Multidisciplinary Team Research." *Social Forces* 33 (4): pp. 367–74.

Böhme, Gernot. 1995. *Atmosphäre: Essays zur neuen Ästhetik*. Frankfurt am Main: Suhrkamp.

——. 2006. *Architektur und Atmosphäre*. München: Fink, Wilhelm.

Boje, Axel. 1971. *Open Plan Offices*. London: Business Books.

Bonetta, Laura. 2003. "Do You Want to Work Here? The Architects behind a New Generation of Laboratories Believe Their Designs Can Stimulate Good Science." *Nature* 424 (August): pp. 718–20.

Bouberkri, Mohamed, I. Cheung, K Reid, N. Kuo, C. Wang, and P. Zee. 2014. "Impact of Workplace Daylight Exposure on Sleep, Physical Activity, and Quality of Life." *Journal of Clinical Sleep Medicine* 10 (6): pp. 603–11.

Bourdieu, Pierre. 1977. *Outline of a Theory of Practice*. New York: Cambridge University Press.

——. 2004. *Science of Science and Reflexivity*. Cambridge: Polity Press.

——. 2018. "Social Space and the Genesis of Appropriated Physical Space." *International Journal of Urban and Regional Research* 42 (1): pp. 106–14.

Bourdieu, Pierre, and Loïc Wacquant. 1992. *Réponses. Pour une anthropologie réflexive*. Paris: Seuil.

Boyce, Peter R. 1974. "User´s Assessments of a Landscaped Office." *Journal of Architectural Research* 3: pp. 44–62.

Boyer, Dominic. 2015. "Reflexivity Reloaded: From Anthropology of Intellectuals to Critique of Method to Studying Sideways." In *Anthropology Now and Next Essays in Honor of Ulf Hannerz*, edited by Thomas H. Eriksen, Christina Garsten, and Shalini Randeria, pp. 91–110. New York; Oxford: Berghahn Books.

Bradley, Raymond T. 1982. "Ethical Problems in Team Research: A Structural Analysis and an Agenda for Resolution." *The American Sociologist* 17: pp. 87–94.

Bredekamp, Horst, and Wolfgang Schäffner, eds. 2015. *Haare hören – Strukturen wissen – Räume agieren. Berichte aus dem Interdisziplinären Labor Bild Wissen Gestaltung*. Bielefeld: transcript.

——. 2017. Das Exzellenzcluster verteidigt eine interdisziplinäre Idee von Universität im weitesten Sinn. Interview by Ljiljana Nikolic. Accessed September 21, 2018: https://www.hu-berlin.de/de/pr/nachrichten/archiv/pm1707/nr_170703_00.

Brookes, Malcolm J., and Archie Kaplan. 1972. "The Office Environment: Space Planning and Affective Behavior." *Human Factors: The Journal of the Human Factors and Ergonomics Society* 14 (5): pp. 373–91.

Brown, Tim. 2009. *Change by Design. How Design Thinking Transforms Organizations and Inspires Innovation*. New York: Harper Collins Publishers.

Burghardt, Manuel, and Christian Wolff. 2014. "Digital Humanities: Buzzword oder Strukturwandel in den Geisteswissenschaften?" *Blick in die Wissenschaft* 23 (29/14): pp. 39–46.

Butcher, Clare, and Angela Plohmann. 2009. *The Future of the Lab*. Eindhoven: Baltan Laboratories.

Camic, Charles, Neil Gross, and Michèle Lamont, eds. 2011. *Social Knowledge in the Making*. Chicago: University of Chicago Press.

Clearwater, Yvonne. 1980. "User's Assessment of a Landscaped Office." PhD, Davis: University of California.

Clifford, James, and George E. Marcus, eds. 1986. *Writing Culture. The Poetics and Politics of Ethnography*. Berkeley: University of California Press.

Collier, John Jr., and Malcom Collier. 1987. *Visual Anthropology: Photography as a Research Method*. Albuquerque: University of New Mexico Press.

Crow, Gary, Linda Levine, and Nancy Nager. 1992. "Are Three Heads Better Than One? Reflections on Doing Collaborative Interdisciplinary Research." *American Educational Research Journal* 29 (4): pp. 737–53.

Dalton, Nicholas S., Holger Schnädelbach, Mikael Wiberg, and Tasos Varoudis, eds. 2016. *Architecture and Interaction. Human Computer Interaction in Space and Place*. Heidelberg: Springer International Publishing.

Dangschat, Jens S. 2014. "Räumliche Daten." In *Handbuch Methoden der empirischen Sozialforschung*, edited by Nina Baur and Jörg Blasius, pp. 973–79. Wiesbaden: Springer Fachmedien.

Delitz, Heike. 2009. *Architektursoziologie*. Bielefeld: transcript.

——. 2010. *Gebaute Gesellschaft: Architektur als Medium des Sozialen*. Frankfurt am Main: Campus Verlag.

Dirksmeier, Peter. 2009. "Eine Methodologie der reflexiven Fotografie." In *Urbanität als Habitus. Zur Sozialgeographie städtischen Lebens auf dem Land*, by Peter Dirksmeier, pp. 151–84. Bielefeld: transcript.

——. 2013. "Zur Methodologie und Performativität qualitativer visueller Methoden – Die Beispiele der Autofotografie und reflexiven Fotografie." In *Raumbezogene qualitative Sozialforschung*, edited by Eberhard Rothfuß and Thomas Dörfler, pp. 83–101. Wiesbaden: Springer VS.

Döring, Jörg, and Tristan Thielmann, eds. 2009. "Mediengeographie: Für eine Geomedienwissenschaft." In *Mediengeographie. Theorie – Analyse – Diskussion*, pp. 9–64. Bielefeld: transcript.

Duffy, Francis. 1997. *The New Office*. London: Conran Octopus.

Duffy, Francis, Colin Cave, and John Worthington, eds. 1976. *Planning Office Space*. Architectural Press.

Duffy, Francis, Andrew Laing, and Vic Crisp. 1992. "The Responsible Workplace." *Facilities* 10 (11): pp. 9–15.

Duffy, Francis, and Alfons Wankum. 1966. *Office Landscaping: A New Approach to Office Planning*. London: Anbar Publications.

Eaton, Joseph. 1951. “Social Processes of Professional Teamwork.” *American Sociological Review* 16 (5): pp. 707–13.

Eberle, Julia, Karsten Stegmann, Frank Fischer, Alain Barrat, and Kristine Lund. 2017. “Finding Collaboration Partners in a Scientific Community: The Role of Cognitive Group Awareness, Career Level, and Disciplinary Background.” In *Proceedings of the 12th International Conference on Computer Supported Collaborative Learning*, pp. 519–26. Philadelphia.

Edinger, Eva-Christina. 2015. *Wissensraum, Labyrinth, symbolischer Ort: Die Universitätsbibliothek als Sinnbild der Wissenschaft.* Konstanz München: UVK Verlagsgesellschaft.

Elzeyadi, Ihab M.K. 2011. “Daylighting-Bias and Biophilia: Quantifying the Impact of Daylighting on Occupant Health.” *School of Architecture & Allied Arts - University of Oregon, Eugene, OR - USA*. Accessed April 20, 2019: https://www.usgbc.org/sites/default/files/OR10_Daylighting%20Bias%20and%20Biophilia.pdf.

Emerson, Lori, Jussi Parrika, and Darren Wershler. 2019. “What Is a Media Lab? Situated Practices in Media Studies.” 2019. Accessed May 15, 2019: http://whatisamedialab.com/.

Farias, Ignacio, and Alex Wilkie, eds. 2016. *Studio Studies: Operations, Topologies and Displacements.* London ; New York: Routledge, Taylor & Francis Group.

Felt, Klaus, Helga Taschwer, and Claudia Nowotny. 1995. *Wissenschaftsforschung. Eine Einführung.* Frankfurt am Main: Campus Verlag.

Frietsch, Ute, and Jörg Rogge, eds. 2013. “Digitalisierung.” In *Über die Praxis des kulturwissenschaftlichen Arbeitens. Ein Handwörterbuch*, pp. 113–18. Bielefeld: transcript.

Furney, Lester. 1950. “Co-Operation in Scientific Research.” *The Journal of Higher Education* 21 (2): pp. 66–71.

Galison, Peter. 1999. “Trading Zone: Coordinating Action and Belief (1997, abridged 1998).” In *The Science Studies Reader*, edited by Mario Biagioli, pp. 137–60. London: Routledge.

Galison, Peter, and Emily Ann Thompson, eds. 1999. *The Architecture of Science.* Cambridge, Mass: MIT Press.

Garfinkel, Harold. 1973. “Studien über die Routinegrundlagen von Alltagshandeln.” In *Symbolische Interaktion. Arbeiten zu einer reflexiven Soziologie*, edited by Heinz Steinert, pp. 280–93.Stuttgart: Klett.

Geipel, Kaye. 2010. “Von Tokyo nach Venedig.” *Bauwelt*, no. 33.2010: pp. 14–17.

Germer, Kerstin. 2019. “Ein Bericht aus der interdisziplinären Wissensvermittlung.” In *Experimentieren. Einblicke in Praktiken und Versuchsaufbauten zwischen Wissenschaft und Gestaltung*, edited by Séverine Marguin, Henrike Rabe, Wolfgang Schäffner, and Friedrich Schmidgall, pp. 263–74. Bielefeld: transcript.

Gieryn, Thomas F. 2002. “What Buildings Do.” *Theory and Society* 31: pp. 35–74.

Glaser, Barney G., and Anselm L. Strauss. 1967. *The Discovery of Grounded Theory. Strategies for Qualitative Research.* Chicago: Aldine.

Goffman, Erving. 1971. “The Territories of the Self.” In *Relations in Public: Microstudies of the Public Order*, pp. 28–61. New York: Basic Books.

Gottlieb, Alma. 1995. “Beyond the Lonely Anthropologist. Collaboration in Research and Writing.” *American Anthropologist* 97 (1): pp. 21–26.

Götz, Norbert, and Janne Holmén. 2018. “Introduction to the Theme Issue: ‘Mental Maps: Geographical and Historical Perspectives.’” *Journal of Cultural Geography* 35 (2): pp. 157–61.

Hagstrom, Warren O. 1964. “Traditional and Modern Forms of Scientific Teamwork.” *Administrative Science Quarterly* 9 (3): pp. 241–63.

Hall, Edward T. 1969. *The Hidden Dimension.* New York: Anchor Books

Hannerz, Ulf. 1998. “Other Transnationals: Perspectives Gained from Studying Sideways.” *Paideuma: Mitteilungen zur Kulturkunde* 44 (Anthropology and the Question of the Other): pp. 109–23.

Hanson, Alice. 1978. “Effects of a Move to an Open Landscape Office.” *Dissertation Abstracts International* 39 (6): 3046B.

Hara, Hiroshi. 2004. *Discrete City.* Vol. 1–4. Tokyo: TOTO Shuppan.

Harrison, Andrew, Paul Wheeler, and Carolyn Whitehead, eds. 2004. *The Distributed Workplace. Sustainable Work Environments.* London; New York: Spon Press.

Harrison, Rodney. 2013. “Reassembling Ethnographic Museum Collections.”In *Reassembling the Collection: Ethnographic Museums and Indigenous Agency*, edited by Rodney Harrison, Joshua A. Bell, and Sarah Byrne, pp. 3–38. Santa Fe: School for Advanced Research Press.

Heath, Christian, Hubert Knoblauch, and Paul Luff. 2000. “Technology and Social Interaction: The Emergence of ‘Workplace Studies.’” *British Journal of Sociology* 5 (2): pp. 299–320.

Hillier, Bill. 1996. *Space Is the Machine: A Configurational Theory of Architecture.* Cambridge: Press Syndicate of the University of Cambridge.

Hillier, Bill, and Julienne Hanson. 1984. *The Social Logic of Space.* Cambridge: Cambridge University Press.

Hoffmeister, Anouk, Séverine Marguin, and Cornelia Schendzielorz. 2018. “Feldnotizen 2.0. Über Digitalität in der ethnographischen Beobachtungspraxis.” Edited by Martin Huber and Sybille Krämer. *Zeitschrift für digitale Geisteswissenschaften* Sonderband 3 (Wie Digitalität die Geisteswissenschaften verändert: Neue Forschungsgegenstände und Methoden): Article 3.

Holmes, Douglas R., and George E. Marcus. 2008. “Collaboration Today and the Re-Imagination of the Classic Scene of Fieldwork Encounter.” *Collaborative Anthropologies* 1 (1): pp. 81–101.

Ingold, Tim. 2013. *Making: Anthropology, Archaeology, Art and Architecture.* London; New York: Routledge.

Interdisciplinary Laboratory. 2019. “About Us.” An Interdisciplinary Laboratory Image Knowledge Gestaltung. 2019. Accessed May 15, 2019: https://www.interdisciplinary-laboratory.hu-berlin.de/en/bwg/ueber-uns/.

Ishigami, Junya. 2014. *How Small? How Vast? How Architecture Grows.* Edited by Chinatsu Kuma. Translated by Pamela Miki and Arthur Binard. Ostfildern: hatje cantz.

Ives, R.S., and R. Ferdinands. 1974. “Working in a Landscaped Office.”*Personnel Practice Bulletin* 30 (2): pp. 126–41.

Jäger, Georg 1997. “Experimentell.” In *Reallexikon der deutschen Literaturwissenschaft*, 3 Vols.: Neubearbeitung des Reallexikons der deutschen Literaturgeschichte. Vol. 1. Berlin; New York: De Gruyter.

Jany, Susanne. 2015. “Operative Räume. Prozessarchitekturen im späten 19. Jahrhundert.” *Zeitschrift für Medienwissenschaft: Medien/Architekturen* 12: pp. 33–43.

Katan-Schmid, Einav. 2019. “Playing with Virtual Realities. A Practice-Based-Research Experiment in Dancing with Technology.” In *Experimentieren. Einblicke in Praktiken und Versuchsaufbauten zwischen Wissenschaft und Gestaltung*, edited by Séverine Marguin, Henrike Rabe, Wolfgang Schäffner, and Friedrich Schmidgall, pp. 93–106. transcript.

Keller, Reiner, and Angelika Poferl, eds. 2018. *Wissenskulturen der Soziologie.* Weinheim; Basel: Beltz Juventa.

Kleining, Gerhard. 1986. “Das qualitative Experiment.” *Kölner Zeitschrift für Soziologie und Sozialpsychologie* 38 (4): pp. 724–50.

Knoblauch, Hubert. 1997. “Die kommunikative Konstruktion postmoderner Organisationen. Institutionen, Aktivitätssysteme und kontextuelles Handeln.” *Österreichische Zeitschrift für Soziologie* 2: pp. 6–23.

———. 2018. “Von der reflexiven Methodologie zur empirischen Wissenschaftstheorie.” In *Handbuch Interpretativ Forschen*, edited by Leila Akremi, Nina Baur, Hubert Knoblauch, and Boris Traue, pp. 226–44. Weinheim: Beltz Juventa.

Knorr Cetina, Karin. 1981. *The Manufacture of Knowledge. An Essay on the Constructivist and Contextual Nature of Science.* Oxford: Pergamon Press.

———. 1999. *Epistemic Cultures. How the Sciences Make Knowledge.* Cambridge, Mass.; London: Harvard University Press.

———. 2001. “Laboratory Studies. The Cultural Approach to the Study of Science.” In *Thousand Oaks* [a.o.]: Sage Publ.

———. 2012. “Skopische Medien: Am Beispiel der Architektur von Finanzmärkten.” In *Mediatisierte Welten: Beschreibungsansätze und Forschungsfelder*, edited by Friedrich Krotz and Andreas Hepp, pp. 167–95. Wiesbaden: VS Verlag für Sozialwissenschaften.

Kockelkorn, Anne. 2008. “Bürolandschaft - Eine vergessene Reformstrategie der deutschen Nachkriegsmoderne.” *ARCH+*, no. 186/187: pp. 6–7.

Kojima, Kazuhiro. 2007. "Fluid Direction." In *Kazuhiro Kojima / CAt*, pp. 134–43. 2G 43. Editorial Gustavo Gili.

Konnikova, Maria. 2014. "The Open-Office Trap." *The New Yorker*, January 7, 2014. Accessed May 28, 2019: https://www.newyorker.com/business/currency/the-open-office-trap.

Kühl, Stefan. 2009. "Experiment." In *Handbuch Methoden der Organisationsforschung. Quantitative und qualitative Methoden*, edited by Stefan Kühl, Petra Strodtholz, and Andreas Taffertshofer, pp. 534–58. VS Verlag für Sozialwissenschaften.

Laing, Andrew, Francis Duffy, Denice Jaunzens, and Steve Willis. 1998. *New Environments for Working. The Re-Design of Offices and Environmental Systems for New Ways of Working.* Taylor & Francis.

Lange, Wolfgang, and Armin Windel. 2013. *Kleine ergonomische Datensammlung.* 15th updated edition Köln: TÜV-Media.

Läpple, Dieter. 1991. "Essay über den Raum. Für ein gesellschaftswissenschaftliches Raumkonzept." In *Stadt und Raum: Soziologische Analysen*, edited by Hartmut Häusermann, pp. 157–207. Pfaffenweiler: Centaurus-Verl.-Ges.

Latour, Bruno. 1987. *Science in Action: How to Follow Scientists and Engineers through Society.* Cambridge, Massachusetts: Harvard University Press.

——. 1997. "Trains of Thought: Piaget, Formalism, and the Fifth Dimension." *Common Knowledge* 6 (3): pp. 170–91.

Latour, Bruno, and Steve Woolgar. 1979. *Laboratory Life. The Construction of Scientific Facts.* Beverly Hills: SAGE Publications.

Livingstone, David N. 2003. *Putting Science in its Place: Geographies of Scientific Knowledge.* Science.Culture. Chicago: University of Chicago Press.

Löw, Martina. 2001. *Raumsoziologie.* Frankfurt am Main: Suhrkamp.

——. 2008. "The Constitution of Space: The Structuration of Spaces Through the Simultaneity of Effect and Perception." *European Journal of Social Theory*11 (1): pp. 25–49.

Luszki, Margaret Barron. 1958. *Interdisciplinary Team Research. Methods and Problems.* New York: New York University Press.

Lynch, Kevin. 1960. *The Image of the City.* Cambridge, Massachusetts: Technology Press.

Marcus, George E. 1995. "Ethnography in/of the World System: The Emergence of Multi-Sited Ethnography." *Annual Review of Anthropology* 24: pp. 95–117.

Mareis, Claudia. 2010. "Entwerfen – Wissen – Produzieren. Designforschung im Anwendungskontext." In *Entwerfen – Wissen – Produzieren. Designforschung im Anwendungskontext*, edited by Claudia Mareis, Gesche Joost, and Kora Kimpel, pp. 9–32. Bielefeld: transcript.

——. 2019. "Entwerfen Um 1960. Methodische Objektivität zwischen Kalkül und Intuition." In *Experimentieren. Vergleich experimenteller Kulturen in Wissenschaft und Gestaltung*, edited by Séverine Marguin, Henrike Rabe, Wolfgang Schäffner, and Friedrich Schmidgall, pp. 323–40. Bielefeld: transcript.

Marguin, Séverine, Henrike Rabe, Wolfgang Schäffner, and Friedrich Schmidgall, eds. 2019. *Experimentieren. Vergleich experimenteller Kulturen in Wissenschaft und Gestaltung.* Bielefeld: transcript.

Mastrandrea, Rossana, Julie Fournet, and Alain Barrat. 2015. "Contact Patterns in a High School: A Comparison between Data Collected Using Wearable Sensors, Contact Diaries and Friendship Surveys." *PLOS ONE* 10 (9): e0136497. Accessed May 28, 2019: https://journals.plos.org/plosone/article?id=10.1371/journal.pone.0136497

Mauthner, Natasha, and Andrea Doucet. 2008. "'Knowledge Once Divided Can Be Hard to Put Together Again': An Epistemological Critique of Collaborative and Team-Based Research Practices." *Sociology* 42 (5): pp. 971–85.

McDonnell, Terence E. 2010. "Cultural Objects as Objects: Materiality, Urban Space, and the Interpretation of AIDS Campaigns in Accra, Ghana." *American Journal of Sociology* 115 (6): pp. 1800–1852.

Mejía, G. Mauricio, Roger F. Malina, and Andres Roldan. 2017. "Towards an Inventory of Best Practices for Transdisciplinary Collaboration." In *Proceedings of the 23rd International Symposium on Electronic Art - ISEA 2017*, pp. 681–87. Manzaniles.

Merkel, Janet. 2019. "'Freelance Isn't Free.' Co-Working as a Critical Urban Practice to Cope with Informality in Creative Labour Markets." *Urban Studies* 56 (3): pp. 526–47.

Metha, Ravi, Rui (Juliet) Zhu, and Amar Cheema. 2012. "Is Noise Always Bad? Exploring the Effects of Ambient Noise on Creative Cognition." *Journal of Consumer Research* 39 (4): pp. 784–99.

Milgram, Stanley. 1963. "Behavioral Study of Obedience." *The Journal of Abnormal and Social Psychology* 67 (4): pp. 371–78.

Mol, Annemarie. 2003. *The Body Multiple Ontology in Medical Practice.* Durham: Duke University Press.

Moravánszky, Ákos, and Albert Kirchengast. 2011. *Experiments: Architektur zwischen Wissenschaft und Kunst / Architecture between Sciences and the Arts.* Berlin: Jovis Berlin.

Müller, Agnes Katharina. 2018. *Coworking Spaces. Urbane Räume im Kontext flexibler Arbeitswelten.* Habitat - International. Schriften zur internationalen Stadtentwicklung. Berlin: LIT Verlag.

Müller, Hans-Peter. 2014. *Pierre Bourdieu. Eine systematische Einführung.* Berlin: Suhrkamp.

Nardi, Bonnie A., and Steve Whittaker. 2002. "The Place of Face-to-Face Communication in Distributed Work."In Distributed Work, edited by Pamela Hinds and Sara Kiesler, pp. 83–112. Cambridge, MA: *MIT Press.*

Nielsen, Jakob, and Kara Pernice. 2010. *Eyetracking Web Usability.* Berkeley: New Riders.

Niewöhner, Jörg. 2014. "Raum: Anthropologische Perspektiven."In *Theorien in der Raum- und Stadtforschung*, edited by Jürgen Oßenbrügge and Anne Vogelpohl, pp. 14–23. Münster: Westfälisches Dampfboot.

——. 2016. "Co-Laborative Anthropology: Crafting Reflexivities Experimentally." Accessed May 28, 2019: https://edoc.hu-berlin.de/handle/18452/19241.

Niewöhner, Jörg, and Ruzana Liburkina. 2017. "Laborstudien - Einführung."In *Science and Technology Studies. Klassische Positionen und aktuelle Perspektiven*, edited by Susanne Bauer, Torsten Heinemann, and Thomas Lemke, pp. 173–97. Berlin: Suhrkamp.

Nobuyuki, Yoshida. 2003. *Office Urbanism.* The Japan Architect 50. Tokio: Shinkenchiku.

Oldham, Greg R., and Daniel J. Brass. 1979. "Employee Reactions to an Open-Plan Office: A Naturally Occurring Quasi-Experiment." *Administrative Science Quarterly* 24 (2): pp. 267–84.

Oswalt, Philipp. 2015. "Wissen - Nichtwissen - Entwerfen." In *Haare hören – Strukturen wissen – Räume agieren. Berichte aus dem Interdisziplinären Labor Bild Wissen Gestaltung*, edited by Horst Bredekamp and Wolfgang Schäffner, pp. 145–58. Bielefeld: transcript.

Parrika, Jussi. 2016. "The Lab as a Symptom." Machinology Machines, Noise, and Some Media Archaeology by Jussi Parikka. May 10, 2016. Accessed May 15, 2019: https://jussiparikka.net/2016/05/10/the-lab-as-a-symptom/.

Parthey, Heinrich, and Klaus Schreiber, eds. 1983. *Interdisziplinarität in der Forschung. Analysen und Fallstudien.* Berlin: Akademie Verlag.

Penn, Alan, and Bill Hillier. 1992. "The Social Potential of Buildings: Spatial Structure and the Innovative Milieu in Scientific Research Laboratories."In *Corporate Space and ArchitectureInternational Symposium Proceedings*, pp. 38–43. Transports: Paris

Penn, Alan, and Alasdair Turner. 2002. "Space Syntax Based Agent Models." In *Pedestrian and Evacuation Dynamics*, edited by Michael Schreckenberg and Som Deo Sharma, pp. 99–114. Heidelberg: Springer.

Pflüger, Jessica. 2013. *Qualitative Sozialforschung und ihr Kontext. Wissenschaftliche Teamarbeit im internationalen Vergleich.* Wiesbaden: Springer.

Platt, Jennifer. 1976. *Realities of Social Research. An Empirical Study of British Sociologists.* London: Sussex University Press.

Plohmann, Angela, ed. 2012. *A Blueprint for a Lab of the Future.* Eindhoven: Baltan Laboratories.

Rabe, Henrike. 2016. "Informal Spaces in Laboratories." In *New Laboratories. Historical and Critical Perspectives on Contemporary Developments*, edited by Charlotte Klonk, pp. 121–46. Berlin; Boston: De Gruyter.

Reckwitz, Andreas. 2002. "Toward a Theory of Social Practices. A Development in Culturalist Theorizing." *European Journal of Social Theory* 5: pp. 245–65.

Rheinberger, Hans-Jörg. 2001. *Experimentalsysteme und epistemische Dinge. Eine Geschichte der Proteinsynthese im Reagenzglas.* Frankfurt am Main: Suhrkamp.

——. 2008. "Experimentelle Virtuosität." In *Interesse für bedingtes Wissen. Wechselbeziehungen zwischen den Wissenskulturen*, edited by Caroline Welsch and Stefan Willer, pp. 331–342. München: Wilhelm Fink.

Riegraf, Birgit. 2018. "Zwischen Exzellenz und Prekarität. Über den Wettbewerb und die bedingte Öffnung der Universitäten für Wissenschaftlerinnen." In *Prekäre Gleichstellung: Geschlechtergerechtigkeit, soziale Ungleichheit und unsichere Arbeitsverhältnisse in der Wissenschaft*, edited by Mike Laufenberg, Martina Erlemann, Maria Norkus, and Grit Petschick, pp. 241–56. Wiesbaden: Springer.

Rogge, Jan-Christoph. 2015. "The Winner Takes it All?" *KZfSS Kölner Zeitschrift für Soziologie und Sozialpsychologie* 67 (4): pp. 685–707.

Sailer, Kerstin. 2018. "Corridors, Classrooms, Classification – The Impact of School Layout on Pedagogy and Social Behaviours." In *Designing Buildings for the Future of Schooling: Contemporary Visions for Education*, edited by Hau Ming Tse, Harry Daniels, Andrew Stables, and Sarah Cox, Chapter 5. London: Routledge.

——. 2019. "Simulieren: Experimente in der Büroraumgestaltung: Konzepte, Herausforderungen und praktische Beispiele aus der Sicht der Architektur." In *Experimentieren. Vergleich experimenteller Kulturen in Wissenschaft und Gestaltung*, edited by Séverine Marguin, Henrike Rabe, Wolfgang Schäffner, and Friedrich Schmidgall, pp. 283–308. Bielefeld: transcript.

Sailer, Kerstin, and Alan Penn. 2009. "Spatiality and Transspatiality in Workplace Environments." In *Proceedings of the 7th International Spcae Syntax Symposium*, edited by Daniel Koch, Lars Marcus, and Jesper Steen, 095:1-11. Stockholm: Royal Institute of Technology (KTH).

Schäffner, Wolfgang. 2010a. "Elemente architektonischer Medien." *ZMK Zeitschrift für Medien- und Kulturforschung: Schwerpunkt Kulturtechnik* 1 (1): pp. 137–50.

——. 2010b. "The Design Turn. Eine wissenschaftliche Revolution im Geiste der Gestaltung." In *Entwerfen – Wissen – Produzieren. Designforschung im Anwendungskontext*, edited by Claudia Mareis, Gesche Joost, and Kora Kimpel, pp. 33–46. Bielefeld: transcript.

——. 2015. "Interdisziplinäre Gestaltung." In *Haare hören - Strukturen wissen - Räume agieren. Berichte aus dem Interdisziplinären Labor Bild Wissen Gestaltung*, edited by Horst Bredekamp and Wolfgang Schäffner, pp. 199–213. Bielefeld: transcript.

Schmidt, Robert. 2008. "Das Zusammenspiel von Habitat und Habitus und die Sozialität der Artefakte: Zur empirischen Rekonstruktion der praktischen Logik von Programmierung und Softwareentwicklung." In *Die Natur der Gesellschaft: Verhandlungen des 33. Kongresses der Deutschen Gesellschaft für Soziologie in Kassel 2006*, edited by Karl-Siegbert Rehberg, Vol. 1 & 2: pp. 1961–67. Frankfurt am Main: Campus Verlag.

——. 2012. *Soziologie der Praktiken - Konzeptionelle Studien und empirische Analysen*. Berlin: Suhrkamp Taschenbuch.

Schulz-Schaeffer, Ingo. 2013. "Scenarios as Patterns of Orientation in Technology Development and Technology Assessment. Outline of a Research Program." *Science, Technology and Innovation Studies* 9 (1): pp. 23–44.

Schulz-Schaeffer, Ingo, and Martin Meister. 2015. "How Situational Scenarios Guide Technology Development - Some Insights from Research on Ubiquitous Computing." In *Practices of Innovation and Responsibility: Insights from Methods, Governance and Action*, edited by Diana M. Baumann, Anne Dijkstra, Camilo Fautz, Julia Guivant, Kornelia Konrad, Harro van Lente, and Silvia Woll. Vol. Studies of New and Emerging Technologies. Berlin: AKA Verlag Berlin.

Schütz, Alfred. 2004. *Der sinnhafte Aufbau der Sozialen Welt: Eine Einleitung in die verstehende Soziologie*. Alfred-Schütz-Werkausgabe 2. München: UVK Verlagsgesellschaft.

Shanken, Edward A. 2010. "The History and Future of the Lab: Collaborative Research at the Intersections of Art, Science, and Technology." In *The Future of the Lab*, edited by Angela Plohmann and Clare Butcher, pp. 16–29. Eindhoven: Baltan Laboratories.

Shepherd, Daniel, Daniel Welch, Kim N. Dirks, and Daniel McBride. 2013. "Do Quiet Areas Afford Greater Health-Related Quality of Life than Noisy Areas?" *International Journal of Environmental Research and Public Health* 10: pp. 1284–1303.

Shobe, Hunter, and David Banis. 2010. "Music Regions and Mental Maps: Teaching Cultural Geography."*Journal of Geography* 109 (2): pp. 87–96.

Shrum, Wesley, Joel Genuth, and Ivan Chompalov. 2007. *Structures of Scientific Collaboration*. Cambridge, Massachusetts: MIT Press.

Sloan, Sa. n.d. "Faa Tenant Gsa Landlord Maslov Love Participation Satisfaction Offices Personal Space Work Production Social Needs Designers Users Product Process." People Space Architecture Company.

Smiley, Sarah L. 2013. "Mental Maps, Segregation, and Everyday Life in Dares Salaam, Tanzania." *Journal of Cultural Geography* 30 (2): pp. 215–44.

Sondermann, Michael, Dagmar Simon, Anne-Marie Scholz, and Stefan Hornbostel. 2008. "Die Exzellenzinitiative: Beobachtungen aus der Implementierungsphase. IFQ-Working Paper No.5." iFQ Institut für Forschungsinformation und Qualitätssicherung . Accessed May 15, 2019: http://www.forschungsinfo.de/Publikationen/Download/working_paper_5_2008.pdf.

Stanley, Liz. 1990. "Feminist Praxis and the Academic Mode of Production." In *Feminist Praxis*, pp. 3–19. London: Routledge.

Steets, Silke. 2015. *Der sinnhafte Aufbau der gebauten Welt. Eine Architektursoziologie*. Berlin: Suhrkamp.

Suchman, Lucy Alice. 1987. *Plans and Situated Actions: The Problem of Human-Machine Communication*. Cambridge; New York: Cambridge University Press.

Sundstrom, Eric, Kring R. Herbert, and David W. Brown. 1982. "Privacy and Communication in an Open-Plan Office: A Case Study." *Environment and Behavior* 14 (3): pp. 379–92.

Terras, Melissa, Julianna Nyhan, and Edward Vanhoutte, eds. 2013. *Defining Digital Humanities. A Reader.* New York: Routledge.

Thierbach, Cornelia. 2016. "Doing Space. Die Rolle von Raum im Alltag von Wissenschaftlern eines Exzellenzclusters." In *Wissen – Organisation – Forschungspraxis. Der Makro-Meso-Mikro-Link in der Wissenschaft*, edited by Nina Baur, Cristina Besio, Maria Norkus, and Grit Petschick, pp. 372–401. Weinheim: Beltz Juventa.

Traue, Boris. 2013. "Visuelle Diskursanalyse. Ein programmatischer Vorschlag zur Untersuchung von Sicht- und Sagbarkeiten im Medienwandel." *Zeitschrift für Diskursforschung* 2 (1): pp. 117–36.

Tschumi, Bernard. 1994. *Event-Cities*. Cambridge, Massachusetts: MIT Press.

Turner, Alasdair, Maria Doxa, David O' Sullivan, and Alan Penn. 2001. "From Isovists to Visibility Graphs: A Methodology for the Analysis of Architectural Space." *Environment and Planning B: Planning and Design* 28 (1): pp. 103–21.

Übernickel, Falk, Walter Brenner, Britta Pukall, Therese Naef, and Bernhard Schindlholzer. 2015. *Design Thinking. Das Handbuch*. Frankfurt am Main: Frankfurter Allgemeine Buch.

Veldhoen, Erik, and Bart Piepers. 1995. *The Demise of the Office: The Digital Workplace in a Thriving Organisation*. Rotterdam: William Stout Architectural Books.

Venturi, Robert, Denise Scott Brown, and Steven Izenour. 1972. *Learning from Las Vegas*. Cambridge MA: MIT Press.

Westphal, Wilhelm H. 1968. *A Short Textbook of Physics. Not Involving the Use of Higher Mathematics*.Translated by Eswald Osers. Berlin; Heidelberg; New York: Springer.

Wikipedia contributors. n.d. "Desktop Metaphor." Wikipedia, The Free Encyclopedia. Accessed February 22, 2019: https://en.wikipedia.org/w/index.php?title=Desktop_metaphor&oldid=897551627.

Winnacker, Ernst-Ludwig. 2005. "Die Exzellenzinitiative: Hoffnung auf den großen Wurf." *Forschung* 30 (2): pp. 2–3.

Yaneva, Albena. 2009. *The Making of a Building: A Pragmatist Approach to Architecture*. Oxford; New York: Peter Lang.

——. 2010a. "Is the Atrium More Important than the Lab? Designer Buildings for New Cultures of Creativity." In *Geographies of Science*, edited by Peter Meusburger, David Livingstone, and Heike Jöns, 3: pp. 139–50. Dordrecht: Springer Netherlands.

——. 2010b. "The 'Architectural' as a Type of Connector: A Realist Approach to Architecture." *The MIT Press on Behalf of Pespecta* 42: pp. 141–45.

Finn Geipel, an architect, is founding partner at the architecture firm LIN and a Professor of Architecture at Technical University Berlin, where he heads the *Laboratory for Integrative Architecture*. Time, openness, adaptability and context-specificity are important themes in his work, as illustrated by architectural and urban projects including *Alveole 14*, *Cité du design* and *Grand Paris Métropole Douce*. He holds a position as a Principal Investigator at the Cluster of Excellence *Matters of Activity* of the Humboldt-Universität in Berlin, and held numerous visiting professorships, including one at MIT.

Séverine Marguin is a sociologist heading the methods lab in the Collaborative Research Center 1265, *Re-Figuration of Spaces*, at the Technical University Berlin. After completing her doctorate on artist collectives in Paris and Berlin, she worked as a researcher on the project *Architectures-Experiments* at the Cluster of Excellence *Image Knowledge Gestaltung* of the Humboldt-Universität in Berlin. Her research focuses on science studies, collectivity, interdisciplinarity, visual research methods and experimentalization. She is co-founder of *ARCHIEXP*, a studio for interdisciplinary spatial research and design.

Henrike Rabe is an architect and doctoral researcher at the *Laboratory for Integrative Architecture* at Technical University Berlin. She studied architecture in Berlin and Toulouse, and worked with *Kazuhiro Kojima+Kazuko Akamatsu/CAt* (Tokyo) and *Brisac Gonzalez* (London). She conducted empirical and historical research on the spaces and practices of knowledge within the project *ArchitecturesExperiments* at the Cluster of Excellence *Image Knowledge Gestaltung* of the Humboldt-Universität in Berlin. She is co-founder of *ARCHIEXP*, a studio for interdisciplinary spatial research and design.

Friedrich Schmidgall, an interaction designer, heads the Open Lab and acts as a consultant for interdisciplinarity at the Einstein Center *Digital Future* at the Technical University Berlin. He studied industrial design in Saarbrücken and interaction design at *Weißensee Kunsthochschule Berlin*. He explored the influence of physical and digital spatial configurations on interdisciplinary work within the project *ArchitecturesExperiments* at the Cluster of Excellence *Image Knowledge Gestaltung* of the Humboldt-Universität in Berlin. He is co-founder of *ARCHIEXP*, a studio for interdisciplinary spatial research and design.

Fabian Scholz, architect, is partner at the architecture firm *0101*. After studying at Technical University Berlin, Sangath Ahmedabad and EPFL Lausanne, he worked with Fernando Menis, *SANAA*, *Uberbau* and *LIN*. As a freelance architect, he won one of ten first prizes in the ideas competition for the M20 Museum Berlin and participated in the 2017 Architecture Biennale in Lyon. He taught at the *Laboratory for Integrative Architecture* at the TU Berlin and held the position of a research assistant at the Cluster of Excellence *Image Knowledge Gestaltung* of the Humboldt-Universität in Berlin, where he was part of the project *ArchitecturesExperiments*.

Christian Stein, a literature scholar, linguist and computer scientist, is a post-doc researcher at the Cluster of Excellence *Matters of Activity* of the Humboldt-Universität in Berlin. He studied at the Technical University Braunschweig, completing his doctorate on the "Primacy of Language - Leitmotif and Topology of the Subject in Arno Schmidt" in 2012. Between 2012 and 2018 he was a post-doc researcher at the Cluster of Excellence *Image Knowledge Gestaltung*. Core focuses of his work include semantic networks, modeling interdisciplinarity, spatial theory and an epistemology of interdisciplinary.

Acknowledgements

This publication is based on the research project *ArchitecturesExperiments* (formerly *Architectures of Knowledge*) at the Cluster of Excellence *Image Knowledge Gestaltung. An Interdisciplinary Laboratory* of the Humboldt-Universität in Berlin which was conducted between 2012 and 2018. The project would not have been possible without the support of many people involved:

First and foremost, we would like to thank all participants[1] of the *Experimental Zone* for their involvement in the project, particularly for their understanding and support during the eight rebuilds and for their invaluable commitment and the trust placed in us during the numerous surveys and workshops.

The project owes its foundations to the Principal Investigators, who also provided years of guidance, and we extend our warmest thanks to the following individuals: Prof. Wolfgang Schäffner for his great support of the project, enriching conversations and indefatigable will to continue searching; Prof. Finn Geipel for many inspiring conversations and his advice as regards the conception, design and realization of both the Experimental Zone and experimental settings; Prof. Jörg Niewöhner for his spot-on methodical and theoretical advice; Prof. Bernd Mahr for his encouragement and advice in developing the process model; Prof. Lars Lerup for the joint design of an experimental setting; Prof. Carola Zwick for her support in founding the Experimental Zone and Prof. Jan Roggenkamp for many years of advice as regards data protection.

We would also like to thank the administration of the *Interdisciplinary Laboratory* for its longstanding support, in particular the untiringly helpful Kathrin Bauer, Sandra Bauer, Amaya Steinhilber and Deborah Zehnder, who made the *Experimental Zone* possible in the first place.

We would like to thank the former team members and associates of the research project, namely Julia Blumenthal, Peter Koval, Maria Lisenko, Cornelia Schendzielorz, Fabian Scholz, Christian Stein, Stefan Solleder and Cornelia Thierbach for the fruitful collaboration, for many inspiring discussions and for their valuable contributions to the theoretical, empirical and design work.

The qualitative observation would not have been possible without Alisa Laila Fluhrer and Felicia Haidl, for whose efforts we are very grateful. We would also like to thank Tom Brewe, Sammy Davids, Susanne Friedl, Nikolay Kozhanov, Alexander Struck and Benjamin Thomack for their support as far as the quantitative observation instruments are concerned. And we thank Laura Enghusen, Theodora Georgopoulou, Maren Krause, Patryk Kujawa, Dimitra Megas, Benjamin Meurer, Catherine Slusher and Rasa Weber for their contribution to the design work and the graphical surveys.

In addition, the repeated construction of settings would not have been possible without the advice and help of the workshop staff of the *Interdisciplinary Laboratory*.

Concerning this publication, we are particularly grateful to the following individuals: Kerstin Germer and Sarah Etz for their editorial and coordinating work; Moritz Queisner for his critical comments; Beste Worte GmbH for the professional editing and Katja Gretzinger for the book's wonderful design.

1. For data protection reasons we cannot thank the participants personally here.

Imprint

The Experimental Zone.
An Interdisciplinary Investigation on the Spaces and Practices of Collaborative Research

Authors:
Séverine Marguin
Henrike Rabe
Friedrich Schmidgall

Authors of the guest contribution:
Finn Geipel
Fabian Scholz
Christian Stein

Copy editing:
Beste Worte GmbH

Editorial coordination:
Sarah Etz
Kerstin Germer
Felicia Haidl

Design:
Studio Gretzinger, Berlin

Paper:
Munken Polar Rough

Pre-press, printing, and binding:
Gugler GmbH, Melk

Fonts:
A-Grotesk (Katja Gretzinger)
GT Super (Grilli Type)

ISBN 978-3-03860-148-7

Park Books
Niederdorfstrasse 54
8001 Zurich
Switzerland
www.park-books.com

Park Books is being supported by the *Swiss Federal Office of Culture* with a general subsidy for the years 2016–2020.

This publication was made possible by *Image Knowledge Gestaltung. An Interdisciplinary Laboratory* Cluster of Excellence at the Humboldt-Universität zu Berlin (sponsor number EXC 1027/1) with financial support from the *German Research Foundation* as a part of the Excellence Initiative.

Image Knowledge Gestaltung
Interdisciplinary Laboratory in the Hermann von Helmholtz Center for Cultural Techniques

Sponsored by DFG